Unusual
Punishment

Unusual Punishment

Inside the Walla Walla Prison
1970–1985

Christopher Murray

WSU
PRESS

Washington State University Press
Pullman, Washington

Washington State University Press
PO Box 645910
Pullman, Washington 99164-5910
Phone: 800-354-7360
Fax: 509-335-8568
Email: wsupress@wsu.edu
Website: wsupress.wsu.edu

Library of Congress Cataloging-in-Publication Data

Names: Murray, Christopher, 1948-
Title: Unusual punishment : inside the Walla Walla prison, 1970-1985 /
    Christopher Murray.
Description: Pullman, Washington : Washington State University Press, 2016. |
    Includes bibliographical references and index.
Identifiers: LCCN 2015044944 | ISBN 9780874223347 (acid-free paper)
Subjects: LCSH: Washington State Penitentiary--History--20th century. |
    Prisoners--Washington (State)--Walla Walla--Social conditions--20th
    century. | Prisoners--Civil rights--Washington (State)--Walla
    Walla--History--20th century. | Prison violence--Washington (State)--Walla
    Walla--History--20th century. | Prison wardens--Washington (State)--Walla
    Walla--History--20th century. | Prison reformers--Washington
    (State)--Walla Walla--History--20th century. | Social change--Washington
    (State)--Walla Walla--History--20th century.
Classification: LCC HV9475.W22 W375 2016 | DDC 365/.979748--dc23 LC record
available at http://lccn.loc.gov/2015044944

Cover Photo by Ethan Hoffman. The inmate president of the Bikers' Club riding his
1951 panhead Harley-Davidson in the Big Yard of the Washington State Penitentiary,
September 1978.

For more photos, stories, and audio and video recordings, visit the companion website at
UnusualPunishmentBook.com.

"In the 1970s, for a convict to do his time in fear of dying every day—that's unusual punishment."

Parley Edwards
Former correctional officer,
Washington State Penitentiary

CONTENTS

ILLUSTRATIONS

PREFACE

I was a young architect working for the agency responsible for the state's prisons when I first travelled to Walla Walla, Washington, and went inside the state penitentiary. On a hot July day in 1976 we walked to Eight Wing to hopefully discover an architectural solution to help reduce the number of rapes, beatings, and occasional murders that happened in the gang shower shared by the hundreds of men who lived in the unit.

The plant manager accompanied us as we made our way to the shower room at the far end of the building. On our left, sunlight streamed through broken panes of glass in the tall bays of windows that looked out on the prison wall to the west. Everything had a beaten and dirty appearance. As we walked in front of the ground-floor cells, my eye was drawn to the catwalk high above, where a striking blond wearing a miniskirt strolled past the cells on the topmost tier.

"You mean they let women in here?" I asked the plant manager.

Without looking up, the plant manager said, "That's not a woman."

I was young. I was naive. I'd never been in a prison before. For a while I assumed all prisons were like the penitentiary in Walla Walla.

We didn't find an easy solution to the gang shower problem that day, but I quickly discovered that not all prisons were the same.

The part of the story of *Unusual Punishment* that I personally saw—albeit mainly from a safe distance—was roughly the middle third of the journey. I knew I was witnessing something extraordinary. I told myself, "Someone ought to write a book."

When no one did, I gave myself a sabbatical from my consulting business in 1993. I read fifteen years of newspapers and photocopied every relevant article I could find. I conducted and transcribed scores of tape-recorded interviews. I interviewed convicts and governors, lawyers and politicians, correctional officers, prison administrators, agency heads, and others. After drafting a few chapters, the priorities of raising a family and making a living intervened. I returned to a busy professional life providing consulting services to adult and juvenile correctional agencies in various parts of the country.

Fast forward to 2010, when I retired. With time on my hands, I interviewed more people and reviewed thousands of pages of archived documents. Then I wrote.

The more I wrote the more I realized that the story of the Washington State Penitentiary from 1970 to 1985—despite its many unique qualities—could be seen as a microcosm for the upheaval in prisons that was occurring all across the country, more or less at the same time. Sometimes starting a little earlier, sometimes a little later, virtually all prison systems in the United States saw a gradual (or precipitous) erosion of the autonomy and power of wardens of major prisons replaced by centralized, standards-based, rule-driven, paramilitary organizations. Convicts became "inmates." Guards became "correctional officers." The phrase "inmates are sent to prison *as* punishment, not *for* punishment," became popular in certain circles. The American Correctional Association published its first edition of *Standards for Adult Correctional Institutions*. Staff training became more rigorous.

Over time, formerly powerless inmates gained at least some checks against arbitrary retribution for both major and trivial transgressions. The exercise of political patronage and nepotism in the hiring and promotion of staff became less common. Death, maiming, and disability from medical malpractice, or what the courts called "deliberate indifference," diminished and eventually became rare.

While changes such as these tended to make incarceration somewhat more humane, there were other forces at work. The "war on drugs," declared by President Richard Nixon in 1971, gained momentum as state after state enacted laws mandating long sentences for possession or sale of relatively small quantities of drugs. Ostensibly intended for major drug kingpins, these and similar laws accelerated the long-term trend toward mass incarceration whose effects continue to this day.

A classic paper by sociologist Robert Martinson published in 1974 (popularly known as "nothing works") effectively ended efforts toward adult prisoner rehabilitation in the United States for at least the next fifteen years.[1] The classic list of the goals of incarceration—retribution, incapacitation, deterrence, and rehabilitation—became shorter. The "just deserts" model became the driving force in adult corrections. Mandatory minimum sentences proliferated and prison sentences, on average, became longer. Like increased admissions, longer sentences drove prison populations ever higher.

The war on drugs, changes in sentencing, and other changes that increased prison admissions and length of stay—as important as they were in shaping the landscape of American prisons today—are not the focus of this book. In fact, in Washington State, the war on drugs had virtually no effect on state prison population levels until the last half of the 1980s, and the state's 1981 Sentencing Reform Act, which implemented determinant sentencing, actually caused prison populations to decline briefly during the mid-1980s.

What *Unusual Punishment* does address is the story of the messy opening of what had long been a closed prison culture and the transformation of that culture into something quite different. In Washington State, and in much of the country, a nearly perfect storm of forces drove this sea change. An onslaught of major legal challenges, riots, new attitudes in the prisoner population, proliferating drug use, and strong public sector unions combined to put the old order on the defensive, and ultimately to overwhelm it.

Growing out of the civil rights movement, and preceded by legal action to improve conditions for people held in giant mental health hospitals across the country, state and federal courts began to abandon their hands-off attitude toward state prison systems. Perhaps the earliest major conditions-of-confinement case occurred in the Arkansas prison system in 1970 where the U.S. District Court found that a combination of practices and serious deficiencies were such that "confinement of persons therein amounted to a cruel and unusual punishment."[2] A year later, the New York State practice of sometimes withholding or censoring inmate correspondence to lawyers, elected officials, and high ranking state agency officials relating to complaints about conviction or incarceration was found unconstitutional. In 1972 Judge Frank Johnson declared the indifferent, ineffective, and grossly understaffed health care system in Alabama prisons to be unconstitutional. After additional litigation, Judge Johnson placed the entire Alabama corrections system under federal court order in 1976. Other cases during the early 1970s introduced the concept of "liberty interest" and due process rights in disciplinary and other decisions regarding prison inmates. These and other decisions affected not just the states directly involved, but all those who wanted to avoid court intervention.

Major riots, starting with the 1971 riot in Attica, New York, in which forty-three people died, shocked the country. Long out of sight and out of mind, prisons became the subject of increased media and public attention and scrutiny. Documented excesses drove policy makers to demand greater oversight and accountability. During most of the 1970s the United States was still a generally liberal nation. (President Richard Nixon proposed a system of subsidized universal health care, founded the Environmental Protection Agency, expanded food stamps, and implemented wage and price controls.) Prison reform was an important political priority in many states.

A changing youth culture with a propensity to challenge authority brought new attitudes to many prisons when members of this new generation were incarcerated. As these attitudes diluted the prevailing prison culture, the long established convict code that valued stability and order began to erode. Some of the new inmates were genuine radicals and revolutionaries, members of the Black Liberation Army, the Weather Underground, the Symbionese Liberation Army, the George Jackson Brigade, and extremist elements of Students for a Democratic Society. These radicals had no more respect for the authority and leadership of the old convict code than they had for the political and corporate leadership of the country. As their numbers increased in prison, the ability of prison administrators, correctional officers, and former convict leaders to maintain stability and order decreased.

Returning from the war in Vietnam, large numbers of young men of an age generally associated with increased criminal behavior returned to civilian life. Many of these returning vets had experimented with drugs in Southeast Asia. Some returned addicted to heroin. Back home they joined a youthful culture where drug use was increasingly common. As drug use proliferated in the general population, so too did it in America's prisons. In general, it wasn't the drug use that was the problem, but the turf battles over the lucrative drug trade, and the extremes to which addicts can resort when their supply runs short.

A robust post-World War II economy brought low unemployment and strengthened trade unions. In the 1960s and 1970s public sector employees increasingly became unionized. In states with laws favorable to organized labor, unions representing correctional workers gained strength and flexed their muscles. While most changes tended to challenge the authority of prison wardens over inmates, strong unions challenged the authority of wardens over their employees. What had often been a system based on patronage and nepotism was put on the defensive.

Altogether, these convergent forces overwhelmed the prevailing method of how prisons were managed all across the country. After years of searching, often resisting, sometimes floundering, a new order emerged. In many jurisdictions, the difference between the old order and the new was like night and day; in others, the difference was more a matter of degree. But everywhere, the unfettered discretion exercised by powerful wardens over inmates and staff alike was broken. The path taken by the Washington State Penitentiary was unique in its details, but not in its overall trajectory.

Before concluding this preface, a word about nomenclature is needed. In the 1970s, most African Americans referred to themselves as "blacks." These were the days of the Black Panthers. The organization at the Washington State Penitentiary representing African Americans was called the Black Prisoners Forum Unlimited. Native Americans called themselves "Indians." Nationally, there was the American Indian Movement, or A.I.M. Their organization at the penitentiary was the Confederated Indian Tribes. Everyone at the penitentiary from the Spanish speaking western hemisphere belonged to the Chicano Club. For the most part, these terms are no longer in vogue. Rather than opt for the currently politically correct terms—which, after all, go in and out of favor—the words used by the inmates, staff, and media during these years are used throughout this book. While it's possible some readers may take offense, this decision avoids the awkward juxtaposition of terms used in quotations with their more modern equivalents.

And, of course, there are people to whom I owe thanks. My consulting business demanded much report writing. Until *Unusual Punishment*, however, I had never written a book or crafted a story line. As with any first, I needed help.

When I had drafted a handful of chapters, my talented school teacher daughter, Breedeen Pickford-Murray, read what I had done, red pen in hand. She found plenty to critique and helped set me on a better course. Other early reviewers included Roxanne Lieb, William Collins, Kathryn Bail, and my wife, Kathleen Gookin. Much to my surprise, members of a history book group I occasionally attend offered to read the first completed draft and provided valuable comments. Knowing next to nothing about prisons, some of them read the book as a case study about organizational change. The Olympia Writers Critique Group—especially group coordinators Alan Shue and Vanessa Palensky, and facilitators Johanna Flynn and Leslie Romer—were consistently supportive and helpful. Syd Boyle, another member of the writers group, did a careful reading of the first proof copy of the manuscript. Finally, the book benefited greatly from the assistance of my first editor, Kathy Carter and, of course, those at Washington State University Press. Thank you one and all.

Of course, there would have been no book—at least not as interesting a book—without the help of the nearly sixty people who shared their memories and insights through recorded interviews. The names of all these people can be found in Appendix B, but I would be remiss if I did not single out Dick Morgan and Robin and Carol Moses for their amazing recall, great storytelling ability, and repeated assistance.

Thanks also to the patient staff of the Washington State Archives. These guardians of history hauled out box after box of old letters, memos, reports, and other documents for me to examine. Thanks to the Aerial Photography Branch of the Washington State Department of Transportation for the excellent aerial photographs. Thanks to former Washington State Penitentiary superintendents Steven Sinclair and James Blodgett for sharing old photographs, slides, and negatives of the penitentiary and of those who lived and worked there. Thanks to Gordon Graham and Instar Performance LLC for permission to quote from Mr. Graham's book, *The One-Eyed Man Is King*; and to Charles Morris for permission to use passages from *A Time of Passion, America 1960–1980*. Finally, a special thanks to Caren and Robert Hoffman for permission to use the photo taken by their late brother, Ethan Hoffman, on the cover of this book. For more about Mr. Hoffman, please see "Ethan Hoffman and the Cover Photograph" at the end of this book.

Timeline

	1969	1970	1971	1972	1973	1974	1975	1976	1977	1978	1979	1980	1981	1982	1983	1984	1985
	Super Custody		Changes			Descent			Nadir		War			Transformation			

OLYMPIA

GOVERNOR			EVANS							RAY				SPELLMAN			*Gardner*
DIRECTOR D.I.	CONTE																
SECRETARY DSHS			SMITH **		**		MORRIS	**	McNUTT	THOMPSON							
DIRECTOR Div A.C.							BRADLEY		VINZANT	TROPP							
SECRETARY DOC													REED				
DIR DOC Prisons Div													*Vernon*		KAUTZKY		

WALLA WALLA

SUPERINTENDENT	MACKLIN				RHAY				VINZANT *		SPALDING		KASTAMA	KINCHELOE			
ASSOCIATE 1			CROWLEY				HARVEY		GENAKOS *		KINCHELOE		*Hanson*				
ASSOCIATE 2			FREEMAN						*	CUMMINS			*Peterson*		*Helgeson*		
ASSOCIATE 3														WOOD			
UNION PRESIDENT	MOSES					CHADEK				EDWARDS			*Piver*				

*** indicates Interim or Acting

Names in *lowercase italics* not mentioned in book

Site Plan: 1970

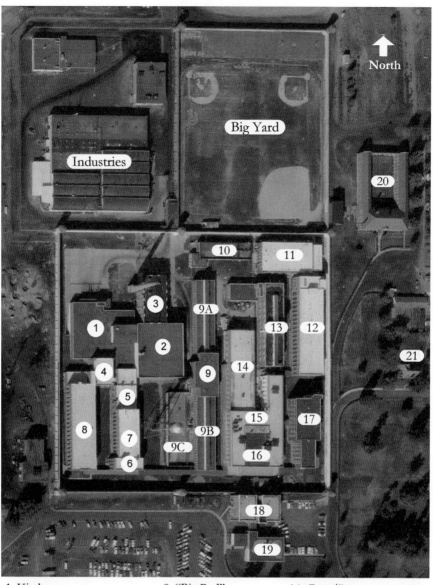

1. Kitchen
2. Dining Halls
3. Power House (not in use)
4. Clothing
5. Chapel
6. Classification & Parole
7. Seven Wing
8. Eight Wing
9. "Big Red"
9A. Admissions
9B. Segregation
9C. Segregation Yard
10. Laundry
11. Auditorium
12. Six Wing
13. Four & Five Wing
14. Gym/Rec
15. Education
16. Central Control
17. Hospital
18. Old Admin
19. New Admin
20. Women's Prison
21. Superintendent's House

PART 1
SUPER CUSTODY
BEFORE 1970

Tower in the middle of the south wall, Washington State Penitentiary

Chapter 1

THE PRISON

IN A BROAD VALLEY in the southeast corner of Washington State, the quiet town of Walla Walla straddles the banks of a small stream. At the western edge of town, north of the railroad tracks, is the town's largest employer: a prison. It's been there, in one form or another, since territorial days. The prison grounds are large—five hundred acres—and one property line extends a half mile along North Thirteenth Avenue. With that much frontage, the choices for an address must have been numerous, but long ago some postmaster with a wry sense of humor decided that the Washington State Penitentiary's address should be 1313 North Thirteenth Avenue.

Approaching this unlucky address from town, North Thirteenth Avenue climbs a gentle grade before reaching the level ground upon which the prison sits. Perhaps one of the prison's nicknames, "the Hill," refers to this little rise, but it's the prison itself that draws the eye.

In the 1960s the ten-acre main compound was surrounded by a twenty-foot-high wall composed of a half mile of stone, brick, mortar, and concrete. Large structures dominated most of the real estate inside the walls. A long building, called "Big Red" by both staff and inmates, ran north-south down the middle of the prison, dividing it in half. Getting its name from the muddy red-brown bricks that made up its nearly five-hundred-foot facade, Big Red housed admissions and segregation. New inmates—or "fish," as the convicts called them—went to admissions when they first arrived. After that, a fish either found or was assigned a permanent cell. If he knew someone with an empty bunk, he could move in. Brothers, other relatives, crime partners, or friends from the neighborhood often shared a cell.

Break a rule, cross the superintendent, be unmanageable for any reason, and an inmate would likely find himself in what convicts called "the hole." This was segregation, or "seg" for short. In the 1960s, a man

3

might stay in segregation for months or even years. Those on death row (a smaller section of segregation) got out only by the gallows or a pardon. In one corner of seg, a half dozen strip cells, with blackout doors and nothing but a hole in the floor for a toilet, were used for disciplinary isolation.

A small, walled recreation yard stood next to segregation. A tower officer observed it all. Once, a ricocheted bullet—meant to stop a fight inside the yard—killed an inmate who wasn't part of the brawl. A man in segregation counted himself lucky if he could see the sky and smell the fresh air for as much as an hour a day.

The eastern half of the institution—sometimes called "East Berlin" by the inmates—included the auditorium, three cellblocks (called "wings" in Walla Walla), the gym, hospital, Central Control, school, and rooms for television and games. West of Big Red were two more cellblocks, the giant kitchen and adjacent dining halls, an abandoned power house, a chapel, and an administrative building used by counselors for the inmates. To the north were the Big Yard and the industries area with its license plate factory, metal shop, laundry, and other areas for work.

South of the main compound, and looking something like a castle, was the old administration building, attached to the wall by a strongly gated entrance. Upstairs, the parole board met to decide men's fate. Downstairs, inmates and visitors gathered under the watchful eyes of a correctional officer. A long table separated inmates from their visitors. A man could hold his wife's hands across the table. A single parting kiss and embrace were the only other forms of touch allowed.

Inmates tended lawns and planted flowers within the prison walls. But the grass was to look at, not to sit on. A man could be "tagged"— given a disciplinary infraction report—for walking on the grass. At night, the shadows of the poorly lit facility competed with each other in overlapping shades of black.

Inside the wings where the inmates lived was a world of gray on gray. The outer walls of the larger wings were a bare concrete shell punctuated by tall, narrow bays of windows with hundreds of panes of glass. Inside, long rows of cells with steel bars and sliding doors were stacked back-to-back, three stories high. A row of cells was called a "tier," or a "deck."

Inside Eight Wing

Two back-to-back tiers made a floor: A and B on the first floor, C and D on the second, E and F on the third. Catwalks in front of the cells provided access to the upper tiers. From the front of the cells to the outer wall was a tall fifteen-foot-wide void running the length of the wing.

At the north end of the long cell house, a large gang shower, with eighteen shower heads suspended from three long metal pipes, filled a tiled room. At the opposite end of the wing, guard stations with their lever boxes for opening and closing cell doors stood at the head of each tier. Metal stairs led to a single door letting inmates in and out of the wing. The first-floor officer controlled the telephone that was the only means of communication with the rest of the prison.

When the sun went down, an officer couldn't see the far end of the tier for want of light. In the morning the stale breath and body odors of four hundred men filled the open space. At the top of the big cell houses the summer temperature could reach 120 degrees or more.

Convicts called their cell their "house." At Walla Walla the largest of these were ten by twelve feet. Twin bunk beds lined the two side walls.

A small sink and lidless toilet were bolted to the back wall. The open bars of the remaining side let in all the noise and smells. Up to four men slept, snored, dressed, and shared the toilet here. There was no room for modesty in a four-man cell.

For many, the best "houses" were the tiny one-man cells in Four and Five Wing. Although each cell was less than fifty square feet, at least you lived alone.

Large or small, the cells shared the anonymity of similarity. Few decorations or special touches distinguished one cell from another. The walls were bare. Everything visible, except perhaps a small family photo, was issued by the state. All personal property, limited to a short list of permitted items, fit within a lock box assigned to each man. Every inmate was expected to make his bed each morning. If a cell wasn't up to standard, an officer ordered the men to make it clean and tidy. Failure to obey an order could land them in the hole.

Crews of inmate workers swept the floors, wiped down the rails, collected and distributed laundry, emptied the garbage, and kept the showers clean. In the 1960s the floors were polished to a gleaming shine, the warden's desktop was like a mirror, and the entire institution was spotless.

Like the cell houses, other buildings were similarly unadorned. Three times a day, two chow halls, with their metal tables and chairs bolted to the floor, fed hundreds of hungry men self-segregated in their various cliques. The tiled floors and hard concrete walls echoed with the sounds of talk and clatter of dishes and metal trays.

Run-down and poorly ventilated, the gym and auditorium helped the inmates pass the time and engage the body and mind.

The bright spot—and everything was relative here—was the education building. Its classrooms could almost pass for normal—as good an environment as any well-used school.

Another benefit for the men who attended class: the teachers were often women. Unless an inmate was confined to the hospital and saw a female nurse, or was lucky and had a visitor, the school was the only place where a woman might be seen. In the 1960s the penitentiary was a world of men.

Chapter 2

THE MEN

ROM A DISTANCE, all the inmates looked the same. Each man wore state-issued jeans, a blue work shirt, and in cold weather, a denim jacket and watch cap. Two sets of clothes and three pairs of socks were issued to each new arrival. Except for the socks, every article of clothing had the inmate's number stenciled on it. Personal clothing was not allowed. Shirts were tucked in, hair cut to regulation length, beards prohibited. In the prison an inmate was known by his number.

The men who called the prison "home" lived in a self-regulated world, a world designed to minimize conflict and smooth the passage of time. The prison's natural leaders—those long-term convicts who had proved themselves through the years—valued calm and order. Walla Walla was for doing time and getting on. A shared set of unwritten rules, the convict code, defined the inmate culture. One of the inmate leaders, who later became a successful businessman and motivational speaker after finally making it on the outside, explained:

> The do's and don'ts that [made] up the convict code [were] clear, and violators [were] subject to instant retaliation by their peers. You don't snitch to the Man, you don't steal from your brother, you don't talk to the Man except on business, you don't prey on the "good convicts," you support opposition to the Man even if it's insane, you don't talk to snitches or child molesters, you don't offend or mistreat women visitors. [1]

Under the convict code, a man could shower and leave his smokes unguarded on top of his well-made bed. His radio, his comb, all his worldly possessions were safe in the prison of the 1960s. There was honor among the thieves.

To the inmates, the correctional officers were "bulls." From a distance, the bulls, like the inmates, all looked alike. Each officer wore his gray blazer unbuttoned over a freshly pressed white shirt and narrow black tie. Matching trousers were creased, black shoes polished to a high shine. An eight-pointed police hat with visor and badge completed the uniform. Like the inmates, all officers had regulation haircuts and clean-shaven faces.

The bulls carried nothing but a whistle and a set of keys—no weapons, no handcuffs, not even a radio. In most situations the officers were outnumbered by at least a hundred to one. They were able to do their jobs only because of a symbiotic relationship between their task of maintaining order and the values of the convict code.

Of course, conflict did occur. The officers could dole out punishment that by today's standards was unquestionably cruel and unusual. An "adjustment committee" frequently banished inmates to strip cells, confining them naked without light or companionship. It may be an exaggeration, but one man was said to have spent eleven years there. Officers administered drugs to control those inmates too difficult to manage in any other way. One former correctional officer explained, "They would bring gallons of Thorazine from the hospital. They used to mix it with the food. They would give them a shot in their gravy, in their coffee, to the point where they would kind of go into a trance and almost freeze in place."[2] Not many received this treatment, but certainly more than medically indicated and none with informed consent. Guards used fire hoses to control groups of unruly inmates. The language of the officers (some of them at least) defined those who were caged as beasts.

While any number of transgressions could send a man to the hole, discipline in the wings might be more direct. A seasoned sergeant who ran a wing would help a new young officer. "I've got a problem with so-and-so," the new recruit might say. The sergeant would ask, "Can you whip him?" If the recruit answered yes, the sergeant replied, "Then you haven't got a problem." If the answer was no, the response was "Hold my keys." The sergeant briefly disappeared, and the problem went away. Even this approach, undeniably rough from today's comfortable vantage, was well within the rules of the day: it was bare fists one-on-one, and either man could lose.

Despite such practices, direct brutality, at least by the definition of the day, was probably rare. Not only rules, but also honor, drew the line: it was cowardly to strike a shackled man.

If the men tended to look alike, blue on one side, gray on the other, so too did the days. There was a predictable regularity in the interactions of the keepers and the kept. Every morning the day shift officers arrived at each wing a little before six o'clock. They unlocked the wing door and relieved the single officer who had been locked in all night without a key with as many as four hundred sleeping inmates. In the larger wings, if it was a weekday, the day shift consisted of a sergeant and two correctional officers—one man per floor. If it was the weekend, the sergeant's day off, or someone's meal break, two officers ran the unit. When this happened, one officer manned the telephone and covered the front door, the two tiers on the first floor, and the doors to the shower, laundry room, barbershop, and janitor's closet. The second officer covered the tiers on the top two floors. To open and close cell doors on the upper tiers, the officer moved from one side of the wing to the other and up and down the stairs.

When the day shift took over, the first order of business was to count the inmates. With the inmates locked in their cells, two officers walked one side of the top floor, preprinted notepads in hand, and wrote down the number of inmates in each cell. As they walked, each inmate stood at the front of the cell, at least one hand clasping a bar. At the end of the tier, the officers added up the number of inmates recorded on their separate notepads. If the numbers agreed, the process was repeated for the other side of the floor and the other floors of the cellblock. When finished, the sergeant or one of the officers called Central Control and reported the count for the unit. The same process was conducted simultaneously throughout the prison, including in the kitchen where inmate workers were cooking the meal and preparing the serving line. If the count cleared—that is, added up to the expected number—the prison day began. If the count didn't clear, no one moved until the discrepancy was resolved. The whole process took about an hour. Count occurred three times a day.

After count cleared, and when the kitchen was ready, an officer in the chow hall telephoned the wings in a preset order and told the unit officer how many inmates to send—usually two tiers at a time. The wing officer called "Chow" and pulled a special lever in the lock box to simultaneously unlock the seventeen cells on one tier. If two tiers were called, the officer repeated the operation for the other side of the wing. With the clang of steel on steel, the inmates manually slid their cell doors open, exited the unit, then moved as a group to the chow hall under the watchful eyes of the tower officers, taking care to stay on the pavement and keep off the grass.

After the last inmate left the building, the outside door was locked. An officer closed the cell doors by going to each lock box and turning a small wheel with a flip-down handle. As the wheel turned, a long steel screw spun around in a metal chase above the cell doors. Gears at the top of each door engaged the spinning screw, and seventeen doors slid slowly closed until they collided with their locks and frames, like seventeen blacksmiths striking steel with hammers.

This process was repeated until the entire institution was fed, which took about an hour and a half. When an inmate finished eating, he could go to his prison job, return to his cell, or go to the Big Yard or other recreation area.

An officer racking doors

The rest of the day was similarly structured. Every morning the "sock man" came down the tier. This was an inmate who swapped out clean socks for dirty socks hung over the bars at the front of each cell. Once a week, a "sweeper" picked up bags of dirty clothes and carried them to large hampers on the ground floor for transport to the laundry. On another day, the sweeper gathered bed linens and towels. Movement in and out of the wing occurred once an hour, on the hour. There were call-outs for the pill line, school, visiting, work, and various appointments.

It was a decades-old system designed to instill dependence. Officers and convicts alike called this mode of operating "super custody."

In his lilting Irish accent, the prison's Catholic priest described the days of super custody. "Any little bit of responsibility [the inmate] might have possessed—we took it away from him," he said. "We'll tell you when to get up. We'll tell you when to go to chow. We'll tell you whether you can wear your shirt inside or outside your pants. We'll tell you the length you can cut your hair. We'll tell you when to shave. We'll tell you when to breathe almost."[3]

For many inmates, this regimented lifestyle had its comforts. "The old system was beautiful for doing time," said one inmate. "You didn't have to think about nothing. Everything was provided for you. Every decision was made....You could float along for months and months and never have to think at all."[4]

Chapter 3

THE WARDEN

THROUGHOUT THE 1960s, at prisons across the country, the warden made the rules. He was also the policeman, prosecutor, judge, jury, and executioner. His reach extended to convicts and staff alike. Such was B. J. Rhay. Variously known as Bob, Bobby, B. J., warden, superintendent, and Mr. Rhay, Warden Rhay had less kindly names as well. But these were never mentioned to his face. At least, not at first. For most of his twenty years as superintendent, he was King of the Hill. And in the first fourteen years, he had enjoyed the predictable monotony of each prison day.

As warden, Rhay could order an inmate be taken to segregation and—in his words—be "buried so deep they'd have to pipe sunshine to him."[5] If an officer offended, two others escorted him to the gate. At Walla Walla, the final words in an officer's career might be those of Warden Rhay: "Get off my hill."

If such incidents conjure a picture of a fearsome man, that would not be B. J. Rhay. A slender six-footer, Rhay could fill a room—occasionally through his fine, hot temper, but more often through charisma and a smile. Confident, direct, or devious as suited his needs, he could toss off sound bites long before that phrase had meaning. Standing there in his well-pressed suit, he looked taller than he really was. If he was your friend, he was very much your friend. And like a politician, Rhay had many friends.

Rhay never shrank from power. He would walk the breezeways and yards alone and chat with the convicts he met. Those in disfavor could feel his sting for years. Once he shot two men as they tried to escape. But despite his toughness, Rhay preferred the carrot to the stick. While the twentieth-century dungeon known as the hole played its part, small freedoms (and larger ones, too) could buy a lot when convicts had so little.

Rhay's control of staff was similarly firm. Even though a citizen's initiative created a civil service personnel system that did away with the worst abuses of the 1950s, staff had few protections. Rhay promoted and protected his friends, and he discouraged or discharged his foes. Some say that when he was at his height, Rhay was a better con than the craftiest convict who ever walked the breezeway. He was master of the game.

In his private life, Rhay grazed his quarter horses in the shadow of the prison wall and raced them at the county fair. He raised his seven daughters in the warden's house where years before, in front of the hearth, he had married a previous warden's daughter. He rubbed elbows with the wealthy farmers and hobnobbed with the town elite.

A Walla Walla native, Rhay was a hero before he was a warden. Leaving college in 1941, he trained as a fighter pilot, then saw action in World War II on seventy-seven missions over North Africa, the Asian Pacific, and Europe. "Three Thunderbolts and a Mustang, that's what I flew," he said.[6] In combat he used a trick he called a "lazy yaw." Nonchalantly drifting to one side or the other, he'd lull the enemy into carelessness, pretending not to notice. Then he'd strike. He returned to Walla Walla in '45, a decorated ace with seven kills. For thirty years a weekend warrior, he was current through the F-100, the Air Force's first jet fighter to reach supersonic speed.

After the war, Rhay got a job at the Hill. He worked as a tower officer, then left to complete his war-interrupted studies at Whitman College. His job prospects brightened with his degree in sociology—not to mention his marriage to the warden's daughter. He returned to the Hill and remained there until his father-in-law, thanks to a change in the occupant of the governor's mansion, joined the ranks of the unemployed. Rhay too was dismissed, only to resurface in New York as an investigator for Erle Stanley Gardner's *Court of Last Resort*, a 1950s radio and TV show dramatizing cases of people wrongly accused or unjustly convicted.[7] Heady stuff for a small-town boy.

Rhay returned to Walla Walla—and to the penitentiary—in 1954, this time for good. After starting a reception/guidance unit at the pen, he was promoted to associate superintendent for treatment and then to superintendent. Rhay prided himself on being the first civil service superintendent in the state of Washington. But his party affiliation—conservative Democrat—must have pleased Governor Albert Rosellini, also a Democrat.

Rhay had friends both high and low. This circle of friends grew and strengthened until he became a formidable political force in his own right. The counties of sparsely populated eastern Washington have always had to present a united front to accomplish anything in a state legislature dominated by Seattle and urban Puget Sound. It was with politicians from his native southeast Washington that Rhay was most allied. He hunted and fished with his legislative friends. He entertained them and was entertained by them. The benefits of these relationships were all the greater for the genuine affection and admiration that flowed in both directions. These friendships and loyalties sustained Rhay long after his crown had slipped in the eyes of most citizens of the state.

In the 1960s Rhay could dispense favors for information or compliance, and reserve his temper for times that really mattered. The convict culture supported the warden's style. Rhay's control of the inmates was measured by his control of a few of their leaders. If the right six to ten men were on his side, Rhay could manage eighteen hundred convicts.

Of course Rhay was not alone. Two associate superintendents—one for custody and one for treatment—did much of the day-to-day work. His chief of custody managed the officers and put the fear of God into the inmate population. His associate for treatment managed all but a handful of the remaining staff and did the nitty-gritty administrative work. Rhay was the public face of the penitentiary and the "good cop" as he walked the breezeways.

William P. Macklin was chief of custody for most of Rhay's early years. Runner-up for the superintendent position that Rhay won, Macklin was a hard-line, old-guard disciplinarian. If Rhay was the carrot, Macklin was the stick. As Macklin's one-time clerk put it, "He ran the penitentiary with an iron fist....He'd walk in the front door in the morning and the inmates would run one way and the staff would run the other."[8] Every day Macklin ran his snitch line. He'd call for a group of inmates, including his regular informants and others selected as cover to hide the identity of those who snitched. One by one they'd come to see him. To those who were not his favored informants, he might say, "Why do you think I've asked you here? What do you think you've done wrong?" Sometimes Macklin knew. Sometimes he fished. Using the information he gathered from his snitches, Macklin would reel in a new batch of troublemakers each evening and lock them up in segregation.

Like a good caricature, one inmate's story paints a telling, if not wholly accurate, picture of the chief of custody. According to the inmate, the "Macklin barometer" was his cigar. "If his cigar was in the left side of his mouth, he was listening. If it was dead center, he was still listening, but very doubtful. If it was shifting from one side to the other, the prisoner was lying and Macklin was madder than hell about it. And if Macklin bit the thing, the con was dead in the water!"[9] Less colorful, but presumably closer to the truth, were Macklin's frequent last words at the disciplinary hearings he chaired: "Ten days isolation, twenty days seg."

Until staff proved themselves, Macklin intimidated them as well. According to one longtime penitentiary employee, if Macklin asked to see you, "that was a command performance. Bill Macklin was *the man.* Everybody just kind of knew that."[10] Another officer implied that Macklin may have intimidated even Rhay. This officer overheard Macklin say to the superintendent, "You take care of the politicians. Leave my prison alone."[11]

Behind the scenes and in the backup role was Bob Freeman, the associate superintendent for treatment during most of Rhay's years. Self-effacing, ever loyal, Freeman played his quiet part. He was perhaps the smartest man at the Hill. It was Freeman who built the well-regarded education program. He wrote the memos and oiled the machine when the superintendent was otherwise engaged. It was Freeman who authored the journal articles and served on national committees. Thoughtful and cool, Freeman could keep a steady head when others, including Rhay, were getting hot.

In the 1960s these three—Rhay, Macklin, and Freeman—had the bases covered. They were as politically correct as you could be in the last days of the absolute warden. Like a stool with three legs, this team was strong in its parts. And the ground beneath their feet—the prison and the culture it contained—seemed as fixed as the broad shade trees that comforted the quiet town of Walla Walla in its hot and lazy summers.

Chapter 4

THE REFORMERS

THREE HUNDRED MILES to the west of Walla Walla—three-sixty if the weather has closed the pass—is Olympia, capital of Washington. Here, at the foot of Puget Sound, the governor makes his home, the agencies keep their offices, the legislature comes and goes. Even today, with airplane service and better freeways, a long day's journey is needed to put Olympia and Walla Walla people face-to-face.

In the 1960s, adult corrections was a division within the Department of Institutions. The entire division consisted of three major institutions plus a couple of forest camps. Of the three, Walla Walla was the largest and most remote. The division had a director, two assistants, and a secretary. In theory, they oversaw it all. But with such a small staff, the other meaning of oversight was probably closer to the mark.

Daniel J. Evans was governor of the state for three consecutive terms. When he first took office in 1965, civil service prevented the wholesale replacement of state employees, a patronage practice that earlier governors had usually followed after election. But civil service never protected agency heads—members of the governor's cabinet—so Evans would have been within his rights to replace all of them. Yet Evans retained the best of his predecessor's men. Foremost among them was Garrett Heyns, director of the Department of Institutions.

By all accounts, Heyns was an imposing, effective leader. Formidable in authority and intellect, Heyns enjoyed the advantages that sometimes come with age. Already in his seventies when Evans became governor, Heyns was making his mark on his final career. As Heyns's successor put it, "He used to go to legislative committee meetings and some criticism would be made. He would sit back...in his grandfatherly way and... giving them full credit for whatever they were objecting to, in a matter of a few words or sentences, completely destroy any dissident reaction they might have....They didn't challenge what he had to say."[12]

Early in his tenure, Heyns recruited psychiatrist William R. Conte to head the department's Division of Mental Health. In his years in this capacity, Conte led the first great wave of deinstitutionalization of the state's mental health facilities, greatly reducing the number of patients treated there. With increased services and decreased populations, for the first time ever, all three of the state's mental hospitals were accredited at the same time. As populations fell, one entire institution was closed. Caseloads at the other two shrank to a fraction of their former thousands. Heyns gave Conte full credit for these successes. The millions of dollars saved brought attention and admiration from legislators and the governor.

Before long, the bright and energetic Conte, thirty years Heyns's junior, was being groomed to succeed the older man. The two got on well. "Kindred spirits" was the phrase Conte used.

As director, Heyns was responsible for all Department of Institutions programs. But his greatest interest, due to his twenty years of experience in adult corrections, was everything relating to prisons. Heyns made sure that Conte's grooming included guidance on prison issues. To Heyns's teaching, Conte brought his own understanding of human behavior. In Conte's words, "What I learned from Heyns was that the prison setting had the potential for being a social psychiatric setting."[13]

The concepts of social psychiatry and rehabilitation had deep roots for Conte. He had come of age professionally prior to the advent of psychotropic medications, during a time when many psychiatric conditions were considered untreatable. But Conte's experience showed him otherwise. In his years at Colorado state hospitals, in local community clinics, and in his private practice, Conte saw patients improve despite what the textbooks said.

"I was at first unbelieving," said Conte, "because I had learned that these people don't change. [But] I had seen too many examples of people who did. In the overall, I had to believe that [the prison population] was a population that could be reached. I was also convinced that it needed a social psychiatric approach—which to me meant use anybody that you can find, anywhere, who has the capacity and the willingness to give something of himself in the way of communication to an individual, and you can help him."[14]

Conte was not alone in his belief that criminal behavior was a treatable condition. This national movement, known as "the medical model," was enshrined in part in the 1967 report by the President's Commission on Law Enforcement and Administration of Justice, *The Challenge of Crime in a Free Society*. With proper diagnosis and appropriate intervention, criminals could be relieved of their symptoms and society rid of the consequences of criminal behavior.

Governor Evans, too, dreamed this heady dream. Some of his speeches included quotations from Dr. Karl Menninger's *The Crime of Punishment*, an influential book of the day. Evans knew for certain that society could create better outcomes for the men and women sentenced to prison. From the early days of his first administration, he was dedicated to prison reform. In psychiatrist William Conte he had just the man for the job.

State law, long ignored, echoed the same refrain. "Garrett Heyns," said Conte, "was probably the first to point out to me that if one reads the law in most states...you will find reference after reference after reference to rehabilitation as the goal."[15] This was certainly true in Washington State. These statutes, a product of a far earlier era, gave impetus to a new period of reform.

These were halcyon days in Washington State. Booming economic times swelled the state's coffers. In the mental health field, psychotropic drugs made the word "incurable" seem obsolete. Even the unrest in the streets and campuses inspired Evans and his reform-minded cabinet. Optimism prevailed. "Government was fun then," said Evans.[16] Anything seemed possible. But Garrett Heyns, in his decades of experience, had seen the tide turn a number of times. He counseled the younger Conte, "You know, you and I had better take advantage of the situation as it is, because never again will administrators have the freedom that we have now."[17]

When Garrett Heyns retired, Evans appointed Dr. William R. Conte director of the Department of Institutions. Conte set out to practice what he preached and to take advantage of the situation as it was.

As the 1960s drew to a close, the situation in Walla Walla was an entrenched culture resistant to change. Conte decided he would challenge Rhay to think in new ways about how prisons could be managed.

And soon the tumult in the streets—the demonstrations and the riots, the challenges to authority, the widening use of drugs—would find its way behind the walls. The King of the Hill was about to lose his throne.

PART 2
CHANGES
1970–1973

By the summer of 1971 unprecedented events began to transform the penitentiary. *Courtesy Jim Hartford.*

Chapter 5

THE EDUCATION OF BOBBY RHAY

To BILL CONTE the strategy was clear: while much had to be done elsewhere, the road to prison reform led through B. J. Rhay. In the small world that was adult corrections in Washington, Rhay was the natural leader. Not only was he senior warden, he was strong and independent. Well entrenched before Conte became director, he was beholden to no one in the current administration. Where Rhay went, the others would follow.

This strategy was not without hope; Rhay had implemented reforms before. Well educated by corrections standards of the day, he'd worked to expand programs and treatment even before he became warden. With Bob Freeman, his associate superintendent for treatment, at his side, he implemented real gains in prisoner education and other programs in the 1960s. But implementing his own ideas was one thing; following the lead of someone else was another matter. How would Rhay react to ideas proposed by Conte, a man who, in Rhay's words, had "never walked the line"?[1]

Conte recalled an all-night conversation with Bob Rhay in November 1969 as a pivotal event. Conte was at the penitentiary part of the day, but felt the real business was his lengthy one-on-one with Rhay beginning in the evening and ending as the sun brightened the morning sky. Conte described the content of their conversation in a letter some years later:

> One thing stands out in my mind very clearly. It was my prediction that something horrible could occur in Walla Walla…and that I thought it was within our power to prevent it. That prevention, of course, rested on our developing humane treatment.
>
> Rhay may have been kidding me, but by the time our night was over, I had the feeling that he was understanding what I was saying and that he

was becoming enthusiastic. Here, for the first time, someone had come to his territory with new ideas and they were challenging.…At that point I asked him if he would consider going on a trip to Europe and visiting the leading correctional facilities there.…He was immediately intrigued.… When we parted company at the door…we had a long handshake and I recall that he held my elbow with his left hand.…I felt that I had conquered my greatest challenge. [2]

Private funding was secured from two Seattle foundations, and Rhay began his unusual European tour in April 1970. Conte was pleased. In his words, the education of Bobby Rhay "was exclusively the aim of the trip—to open his eyes and let him see that there was another way of doing things."[3]

Years later, at his home in Walla Walla, Rhay didn't remember this all-nighter with Conte. But in his written report about his European tour, he referred to a private conversation with Conte in the fall of 1969 as the origin of the tour idea.[4] This report, written shortly after his return, is as good a look at what Rhay learned as we can get.

"It was agreed in the formative phase of this project that the basic purpose of the tour would be to study the newest ideas and practices in the correctional field," Rhay wrote. To this end, the tour took him to England, France, Holland, Denmark, Norway, and Sweden. "My real search for innovation and new ideas began in [Denmark and Holland]. There I found…many interesting ideas being applied to the corrections process."[5]

Rhay wrote enthusiastically—perhaps enviously—of the small size of the European institutions he saw. "Our large-size prisons create custodial problems while the small-size European institutions minimize custodial problems," he wrote. The small size also "lends itself…to more effective treatment." He was struck by the relatively short sentences imposed for most offenses, and noted in his conclusion that "most of the institutions visited were more comparable to our city and county jails than [to] our state or federal institutions." These differences, significant as they were, didn't seem to affect the ideas about prison reform that Conte was contemplating.

Among the new ideas that Rhay encountered were lack of censorship of inmate mail; policies that allowed visitors to freely meet with inmates, not only in a visiting room but at their prison jobs or in their cells; weekend furloughs where "no one cared if [prisoners] stopped at the local pub, visited their families, or saw their girlfriends"; decriminalization of certain crimes; and what Rhay called "the democratization process." The latter was a leveling of differences between prisoners and officers that brought prisoners, in a limited way, into the day-to-day decisions of how the institution was run. In the eyes of a typical American warden in 1970, these practices were not only new, but almost unimaginable.

While Rhay would eventually back away from advocacy of virtually all the reforms later unleashed, his words were less equivocal following his return in the summer of 1970. "Undoubtedly the most impressive ideas abroad in the field of crime and punishment in Western Europe today are movements toward decriminalization and democratization," he wrote. "If progress continues to be made in these two areas, corrections will move forward to a new and humane level of achievement." Rhay concluded by stating that "Holland has the most advanced corrections program because of their emphasis on personal freedom, human dignity and individual worth."[6]

Conte was pleased. After talking with Rhay when he first returned, "I called [one of the donors who supported the trip] and said, 'You may never have invested three thousand dollars that has such far-reaching consequences as this trip.'" According to Conte, the donor replied, "Well, that's good. I haven't done too well in my business lately. It's nice to know that something's working out."[7]

Conte continued to see that things worked out. Rhay's education in correctional reform continued, now in concert with other wardens and key correctional staff at a series of internal adult corrections leadership conferences in the summer and fall of 1970. Ideas near and dear to Conte, now at least described and understood by Bobby Rhay, were included in the agendas of these conferences. The end of mail censorship, providing telephones for prisoners to use, and development of "resident government" all appear on the programs and meeting minutes from these conferences.[8]

Sometime during these same months, Rhay began a program at the penitentiary called "Pride in Culture." Perhaps he was moved by

ideas he encountered on his European tour, including those promoting communication between inmates and the administration. Whatever the cause, Rhay began to meet once or twice a week with groups
of minority inmates—blacks, Chicanos,[9] and Native Americans—along
with minority representatives from the community. In Rhay's mind, the
purpose of these meetings was to promote awareness of the cultural history of each group. He called it "a history teaching program."[10] Rhay
also viewed these meetings as a personal opportunity to learn about civil
rights and issues important to many of the inmates in his prison.[11]

For the minority groups in the prison, meeting with the superintendent was an opportunity to air their grievances. This was especially true
for African Americans. Prior to the Pride in Culture program, attempts
by black inmates to discuss issues within the institution had resulted in
disciplinary infractions for "unlawful assembly," trips to the hole, and
an order by associate superintendent Macklin "not to ever meet again."[12]

Rhay may have learned from the Pride in Culture meetings, but his
concept that it was a history teaching program was never realized. The
minority groups began to organize. The blacks initially called their organization the United Front. Later they called it the Black Prisoners Forum
Unlimited, or B.P.F.U. The Native Americans became the Confederated
Indian Tribes (CIT), and the Chicanos became United Chicanos (UC).

This was new. Until Pride in Culture, the only recognized organizations in the penitentiary were sports teams and benign groups like
the Junior Chamber of Commerce, Jaycees, and Toastmasters. Now, the
organizations that grew out of Pride in Culture were based on race and
ethnicity at a time when racial consciousness in the United States was
increasingly politicized and radical. These were no longer the passive-
resistance days of the early civil rights movement; these were the days
of the Black Panthers, the United Farm Workers, and an increasingly
assertive group representing Native Americans, the American Indian
Movement.

On both sides of the bars, the stage was set to move from talk to
action.

Chapter 6

SUPERAGENCY

A<small>T APPROXIMATELY THE SAME TIME</small> B. J. Rhay left for his tour of prisons in Europe, the Washington State legislature enacted into law the most ambitious reorganization of social services in the state's history, the creation of the Department of Social and Health Services (DSHS).

The 128-point type on the front page of the March 1970 edition of the *Washington Public Employee* left no doubt that organized labor was enthusiastic about what the legislature had just done. The headline crowed, "41ST LEGISLATURE...IT WAS GREAT." A feature article in the paper explained the reasons for labor's enthusiasm. First, twelve thousand state employees, who formerly worked for five separate agencies, were now organized in a single superagency under one agency head (the Secretary of DSHS), one office of human resources, and one personnel director. Organized labor understood the statewide implications of this consolidation of power: hiring and firing would become more standardized and bureaucratic, and their members would be better protected from arbitrary decisions.

The implications at the local level were perhaps more profound. Before the creation of DSHS, authority to hire and fire was widely dispersed. Bob Rhay, along with other institution heads, had long been responsible for appointing, promoting, disciplining, and firing employees. Although the unbridled power of wardens and others was somewhat curtailed by a citizens' initiative in 1960, it was unusual for personnel matters to be elevated to the attention of Olympia. With the creation of DSHS and centralization of personnel matters, no longer would "Get off my hill" suffice as a way to fire someone. Friends and relatives could no longer be hired or promoted unless Olympia gave the okay. In one fell swoop, some of the most effective tools Rhay had for controlling and managing employees were gone.

The second reason organized labor was enthusiastic had to do with another provision in the statute that created DSHS. Prior law required bargaining units to be established at each institution and contract negotiations to be conducted locally. Rhay and his associate superintendents bargained with a small local union and developed a contract unique to the penitentiary. In an amendment to the law requested by the Washington Federation of State Employees, the union obtained the right to establish statewide bargaining units.[13] Not only was the relationship between Rhay and his employees suddenly altered, so too was the relationship between Rhay and the union.

Conte was concerned. Before the legislature finished its deliberations, he wrote to the governor's staff attorney and argued that

> placing one person [i.e. the secretary of DSHS] as appointing authority over one-half of the state employees…makes every appointment subject to attack by political appointees and makes every issue a statewide issue for the union. As it stands now, literally thousands of personnel transactions are handled locally and their potential as political tools against the administration is greatly diluted. The proposed system makes it much easier for the Union to accomplish its mission and to bring all of its pressure to bear on the Governor.…[Furthermore,] although the authority would be delegated, every superintendent and every employee would know that every appointment and every issue could be decided at the top.…Union members could acquire an attitude of no respect for their institutional administration since the decision would be so easily reversed by pressure applied at the right place.[14]

Conte's letter to the governor's attorney had no effect.

The new superagency was written into law, but how the agency would operate was far from clear. Governor Evans had a vision of what he wanted, but DSHS was one of the first superagencies in the nation. "As I remember," said Evans, "we did not have much of anyplace else to look for advice and experience."[15] To help with the transition, six months were spent in planning and incremental implementation before the official inauguration of DSHS on January 1, 1971.

Evans appointed Sid Smith to be the first secretary of the new agency. Smith had worked in manpower planning and human relations at Boeing, was a lobbyist for the Association of Washington Industries, and served as director of the Department of Employment Security and director of the Department of Public Assistance for Evans. Smith asked Conte to be his deputy, and Conte accepted.

When asked whether he thought Conte wanted to be secretary, Smith replied, "I think I'm right in saying that every single director...[who] reported to the governor thought that they ought to be secretary. Conte and the others—the 'professionals,' so called—probably did not understand how a business person could come in there and possibly run a social service agency."[16]

Given the organizational structure of DSHS in the early years, a business person was probably the *only* one who could have run the agency. Instead of the usual vertical organization, where all the expertise needed to operate a function like adult corrections was hierarchically arranged within a division, the new superagency was divided into three primary areas: program development, management services, and service delivery.

Program development was responsible for working with the legislature, the federal government, and statewide advisory committees for every function within DSHS. Staff in this area helped propose legislation and write descriptions of the programs to be implemented. The management services area was responsible for administrative matters like budgeting, accounting, and facilities planning and maintenance. For purposes of service delivery, the state was divided into regions, each with its own administrator. People in service delivery were to take the program descriptions (written by program development) and the money (figured out by management services) and then implement the programs. As Smith put it, he'd say to the regional administrators, "Here are the programs all written down, here is the basis in law for them, here's your money. Now go deliver the darn thing."[17] At least, that was the theory.

In practice, people from different programs were lumped together into program development and told to report to bosses who did not necessarily know anything about any of the programs. Meanwhile, other people who had historically worked closely together were scattered about in service delivery or management services.

Dividing an agency into program development, management services, and service delivery might work in manufacturing, but it was totally foreign to the social service workers and others in the new super-agency. Governor Evans, who was trained as an engineer, and Sid Smith, who came from Boeing, may have understood it, but almost everyone else was confused. On the other hand, the immediate effect of creating the new superagency was negligible. A six-month transition preserved the operations of the old Department of Institutions while plans were put in place for the official inauguration of the Department of Social and Health Services.

Still in charge, Conte pressed for prison reform.

Chapter 7

THE FOUR REFORMS

THEY MAY NOT REMEMBER THE DATE, but those who were there remember what happened on November 18, 1970. On that day Bill Conte and others spoke at the Seattle Center at a lengthy press conference called a "Discussion in Depth." Rhay and Bob Freeman drove over from Walla Walla to hear it. After months of discussion and circulated drafts of proposals, four major changes in inmate rights were publicly announced. Rhay, in his inimitable style, recalled it this way: "Bang! Bang! Bang! Bang! You've got four reforms. Now implement them."[18]

It didn't happen quite that way. While prison staff may have been alarmed (and inmates delighted), Rhay and the other wardens had no reason to be surprised.

Abolition of strip cells, an end to mail censorship, phasing in telephone service for prisoners, and implementation of resident government—these were the four reforms. Each was discussed in a series of adult corrections leadership conferences in July and October, and each was the subject of memoranda sent to all wardens two weeks prior to the press conference. The paper trail shows drafts of these memoranda circulating among the wardens for several months prior to their formal issue on November 6, 1970.

The first memorandum said, in its entirety, "Effective immediately, all use of strip cells (quiet cells) in adult correctional institutions is discontinued."[19] A second memo outlined new regulations for inmate mail, including these statements: "All incoming mail will be opened. It will not be read....The purpose of opening the letters will be solely for the purpose of removing...contraband....No outgoing mail will be censored."[20] Two other memoranda provided rules for implementing telephone service for prisoners and identified ten "essential elements of resident government."[21]

The press conference at the Seattle Center was a public announcement of initiatives that had been in the works for months and had actually been implemented several weeks before. In fact, in a 1972 recorded interview, Rhay noted that penitentiary staff were meeting in his conference room to discuss how to implement an end to mail censorship at the very time Conte made the public announcement.[22] Rhay and the other wardens may not have liked what Conte said, but they couldn't have been surprised.

Conte began the news conference by reminding his audience of his philosophy of corrections—the subject of another "Discussion in Depth" the year before. "The time during which a client is assigned to a correctional endeavor must be held in sacred trust by the corrections staff," he said. "Everything done to, for, about, or with the individual must have as its primary purpose the successful return of that individual to productive and responsible citizenship."[23]

He followed this introduction with a description of the four reforms, then concluded by saying,

> When I announced the philosophy of corrections a year ago, I made the comment that a prison is the most unlikely treatment setting. I noted that it was isolated and isolating, and that it did not have all of the avenues of communication which were needed, and it did not have all of the services which were required. I address you this morning, almost a year later, with confidence that we have taken significant steps toward improving [the prison as a] treatment center. It becomes a bit more likely setting for effective treatment than it has ever been before.[24]

Conte acknowledged that the reforms brought many challenges and voiced trepidation about some of their possible consequences. In discussing an end to mail censorship, he said, "I think all of us in the administration of correctional programs recognize that this move is accompanied by certain risks." He noted that victims, among others, might receive mail from inmates. "I freely admit that this gives me a great deal of distress." With regard to telephones, Conte noted similar concerns: "I would be less than honest...if I did not admit some anxiety in this development," he said. "Not all individuals will respect this privilege and use it appropriately." But true to his training as a psychiatrist and his belief that a prison could be a "social psychiatric setting," Conte concluded that "when there is an inappropriate use of a privilege, it may become a useful topic in conversation in a counseling program, [and] hopefully that difficult experience may be used to…therapeutic advantage."[25]

Conte voiced no real concern over the potential risk of resident government. But while all the reforms had a rocky ride, none was bumpier than resident government at Walla Walla. Perhaps Conte was reassured by the list of "essential elements" for resident government, one of which stated, "It is understood that the final responsibility and authority for the operation of an institution is vested, by law, in the superintendent. He will have veto powers [over resident government decisions]."[26]

Donald Horowitz, Conte's senior assistant attorney general during the transition from the Department of Institutions to the Department of Social and Health Services, shared the podium with Conte that November day. Horowitz came to the job through connections he made when he clerked for the state supreme court after graduating from Yale Law School in the late '50s. One of the justices he knew told him the attorney general was looking for a lawyer interested in social issues to head up the legal services division for the new department. When DSHS secretary designate Sid Smith interviewed Horowitz, Smith told him he wanted a "do guy" instead of a "don't guy"; he wanted an activist who could figure out how to do things legally, not a lawyer who would tell them why things couldn't be done. It was just what Horowitz wanted, and he took the job.[27]

Horowitz must have been wearing his activist hat when he took the podium after Conte and declared, "Power to the people—resident government!"[28]

Rhay and Freeman returned to Walla Walla. Rhay recalled that when he got back, the officers were asking, "What power did I have before that I don't have now?" and the inmates were asking, "What power do I have now that I didn't have before?"[29] The inmates were the first to figure it out.

Chapter 8

THE CHRISTMAS STRIKE

FOLLOWING CONTE'S NOVEMBER announcements, staff were confused, and the inmates delighted. The latter pushed the envelope. In December 1970, less than a month after the "Discussion in Depth" press conference in Seattle, a group of penitentiary inmates left their prison jobs as janitors, kitchen workers, maintenance workers, and so forth, returned to their cells, and began a sit-down strike. Ostensibly it was about haircut rules and prohibition of beards. According to Warden Rhay, most of the other inmates joined the strike, and within an hour the prison was locked down. Rhay told the press that "the so-called shaving dispute has been underway for some time."[30]

It quickly became apparent that hair was not the only issue. Making full use of their newfound freedom to send mail without fear of censorship, several inmate leaders sent "Dear Friends" letters to various newspapers. The strike was not about haircuts, they wrote, but rather a peaceful demonstration about conditions at the prison. The grievances were many: indifferent medical care, unqualified parole board members, use of segregation and isolation as punishment, restrictions on inmates working on legal matters, lack of minority counselors, a "kangaroo court" for reviewing inmate infractions, restrictions on contact with visitors, de facto segregation of inmate housing and jobs, and poor communication with the administration.[31]

Back in Olympia, Bill Conte also received letters. "I don't know if you are aware of it, but to a great number of men in here you have become almost a hero," an inmate leader told him in a letter written several days before the strike.[32]

The inmate leader had been writing to Conte for several weeks. When an issue was raised, Conte would write back and note that such matters should be resolved locally. "Nothing in this letter should be construed as any lack of interest on my part in the subject of your petition,"

Conte wrote in one such reply. "However, we have established a chain of communications via the resident governmental process and I believe that for me to take on any study of [your issues] at this point is to circumvent the opportunity for adequate communications…in your institution."[33] Each time, the inmate would—either wishfully or craftily—interpret Conte's expression of interest as encouragement to continue to ask for help.

Conte received the inmates' list of grievances at the same time the newspapers did. In their cover letter, the inmates wrote, "Your immediate assistance in the form of a personal visit will mean a lot to all residents involved and concerned."[34]

Behind the scenes, Conte told Rhay to negotiate an end to the strike. "For God's sake, settle it before Christmas," is what Bob Freeman remembers Conte saying. Exact words aside, "that's entirely accurate," confirmed Conte many years later. "I had visions of the people from the First Methodist Church going to their bishop and saying, 'Can you imagine, on Christmas Day these people in prison have to be locked in their cells!'"[35] But Conte's wish to have it settled by Christmas went unanswered.

As the strike progressed, Conte was in frequent communication with Rhay. His notes from the time indicate a flurry of calls, telegrams, meetings, and letters. "I stand ready to help you in any way I can," he wrote the day the strike began. "I would be willing to come to Walla Walla and meet with staff on all the shifts if it would be supporting of you and them. You say the word and we (any of us) will be available to help."[36]

Two days later, the day before Christmas, Conte replied by teletype to the inmates' request for a visit. In a strategy that Conte says was reviewed and approved by the governor's chief of staff, he wrote, "Your invitation for me to meet with you coincides with a request Mr. Rhay made when he was in Olympia on December 17.…My present plans call for my coming to Walla Walla early in January and I have set a tentative date for January 8 in the hope conditions will be right for a constructive conference."

Conte cautioned the inmates that change would not occur overnight. "You must move quickly and in concert with Mr. Rhay to fully implement the resident government mechanism because it is *the* procedure which has been created to accomplish the necessary communications for decision making." Finally, he noted: "It is my hope that this letter may contribute to an early resolution of the protest and dead lock."[37] Privately, Conte told Rhay that if the strike was not settled by New Year's Day, "we would have to come over and settle it" for him.[38]

Rhay began to negotiate with the Inmate Advisory Council (a weak predecessor to the Resident Government Council that was to follow). After several days of talks, Rhay expressed optimism to the press that progress was being made. Agreement was reached on a number of issues, and ultimately the issue of haircuts and beards was referred to Don Horowitz for legal opinion. On New Year's Eve, a few hours before the deadline Conte had imposed, the inmates began to vote. One housing unit refused to participate until parts of the settlement agreement were broadcast over a local radio station. By nine thirty in the evening it was over. Voting 757 in favor to 233 against, the inmates agreed to shave their beards and end the ten-day-old strike.

The inmate population was jubilant. "The days of the old-fashioned riots are gone. We can get what we want—what we need and have coming—just by growing that goddamn hair!" proclaimed an article in the prison's underground newspaper, the *Bomb*.[39]

After the strike, Horowitz issued an informal legal opinion. In what can only be characterized as a creative interpretation of law, he concluded that inmates could sport beards and let their hair grow long. "I knew the answer [Conte] wanted," said Horowitz. "I was young. It was a little bit of show biz....I didn't mind being out front."[40]

Soon, the barbers at Walla Walla had less to do. In addition, inmates with funds or connections had items of personal clothing sent to them so they wouldn't have to dress like everyone else. The penitentiary was getting colorful.

Conte came to Walla Walla and met with the inmate leaders on January 8, 1971. In his statements to the press he said, "All the people I talked to were aware that my visit was not to make any changes or definitive decisions, because changes and decisions are the responsibility of the superintendent in collaboration with the inmate advisory council and the staff....I was here to listen and to make certain the population of the institution knew their concerns had been heard by me."[41]

Conte was always careful with his words. How his actions were interpreted by others was another matter. More than twenty years after the fact, Bob Freeman was still bitter. Speaking of the effect this meeting had on Superintendent Rhay, he fumed, "If you don't think that deballed him...." Now, according to Freeman, the inmates were saying, "Why should we deal with this administration when we can deal directly with Olympia?"[42] In fact, the Christmas strike was the first in a long series of occasions when Rhay's once unquestioned authority was challenged by inmate appeals to administrators and politicians in Olympia.

Chapter 9

New Beginnings

I N THE LIBERALIZED ENVIRONMENT at the penitentiary, tensions rose on both sides of the bars. One month into the new year of 1971, Calloway R. Dickens, a thirty-six-year-old black man convicted of grand larceny, was found dead in a pool of blood in the dressing room of the prison recreation building. He'd been stabbed twice, once directly over the heart. In a front-page article, the local paper told the man's history just like any other: born February 26, 1934, in Lake Charles, Louisiana; a member of the Baptist church; a meat cutter and construction worker for a number of years; survived by his wife, two daughters, two sons, his parents, and a brother.[43] Such detail became a nicety soon forgotten as the body count began to grow. Within four months, two more were killed.

"Oh God, we didn't know what a death was until this thing," groaned Rhay.[44] In fact, murder *was* a new thing at the penitentiary—at least on the scale that was to follow. At the toughest joint in the state, there had been three murders throughout the previous ten years.[45] By May 1971, that total had already been matched.

Correctional officers, contrary to their usual reticence, began to air their complaints in public. "There's no clear-cut defined policy," said one officer. "You see a guy [act] out with something and we don't know if we're supposed to tag him (write out a rule infraction memo) or not." Officers complained that superiors up the chain of command had rescinded tags for reasons unknown.[46]

"The prisoners act contemptuous towards us," said another officer. "There are more blow-ups in people's faces."[47]

More ominously, the inmates were becoming armed. The three dead men had all been stabbed by knives fashioned in the prison shops or smuggled in by means unknown. "No job or any money is worth the risk," said an officer who had recently quit. The newspaper said that at least thirty other men—more than 10 percent of the workforce—would resign if they could find another job.[48]

The means for inmates to fashion weapons had long been available. The metal and license plate shops had the materials and tools to craft effective sharp-edged blades. With few staff and many inmates, working unseen on some clandestine project or grabbing an object to use as a club was always easily done. And in the early '70s, before the advent of metal detectors, there were no special complications to moving metal contraband about. Besides, a baseball bat could be a club, a length of wire a garrote; a pointed piece of wood or plastic could do real damage.

The means had always been there—why now the will?

The old method of control, with its omniscient, heavy hand, was brutally efficient at managing convicts. Movement occurred by cell house tier. No one loitered or strayed from predefined paths. Groups met only if sanctioned by the associate superintendent for custody, Bill Macklin.

This was not control just for the sake of control: it limited opportunities to conspire and for groups to operate in unison; it kept those apart who needed separation; it defined every aspect of the day and, for those who followed the rules, made life easier for officers and inmates alike.

Then, in the weeks following the Christmas strike, the rules became less clear. Simple forms of disobedience, like not making a bed, led to bolder acts of defiance. Men congregated in groups of their own choosing. Inmate movement occurred in random ways. Unpopular jobs stopped being done. Orders were ignored.

As inmates tested the limits of their freedom, individuals and groups that had previously been separated by conscious design now occupied the same space. But like oil and water, they never really mixed. Blacks and other minorities encountered white supremacist inmates and more common forms of prejudice from officers and inmates alike. "Small bands of inmate predators began to roam the institution," wrote one former convict. "Beatings and robberies began to take on racial tones."[49] Blacks, who were outnumbered nearly four to one in the prison, "made a pact that, if one was attacked, others would come to his defense."[50]

According to an inmate leader, Macklin inserted himself into this mix. "This [was] Macklin's old game: grab a few guys, talk to them, and push them back out in the population. They stir a little trouble here and there and gradually [tension] builds up."[51] Whether Macklin actually played this game or not, the convicts believed he did. The convicts also believed that many in the prison administration—not just Macklin—needed a major incident to keep inmate self-government from happening.[52]

On March 21, 1971, a spark nearly ignited such an incident. As a television program ended on the stage in the prison auditorium, a young white inmate demanded that the elderly black man assigned to change the channels switch to a certain station. This was not the accepted protocol—the planned schedule could be modified only by a vote of those present. When the black man explained this, the white man struck him. According to an article that appeared in the prison newspaper nearly a year later, "Soon a melee ensued with members of both races becoming involved in a serious brawl." That night other racial conflicts were reported throughout the prison.[53]

The next morning, an inmate barber was waiting for customers when an acquaintance came to him and told him to "bring your stuff" to the auditorium. "Stuff," explained the barber, was "a knife or a chain or a baseball bat or whatever you got." The barber opened his drawer, took out two straight razors, put them in his pocket, and walked to the auditorium. Inside were hundreds of inmates, whites and blacks.[54] When everyone was inside, someone locked the auditorium doors. No one could leave.[55]

Gordy Graham, now (and for many decades) a successful businessman and motivational speaker, had a résumé at the time that included burglar, thief, forger, professional boxer, and longtime convict. In his book *The One-Eyed Man Is King*, written after he was released from prison, he recalled what happened.

> An arrangement was made between black and white leaders to meet in the prison auditorium and "settle" things once and for all. Four hundred inmates armed with knives, clubs, iron bars and baseball bats began to slowly assemble in the dingy, dimly lit auditorium.
>
> There was no attempt by the prison staff to stop the confrontation. They knew it was destined to be a bloody, brutal struggle between human beings, a senseless slaughter....It was first degree insanity....

As I looked around the auditorium I saw black guys who were good guys, friends of mine, who in a minute would be forced to kill me because I was white. I saw white guys who would attack blacks because they were black. Interspersed throughout both groups, I saw the predators, the instigators, men who were filled with hate, their faces gleaming with the sick excitement of the pending battle....

I walked slowly up the narrow stairs to the center of the stage at the front of the auditorium. My heart was pounding and I felt alone and vulnerable. I looked out over the mass of angry, hostile faces, black on one side, white on the other. I began. "What the hell are we doing? Here we are down in this stinking auditorium about to kill each other because we are black and white. The Man has locked the doors and said let the animals prove how responsible they are, that they can govern themselves. Boy, we're going to show them aren't we? Hell, I look around at guys who are my friends, guys who've escaped with me, drunk with me and raised hell with me and because I'm white, they're ready to stick a knife in me. What the hell's going on? This ain't no way to solve our problems." The men were beginning to look at each other. I could sense the tension easing.

A huge barrel-chested black guy, a friend even though we didn't spend a lot of time together, separated from the blacks and climbed the stairs to stand beside me. [Johnnie Harris] was one of the "baddest" dudes in the joint and a leader among the blacks. "Gordy's right, brothers. This ain't no solution. We're playing right into the Man's hands. They put us against each other and they just sit out there and laugh." Other leaders were beginning to join us on the stage. I knew that it was over.[56]

When the guards unlocked the auditorium doors, the men filed out and dumped their weapons into two fifty-five-gallon drums. "You could hear the clanging of metal as knives and steel bars were dumped in the barrels. When everyone was gone...[inmates] picked up the barrels and carried them to the guard's control booth and set them down without a word."[57]

The next day the inmates formed a Race Relations Committee. A month later, after its constitution was approved, the first Resident Government Council (RGC) was elected. The RGC's first two co-presidents were Johnnie Harris and Gordy Graham.

Rhay was surprised. What happened in the auditorium, he said, was "not nearly what we expected."[58] Presumably, he expected the "bloody, brutal struggle" that Graham feared as he climbed the stairs to the auditorium stage.

What was Rhay thinking? Was he was trying to sabotage the reforms, as many inmates believed? Or perhaps it was his idea of a test—a pass/fail test—a roll of the dice with lives at stake. That's what it sounded like when Rhay was interviewed some months later for the prison newspaper. "I think it would have been a mistake for the custody officers to have intervened [while the inmates were in the auditorium]," he said. "If they had, self-government would never have come about as this was something the inmates had to work out for themselves."[59] We'll never know for sure, but on that day, inmate self-government passed the test.

In the following months, when he was clearly sounding like one of the faithful, Rhay would refer to the incident in the auditorium as a turning point in his attitude toward resident government. "I guess that made a true believer out of me, real sudden like," he said.[60]

Chapter 10

RHAY TAKES CHARGE

O NCE RHAY GLIMPSED THE POSSIBILITY that inmate government might work, the pace of innovation quickened. In the aftermath of the incident in the auditorium and formation of the Race Relations Committee, a group of inmates founded Lifers with Hope, a self-help and community service group. While the new organization was open to anyone with a life sentence, its members mainly came from Eight Wing, which was overwhelmingly white.

In April, members of Lifers with Hope staked out a piece of prison real estate as their own. Initially called Lifers' Acre, and later Lifers' Park, it was a bit of grassy land between Seven and Eight Wing that the lifers spruced up. They built a brick-paved walkway, complete with an arched bridge over a small fish pond, and grew flowers and shrubs. Later they added picnic tables. With the cool, green grass and the flowers swaying in the

Lifers' Park—Eight Wing on the left, Seven Wing on the right

breeze, the men lounging on the lawn or playing cards at the picnic tables could almost forget the drab cellblocks and prison walls that enclosed the space. At the north end of the park, the lifers turned a former clothing room into a club room and office for their group.

The lifers had a nice grassy area all their own, but it was restricted to those with a life sentence. No one else had this luxury. Three weeks after the lifers dedicated their acre, and shortly after formation of the Resident Government Council, Rhay addressed the issue in a memo to his associate superintendent for custody, Bill Macklin:

> The grass area adjacent to the water tower is to be designated as a "People's Park area," an area in which the resident population will be free to lay [sic] on the grass in small groups. It is understood that the RGC will be responsible for policing up the area as well as establishing the ground rules under which this People's Park is being open to the resident population.[61]

A bit of grass to lie on—this doesn't seem like a big deal. But this area had been off-limits, and loitering or walking on the grass was against the rules. Furthermore, not everyone thought that letting the RGC be responsible for "policing up" the area was a good idea.

People's Park—Segregation and seg yard in foreground

A copy of Rhay's memo was sent anonymously to Governor Evans. Ominously, a postscript was added in a different typeface:

CONGRADULATIONS [sic] GOVENOR [sic],

WE CONVICTS ARE NOW IN CONTROL

The author of this postscript is not known. Copies of the memo may have been posted in a variety of places to inform staff of the change in policy, so the postscript could have come from anyone with access to a typewriter. The words imply it was from the convicts, but the hint of sarcasm makes that seem unlikely.

And the name—"People's Park"—did the inmates suggest it? Was Rhay aware of its origin? The original People's Park was a plot of land near the University of California campus in Berkeley. It was made famous in 1969 when Governor Ronald Reagan sent in the California Highway Patrol and Berkeley police to retake the vacant university property that had been appropriated by students and local activists. Thousands of protestors and hundreds of police clashed in a violent confrontation. Bricks were thrown and buckshot fired. One person died from the buckshot, another was blinded, and many others, including some police officers, were injured. After a few weeks, the government backed down in response to the public outcry over police tactics, and the land became a park. The "radicals" won a hard-fought battle in Berkeley. The convicts had an easier time in Walla Walla.

Soon, it wasn't just People's Park where the RGC was exercising control. In hand-written notes from a conversation Governor Evans had with the chairman of the parole board, Evans recorded some of the things he was told: the RGC had become the police agency inside the walls, the RGC leaders were very tough, and their enforcement activities had produced several broken jaws.[62]

Gordy Graham, serving the first of two six-month terms as co-president of the RGC, may have been referring to these broken jaws when he said, "Day and night we were called on to quell disturbances....We ran continuous sessions with potential troublemakers, and when all else failed, we would resort to physical force."[63]

While the inmates were creating and pressing for change, so too were Olympia and Bob Rhay. On July 1, 1971, a new law authorizing superintendents to approve inmate furloughs of up to thirty days went into effect. Not to be outdone by the furlough law, Rhay started his own program with the improbable name of "Take a Lifer to Dinner." Under Rhay's program, an inmate could be taken to dinner or lunch by a prison employee at a drive-in, a restaurant, or the employee's home. Several inmates told a newspaper reporter that one of their favorite outings was a scenic drive around the area.[64]

In July, the Confederated Indian Tribes (CIT) was the first of many inmate organizations to hold a banquet inside the prison walls to which guests from the outside were invited. The Walla Walla newspaper covered the event: "The prison's 'big yard,' which normally resounds to the hustle of the Whiteman's [sic] recreation, gave way to teepees and chants as inmate members of the institution's CIT, about a hundred other prisoners and 250 outside guests mingled freely in celebration.... 'Imagine seeing...two teepees set up inside the walls,' marveled Rhay."[65]

In addition to the RGC, Lifers with Hope, and the ethnic organizations, other groups were formed. There was an inmate newspaper, a chess club, a model airplane club, a veterans' group, a car club, a motorcycle club, Alcoholics Anonymous, a musicians' association, a writers' club, rock bands, church groups, and sports teams. The list could go on and on.

To Bill Macklin, a man who had devoted his professional career to building and maintaining a system of prison discipline and control, these developments were both galling and frightening. The parole board chair, who assured Evans he was not a Macklin fan, said Macklin was fearful of narcotics and guns coming into the institution. He characterized Macklin as honestly distressed, not playing games, and very outspoken about the changes that had occurred.[66]

Whether from stress or some other cause, Macklin took sick leave and spent most of the summer of 1971 nursing a serious ulcer.

Throughout the summer, additional inmate banquets were held, furloughs were granted, and lifers went on outings escorted by penitentiary correctional officers. The RGC leaders continued their enforcement activities, and the rash of inmate murders from the previous winter and spring came to an abrupt end.

When problems relating to uncensored mail arose that summer, the RGC publicly came to the aid of Rhay. "One man wrote a very obscene letter to a girl," an official in Olympia told a reporter. "Her parents sent it back to the superintendent and said, 'What are you guys doing? This ought to stop.'"[67] In another incident, a prison inmate sent a pair of prison-made moccasins to a friend in Seattle. The friend carefully opened the package, sewed drugs inside the sole of one of the moccasins, resealed the package, and told the post office to return it to sender. Pornography also came through the mail. "We had someone that was in for screwing...little boys," said associate superintendent for treatment Bob Freeman. "Someone sent him a whole mess of magazines—kiddy porn."[68]

To address these problems, the RGC worked with the administration to help write new regulations placing limited restrictions on incoming and outgoing mail.[69]

The RGC made the news again a few weeks later, when an inmate referendum was held. The inmates reportedly voted five to one in favor of banning drugs and gambling inside the penitentiary. Under the inmate plan, approved by Rhay, first-time violators would be seen by a peer counselor, and repeat violators would spend time in segregation. Rhay told a local newspaper reporter this was the kind of thing he had hoped might result from inmate self-government.[70]

In another remarkable initiative that summer, Rhay began having RGC representatives sit in on his staff meetings.

But the biggest surprise in the summer of 1971 was the abrupt resignation of William Conte. In his letter to the governor he simply said, "For professional reasons, the time has come for me to pursue other interests."[71] A decade later he wrote, "I was convinced that with the developments brought about through the reorganization of state government [and with] the basic control of institutions which the labor unions had acquired...I could not carry the program further."[72]

Conte was gone.

"My God!" recalled DSHS secretary Sid Smith. "Here we are—we've taken all this time and the man that was going to be number two just walks off. The governor threw his hands up. I threw my hands up.... What do we do?"[73]

What Smith did was get the dean of the school of social work at the University of Washington to take over the number two spot for six months. But this was just a stopgap measure and it did nothing to address the need for an experienced leader to advise Smith and the governor on matters dealing with adult corrections.

According to almost everyone, the real void in leadership in corrections was filled by Donald Horowitz, senior assistant attorney general for DSHS. It appears that the only one who disagrees with this assessment is Horowitz. "I suppose that I did what I could to influence policy," he said. But in his words, he was "suggesting" things, not "directing" them.[74]

Horowitz's modesty aside, others saw him as key. "In essence he was an unofficial director of [corrections]," said Smith. Smith's assistant secretary for service delivery during the first years of DSHS had similar recollections. "When I started having my initial exposure to the corrections system, the person doing the most talking about it, and [the person who exercised] the greatest lead with the legislature and a lot of the lead publicly, was Don."[75] Governor Evans himself says that Horowitz "played a much more activist role than you would expect any assistant AG to play in a situation of that kind. He was an active participant in the policy making of the department all the way along."[76]

For all his talents, Horowitz was no expert in corrections. For the next two years—until the arrival of a new deputy secretary for DSHS in August 1973—no one with the clout of top management in Olympia had any direct experience whatsoever working with prisons. For all practical purposes, Rhay was on his own.

Chapter 11

MAKING HISTORY

BILL CONTE WAS GONE, but the four reforms were still in place. Rhay wanted reassurance that what he was doing was what the governor wanted. "I went one-on-one with Evans," Rhay said. "I asked for an interview....I said, 'Governor, here's what's coming down. I want to know from you—[is the direction we're headed] really what you want?' He says, 'Bob, this is the future of corrections. This is what's got to happen in the system.' I said, 'Okay—but understand, here's what could happen.' Chapter and verse, I read it to him. But he said, 'No. This is what I want.' [He] complimented me in the process. He said, 'Without you, I don't think [reform] can happen.'"[77]

"That sounds like Bob Rhay," chuckled Evans as the transcript was read to him. "I think the embellishment would be identifying all of the [future] problems at that point....The details of the discussion I don't remember as well as he might...but I do remember him coming over. We were concerned," the governor said. "We were determined to go ahead. I'd made up my mind that [reform] was something that we ought to do. The question was just how best to get it done and make sure that those who had the responsibility for carrying it out would do so."[78]

Rhay went back to the prison and told his key staff he was going to push forward with reform. "I was kind of fired up....That's when I told them, 'Hey, this is gonna happen. This is what we're going to do.'"[79]

Bill Macklin had had enough. After coming back from sick leave toward the end of August, he resigned. But the cause of his resignation wasn't his health—it was his disgust with the changes at the prison. On Sunday, September 12, 1971, the *Walla Walla Union-Bulletin* printed a front-page article in which Macklin blasted conditions at the penitentiary. Despite what had been a generally peaceful summer, Macklin said, "the prison is now being run by inmates under threat of sit-down, burning, [and] hostages. It is impossible for me to work there and carry out the duties and responsibilities of my office with this type of program.... [The situation is] bound to lead to bloodshed before it's over."[80]

Timing is everything. The very next day, around the world, stark headlines read THIRTY-SEVEN DEAD AT ATTICA.[81] A prison riot in New York had been put down in a hail of bullets. It's doubtful that Macklin's views would have made a difference, but whatever chance he had was drowned in an avalanche of other prison news.

Two days after the Attica headlines, Rhay spoke to an assembly of inmates in the prison auditorium. Contrasting the experience at Attica and Walla Walla, Rhay told the inmates, "It is necessary for the country's correctional administrators to choose between the systems represented by the two systems....And gentlemen," he said, "there are no other alternatives."[82]

Around the country, there was soul-searching about what went wrong at Attica. The deaths there changed everything. Prison administrators, politicians, and journalists were looking for answers. Somehow, word began to spread: "You know, they're trying something really different out in Washington State." Suddenly, B. J. Rhay had a national stage.

The election and installation of the second six-month term of the Resident Government Council (RGC) was held one month after Attica, on October 12, 1971. The event was attended by about one hundred outside guests, including journalists from the *New York Times*, *Newsweek*, and other national media. Rhay was interviewed by CBS News.

"I don't think I need to sell this program any longer," Rhay announced at the installation banquet, where Graham and Harris were reelected co-presidents. "I think we're writing history here."[83]

Newsweek said the penitentiary was "clearly the most innovative, liberal maximum-security prison anywhere in the US." While citing dissenting opinions, including Macklin's, the article concluded, "It's far too soon to tell just what impact the reforms at the Washington State Penitentiary will have, but many penal experts believe they are at the very least a giant step in the right direction."[84]

"If this succeeds as I think it probably will," Rhay told a luncheon group in Walla Walla in early 1972, "what we're doing here will become the correction program throughout the United States."[85]

In a recorded interview in March of the same year, Rhay said, "I think part of this thing is the salvation of corrections....We've got adjustments to make way out there in the future. But the steps we have already taken [are] a lot more in relation to where corrections is going in the future than what we had in the past."[86]

"The most significant thing happening in American corrections today is happening right here in Walla Walla," he said a month later.[87]

Even a year after Attica, when more than a few things had gone sour, Rhay was still upbeat. In an interview with *Life* magazine he said, "I'll tell you, some beautiful things are coming out of this. There's a noticeable lack of tension in there, almost a friendliness. It's not the same anywhere else in the country."[88]

Did Rhay believe what he was saying?

Years later Rhay said, "I thought I could do it then. I really did....I was uncomfortable because I was doing something different....But I had such a strong staff—even though they weren't sold on it either—that I thought I could pull it off."[89]

Vanity also may have played a role. How many people get quoted in the *New York Times*, have their picture in *Life* magazine, or have their voice and image broadcast to millions on the evening news? Surely what Rhay was doing must be important. Why else would the media be covering it?

In the months following the installation banquet, RGC co-presidents Graham and Harris were escorted around the state for public speaking engagements. In early 1972, in what was believed to be a first, both men traveled to Olympia with Bob Rhay to testify at legislative hearings on medical and educational programs and general conditions at the prison. "It was a good political ploy," said DSHS secretary Sid Smith. Speaking of the effect of inmate testimony on the legislators, Smith said, "It helped sell the program. They had them eating right out of their hands."[90]

Rhay thought he could make resident government work. Nonetheless, he was uncomfortable: in the history of adult corrections in America, no maximum security prison had been managed anything like what Rhay was attempting in Walla Walla.

Chapter 12

UNINTENDED CONSEQUENCES

F REE DRUGS FROM PRISON DOCTORS of questionable credentials made life mellow for those who could manipulate the system. But the central office was shocked and put an end to it. Little did they know what would happen next.

"Goose and I, we started out doin' juvenile time together," recalled one inmate. "By the time we hit the walls in 1969…it was kinda like we were already established—like, 'Hey, we know them guys, they're cool, they're all right.' So we got accepted right off the bus."[91]

There were advantages to having friends already in the joint. "Gary or Ron or one of them guys I'd done juvie time with said, 'Man, put a kite in right now for [the prison psychologist].'" (A "kite" is a form used by an inmate to send a written message to staff.) "Tell him you're depressed, you're thinking about suicide, you just come in and you got two life sentences. Tell him you need a little help."

"So I put that kite in….Two weeks after I [arrived], I was on thirty milligrams of Dexedrine in the morning—which is a stimulant—I was on three grains of Seconal at night so I [could] sleep. And then I went over and had a tooth pulled….I'd go up and get a shot of Demerol five times a day."

There were lots of games around hospital drugs. For example, "you could get a quarter-grain morphine shot if somebody in your family died—and somebody in my family died *all the time.* It got to the point I'd go in and I'd tell [the doctor], 'Man, I need a little help. My so-and-so just died.' Doc kinda looked at me and said, 'Didn't they die last month?' 'I don't think so,' I'd say."

In another incident, the same inmate recalled taking advantage of an old sports injury. It didn't hurt, but he had an ankle that would sometimes give a loud pop. "We were out at softball and I went slidin' into second base and [my ankle] went POW….Right away my brain goes to work—quarter-grain shot. 'OW! OW!' And here comes our coach, and he says, 'Man, we need a gurney.' They come out and put me on the gurney—wheel me into the hospital."

The "injured" inmate continued to put on a good show.

"I'll be right back," said the doctor.

The doctor returned with a quarter grain of morphine in a hypodermic.

"Soon as he give me the shot, I got up. 'Thanks, doc, I'll see you later.'"

It apparently wasn't just the doctors who were taken advantage of. The same inmate who tricked the doctor into a quarter grain of morphine talked about tricking a nurse. "We had one guy that was hooked up with one of the gals that was workin' [in the prison hospital]—a nurse." Sex, at least heterosexual sex, is hard to come by in a prison. So the inmate approached her: "You're givin' him some. I want some."

"You know I can't," she protested.

"What? What d'you mean you can't? You can with him."

"I can't," she repeated.

"Okay, how about some Dexedrine?"

"I can do that."

Tricking the doctors and taking advantage of the nurses weren't the only ways to get drugs. Consider the resources the convicts had. As one prisoner said, "They had guys out in population that for a carton of cigarettes could write [the doctors'] names better than they could. You wanted a prescription for something, you could get it," and the pharmacy would fill it.[92]

Many inmates and some staff believe that one prison doctor was a morphine addict and the other a speed junkie. As one inmate put it, this determined which doctor you asked to see: "It all depended on which you liked the best—speed or morphine—Class A narcotic or opiate." Conte himself mentioned "addiction charges" against one of the doctors.[93] There are no other facts to back up this allegation, but Washington State was far from alone in having serious problems with some of its prison physicians and medical staff.

Easy access to drugs through the prison hospital went on until early 1972—one year after the four reforms were started and toward the end of Graham's and Harris's second six-month terms as Resident Government Council co-presidents.

The change started on December 8, 1971, when one of the prison physicians met with RGC leaders. The next day the inmates started a sit-down strike and released an ultimatum demanding major increases in hospital funding and changes in health care staff. "We'll be shuttin' it down, and it's about as serious as a prison difficulty can be," said an RGC member. Furthermore, the spokesman threatened that "it could be rougher than a sit-down strike—we can't predict or direct it, after it's begun."[94]

Simultaneously, one full-time and one part-time doctor announced they were quitting at the end of the month. The dentist said he was leaving in a week. The doctor with the alleged "addiction charge" was on extended sick leave. The doctors claimed they weren't promoting the strike. "Any actions [the inmates] take are entirely on their own," one of them explained.[95]

The inmates gave their ultimatum to the press and mailed it to Governor Evans and others in Olympia. B. J. Rhay learned about it by reading the newspaper. Among the inmates' demands was that the physician who met with them be named chief medical officer, with the power to hire and fire prison medical staff.

Rhay tried to minimize the issue, but inmate grievances about health care at the prison, as well as the doctors' concerns about staffing levels and working conditions, were long-standing and legitimate. Now, with the pending resignations of the doctors, Olympia needed to take action.

DSHS quickly assigned a physician from headquarters to fill in at the penitentiary until permanent staff could be hired. Shortly after he arrived, the new doctor told a legislative committee, "Records that I've looked at indicate many of the residents have been on prescribed drugs—habit-forming ones—for years....Eight out of every ten men who came to me in the first three days I was there asked for drugs. Many had been regularly using Dexedrine and Empirin No. 4, which has codeine in it, and is a tremendously addictive drug."[96] The doctor attributed excessive use of medication to the workload of the previous physician. He speculated, "It was easier for him to just dispense pills than look at the problems."[97]

Corroborating this assessment was a huge reduction in the number of inmates getting meds from the hospital. With fewer than one thousand inmates inside the walls, one report said that during the month before the new doctor arrived, three hundred of them went to the pill line every day; the month after, only twenty-two per day.[98]

The point is, as long as free dope was coming from the prison hospital, the inmates had far less need for illicit drugs. Of course, there have always been drugs that junkies have to have and that no doctor can or will prescribe. But inmates who were satisfied with simpler highs could get them for free just by going to the hospital. No smuggling of contraband, no need for extra cash, no danger of going into debt, no getting busted by the officers—pretty mellow, according to some old-time inmates.

Then it all changed. According to one inmate, "[The doctors] shut everybody off." Without access to free drugs from the hospital, he said, "that's when the dope really started comin' in."[99]

Just as the doctors were shutting off the supply of free drugs, a man called "Cadillac" by convicts and officers alike was sentenced to prison. Cadillac Brown was convicted on a narcotics charge in Seattle and sent to Walla Walla. Prior to this conviction, law enforcement officials said Brown was one of the largest heroin dealers on the West Coast. His main suppliers were from Oakland, California. Not long after he arrived in Walla Walla, Brown was assigned the job of working the switchboard for the inmate telephones. In this capacity, Brown could make unlimited and unlogged long-distance calls anytime he wanted. It's believed that this was when, and how, he set up a narcotics ring at the penitentiary. In any event, heroin began to show up at the prison early in 1972.

Drugs came from all directions. They came through the mail. They came through the visiting room. They came in milk cans brought in from the dairy. They were hidden in sides of beef destined for the kitchen, and in bike parts purchased by the motorcycle shop. They came from volunteers. They came from corrupt staff.

"I mean anything you wanted—it was there," said an inmate who has spent most of his life trying to get high. "There was heroin, crank, weed, hash, morphine, codeine, acid—anything."[100]

Chapter 13

RED FLAGS

URING THE THREE MONTHS following installation of the second RGC, all the stories about Walla Walla were positive. Early 1972 found Bob Rhay enthusiastic about conditions. Murder was gone from the walls, and a stream of drugs flowing into the penitentiary had not yet flooded the prison. Inmates Graham and Harris toured the state and spoke at various functions, saying responsible things. The national media liked what they saw. By the start of the year—an election year for Governor Evans—it looked like prison reform in Walla Walla was going to work.

But the positive phase didn't last. If the penitentiary had been the only issue in the governor's race that year, Dan Evans wouldn't have stood a chance.

Through early February 1972, across the state, 2,049 inmates had spent at least a day or two away from prison while out on furlough. Forty-two had failed to return, but nothing happened to bring adverse attention to the program. Then, on a Saturday evening early in the month, state trooper Frank Noble made what started as a routine traffic stop. An inmate from Walla Walla, out on his second furlough, was behind the wheel. He pulled a gun and shot Noble three times. Noble died at the scene, and the inmate was arrested within the hour.

Evans held a news conference the following Monday. "One incident, however tragic, cannot by itself end a program which has been considered promising," he said.[101]

If his governor could say such a thing in an election year, Rhay could stay the course. Even the inmates rallied and, with the help of the RGC led by Graham and Harris, voted overwhelmingly to tighten the rules for granting furloughs. Rhay and the other wardens converged on Olympia and hammered out new criteria. These were announced by the governor as "an eight-point plan" to tighten the program and "to protect those tools that are necessary to rehabilitate."[102]

Ten weeks after the murder of Trooper Noble, Rhay gave permission for inmate Arthur St. Peter to leave the institution for the evening, accompanied by a prison employee. St. Peter went to the man's home as part of Rhay's "Take a Lifer to Dinner" program. While he was there, St. Peter excused himself to use the bathroom and escaped by way of a window. Two weeks later he was arrested in Tacoma, Washington. He'd been shot ten times, with wounds in the arm, leg, chest, and pelvis.[103]

St. Peter had tried to rob a pawnshop. Robert Taylor and his wife, owners of the pawnshop and victims of prior robberies, both carried .38-caliber revolvers. In the gun battle that ensued, St. Peter killed Taylor and shot Taylor's wife in the back.

Not only was he a lifer, but St. Peter also had a thirty-five-year federal sentence awaiting him if the state of Washington ever decided to grant him parole. In 1961 he had escaped from a tenth-floor jail in Seattle using sheets for a rope. One inmate fell to his death in the escape. St. Peter had tunneled out of Walla Walla in 1964 and held two people hostage before he surrendered. Letting St. Peter out for the evening was "the most flagrant example of bad judgment in prison management I have ever seen,"[104] said a judge who had presided over one of St. Peter's trials.

In the storm of controversy that followed, Evans concurred: it was bad judgment.

In a lengthy letter to the state representative from Walla Walla, Evans wrote, "I agree that public safety must be the primary consideration of correctional programs." But Evans's definition of public safety was shaped by conviction.

> A return to the highly punitive program of incarceration would do nothing to foster public safety because inmates would be returning to their communities unchanged after their release and commit further crimes....Unfortunately, even in the best of well-regulated programs there will be failures, since there are significant risks involved. But we know that almost all persons who are sentenced to prison terms will eventually return to the community. If the prospects of a successful return are improved, then public safety is enhanced.[105]

While Rhay's "Take a Lifer to Dinner" program would stop, the furlough program and other reforms would stay. Although many disagreed with Evans's ideas about corrections, he certainly had courage.

Meanwhile, tensions were rising in the prison. The first two resident government councils had been qualified successes, but now the climate was changing. By the spring of 1972, "the mood behind the shadowing walls began to sour," reported *Life* magazine. Newly admitted inmates who hadn't experienced the days of super custody didn't know "they were supposed to be grateful for the freedom to straggle into the mess hall, to wander out to the half-acre field under the water tower...and to slide through days in their bell-bottoms and earrings," said the article.[106] The men elected to the third resident government council were radicals and revolutionaries far different from their predecessors. They vowed not to cooperate with the administration in the way Johnnie Harris was alleged to have done.[107]

In April, after a hiatus of a year, another inmate was murdered.[108]

In July 1972, in what was described as "Attica weather," Rhay was forced to lock the prison down—the first such action since the Christmas strike of 1970. The lockdown was precipitated by a list of twenty-two demands issued by the Black Prisoners Forum Unlimited (B.P.F.U.) in a document they called "Black Manifesto—22." "We will no longer sit by and let this type of treatment continue," said the manifesto. "If you do not act in a positive manner to correct these problems, then we will have no choice but to take whatever action we feel necessary to correct them ourselves."[109]

DSHS secretary Sid Smith and other senior headquarters administrators came to Walla Walla and participated in the negotiations with the black prisoners. One of the state's concessions was that an old, unused cellblock would become a dedicated meeting place for the B.P.F.U. The blacks called this new meeting place Walter Carter Hall, after a popular black prisoner who had recently died on the third floor of the hospital. The written agreement between Rhay and the B.P.F.U. included Rhay's conditions that "it would not be a closed area in relation to all staff [and] that hours and rules and regulations would have to be agreed upon."[110] With the agreement, the brief lockdown ended. But as with many agreements between Rhay and the inmates during these years, Rhay never enforced these conditions.

By the summer of 1972 many of the groups in the prison were holding annual banquets. The members of Lifers with Hope held theirs in Lifers' Park. The B.P.F.U. used a grassy area behind their new clubhouse. The Bikers' Club, which now had its own club space in an old, abandoned power plant, held banquets in the Big Yard. These events often included hundreds of outside invited guests. During the bikers' banquets, Rhay sometimes allowed outside motorcycle clubs to bring their show bikes into the institution and ride them around the Big Yard.

Bringing hundreds of outsiders inside the walls certainly created opportunities for mischief (and worse). But for the most part, especially in the early years, these social gatherings were lively, fun affairs. At least, that's how Barbara Miller remembers them. The first representative for Prison Legal Services to work inside the walls, Miller brought her teen-age daughter and her six-year-old niece to some of the banquets.

In a world of few women, Miller stood out. Not only was she a great friend of the inmates, she was attractive, vivacious, and smart. Working as a paralegal, she had such credibility with the inmates that both the inmates and administrative officials in Olympia would sometimes ask her to help defuse tensions or mediate disagreements between B. J. and the inmates. Miller became immensely popular with the men inside the walls. This is how she described the inmate banquets:

> People would just socialize. There would be officers commingling. I suspect there [were] some sexual activities. I don't know that. I never saw that....You didn't see people loaded. You didn't see people getting weird....[There] were children all over the place; children just being children and playing and having an opportunity to have a semi-natural few hours with the parent or whatever. I thought they were pretty wonderful.[111]

But turmoil continued. In August, another inmate was murdered. The attack occurred in the darkened prison auditorium while seven hundred men calmly watched a movie. In September and October, two other men were stabbed and severely wounded. The last attack occurred in the RGC office, where the victim had been summoned to appear.

In addition to giving permission for banquets to be held and bikers to ride their choppers around the Big Yard, at some point Rhay authorized the RGC and all the clubs to get keys, often the only keys, to their meeting places. Rhay and associate superintendent Bob Freeman deny doing this. To hear them tell it, the inmates getting keys to the clubs was something that just happened.

Freeman, for example, suggested that the officers gave keys to the inmates on their own initiative. "The inmates would be doing something, or want to do something, and the superintendent would let them," he said. "Pretty soon the inmates are doing about anything they want. The correctional officer didn't know where he [stood]. He didn't know what authority he had....His easiest route was to give the inmates most anything they wanted....I'll bet you on the key thing, it was more or less guards did it."[112]

Not so, according to the plant manager. "I gave the keys to the inmates," he said. "That was on orders from the front end."[113] By "front end," the plant manager meant the administration—in other words, B. J. Rhay.

It doesn't take a corrections expert to understand that giving the inmates the only keys to certain areas of a maximum security prison might lead to problems. Consider, for example, the club room for Lifers with Hope. To get into the room, officers had to negotiate two locked entrances. First there was a locked gate at the south end of Lifers' Park. Sometimes the inmate standing watch at the gate would claim he didn't have the key. When that happened, the inmate walked the sixty or seventy yards to the other end of Lifers' Park, went into the club area, presumably mentioned that officers were on their way, and returned with the key. Once through the gate, the officers walked through the park, then climbed the stairs to the lifers' club room, where they came to another door that might also be locked. This system gave the lifers ample time to hide contraband or stop nefarious activities by the time the officers arrived.

One can only speculate why Rhay permitted the inmates to have the only keys to their club areas. It may be that once a decision was made to allow dedicated space for the various clubs, having inmates control their own doors was the only way the arrangement would work.

Throughout most of the '70s, the penitentiary rarely had enough staff to post a correctional officer on every floor of the big cellblocks, much less at every clubhouse door. Since there was animosity between some of the clubs from the start, keeping nonmembers out of the meeting places was probably a good idea. The only groups with surplus labor to do the job were the clubs themselves.

Whatever the reason, allowing inmates dedicated turf for their club areas and the ability to deny correctional officers access to those areas was an unprecedented decision. According to Anthony Travisono, long-time director of the American Correctional Association, Washington in the 1970s was the only state in the country where this occurred.[114]

While knowledge of the inmates' exclusive control over parts of the prison wasn't part of the political discourse during the race for governor, there was still more bad prison news for Dan Evans. First, in mid-September, a report requested by Olympia was leaked to the local newspaper. It had been written by two officers, three inmates, and the chairman of the penitentiary's Citizens Advisory Council. The article appeared under the headline "Irresponsibility Pervades Prison, Report Charges." The issues described were many: Rhay and Freeman were unresponsive to criticism; administrators and counselors were often loafing; the prison was filthy; correctional officers were apathetic, sometimes watching movies instead of patrolling the wings; petty theft—by officers and convicts alike—was common.[115]

The chairman of the Citizens Advisory Council spoke to the Walla Walla reporter. "One of the main points in the report that we make is that the administration is unresponsive to criticism. Facing up to criticism is humiliating to a certain kind of pride." Rhay and Freeman were "approached by everyone, even immediate subordinates, with caution," said the report. "As a result, criticism is muted and softened because of fear that too direct an approach will result in belligerence and summary dismissal."[116] This was personal. Rhay had never been attacked so publicly.

The same week that the "Irresponsibility Pervades Prison" article appeared, a projectile was fired through the window of Nine Tower, narrowly missing an officer. With half the officers in attendance, the union voted unanimously to ask Rhay to order another lockdown and do a complete shakedown of the institution. Furthermore, if Rhay refused, they would go around him to higher authorities. State and regional union representatives joined the president of the local union as he presented the union motion to the warden. The employees had never been so bold.

Elected officials in the Walla Walla area, some of them no doubt hoping to help their local state representative unseat Evans in the GOP primary later that month, sent damning telegrams about the penitentiary to the governor and gave copies to the press. They agreed with the officers. "Urgently request the influence of your good offices toward the immediate deadlock [i.e. lockdown] and shakedown of the Washington State Penitentiary," stated one telegram. Furthermore, it asserted, "Reliable information indicates presence of firearms, knives and naphtha gas behind the walls....Another Attica could occur."[117]

When Evans prevailed in the Republican primary, former governor Albert Rosellini, his Democratic opponent, took up the call. He blasted Evans for problems in adult corrections and promised that if he were elected, he would keep Rhay but sack those in Olympia responsible for reform.

Steve Chadek, union president at the penitentiary, got both Evans and Rosellini to come to Walla Walla and meet with the union in the weeks before the election. Afterwards, Chadek all but endorsed Rosellini. As one officer slid a Rosellini matchbook to a reporter, Chadek noted that the union couldn't endorse candidates, but "my mind is made up and one candidate is way above the other."[118]

Days before the election, Rosellini charged, "A well-intentioned program called 'prison reform' is jeopardizing your safety—and your child's."[119]

It didn't work. Evans was reelected.

The bad news continued after the election. A few weeks later, the RGC leadership sent a letter to the governor. "As of this date the RGC has been terminated until you, Sir, or your designee will correct the deplorable stalling, chicanery and refusal to cooperate with us by the [prison] administration."[120] In his first meeting with the resigned leadership, Rhay was told that the inmates didn't trust him—they wanted to negotiate with someone else.

The next day, the deputy secretary of DSHS, along with an assistant attorney general for the agency, joined the negotiations. An agreement was reached, and two days later the RGC reconstituted itself. For the second time that year, and the third time in two years, the inmates had successfully gone around Rhay and used Olympia to get what they wanted.

While the rhetoric of the political campaign and the posturing of the inmate leaders was little more than an irritant, the dead bodies didn't lie. By his third term in office, Evans had every reason to know that something had to change.

All this must have affected Rhay as well. Like dry sand draining through an hourglass, hope must have been slipping, too. By '73 Rhay had every reason to feel the accumulated weight of trust betrayed and risk unrewarded.

The coup de grace may have come that spring. Lorraine Taylor, widow of the pawnbroker slain by escaped convict Arthur St. Peter, sued the state, Rhay, and the secretary of DSHS for negligence. In the evidence presented, Rhay's associate superintendent for custody, Art Crowley, testified he would not have let St. Peter participate in the "Take a Lifer to Dinner" program and that he'd told the warden of his misgivings. Others said the classification committee disapproved of the release. Macklin came out of retirement to support the plaintiff. Rhay's strongest supporters were four convicts who claimed St. Peter was a changed man. In the civil suit, which takes ten votes to convict, the twelve-person jury was unanimous: Bob Rhay was personally negligent in allowing St. Peter to escape. Mrs. Taylor was awarded damages of $186,000.

Decades later, it still hurt. "The biggest mistake I ever made," Rhay said. Then, his voice trailing almost to a whisper: "Crowley recommended against it. Oh yeah, one of the mistakes I could have done without."[121]

Chapter 14

UNDER THE RADAR

GORDY GRAHAM, JOHNNIE HARRIS, and other longtime prisoners called themselves *convicts*—not "inmates" and certainly not "residents." To the older generation, the word "convict" expressed an identity; it had a specific meaning and implied a certain lifestyle and set of values. They lived by the convict code. "Inmates" were dependents who lived in institutions. An inmate could be anybody and was therefore nobody. Convicts lived in prison and knew why they were there.

Increasingly, these old convicts found themselves surrounded and replaced by younger men no longer enamored with all aspects of the convict code. New blood was taking over.

An article on prison reform in the inmate newspaper described this "new blood." According to the author, over half of the then 1.3 million people incarcerated in America's jails and prisons "consist of a revolutionary new breed of prisoners…prepared and willing at the slightest provocation to engage in violent and extreme acts against the system, which they see as a total failure, to achieve what they deem as relevant reform."[122]

On the national scene, Black Panther Party leaders Huey Newton, Eldridge Cleaver, and Bobby Seale were committed to, and participated in, armed struggle. These men were heroes to George Jackson as he studied and wrote his letters from a California prison, published in 1970 as *Soledad Brother*. "I met Marx, Lenin, Trotsky, Engels, and Mao when I entered prison and they redeemed me," he wrote.[123] More than 400,000 copies of Jackson's book were sold, not a few of which circulated in America's prisons. In August 1971, when Jackson was killed in an escape attempt in which six hostages died, the radicals considered him a martyr. In September 1971, four days after dozens of inmates and hostages were killed at Attica prison in New York, a radical group called the Weather Underground detonated a bomb near the office of the New York Commissioner of Corrections. By the late '60s and early '70s, all over the country, the radicals and their ideas were going to prison.

But politics was not the only motivation of the new blood taking over the Resident Government Council at the Washington State Penitentiary. As one officer noted, "The people who controlled the drugs and the people who were violent found out that the officers of [the RGC] had somewhat free movement around the institution." The drug kingpins were uninterested in resident government, but "they wanted their people in...to move the drugs."[124]

These changes in the inmate population complicated Rhay's ability to control the prison by controlling the inmate leaders. Not only were the leaders and their followers more radical and confrontational than before, but the elected leaders were not necessarily the real leaders. Furthermore, as the clubs gained membership and power, there were more leaders than ever, and the agendas of these groups were not always the same.

In addition to these changes in the inmate population, there were also changes on the labor front and in the legal arena that contributed to the erosion of Rhay's authority.

With the creation of DSHS came the first statewide contract for correctional employees. When Steve Chadek, the penitentiary's union president, read the contract, he thought, "Holy Toledo! I can't believe some of this stuff. You see, [for the employees, it was] a perfect contract....We didn't want to have to go in there and give anything up....In fact, I had a pretty good policy. Anytime management done anything bad to us...I would turn around and do something bad to them—using the contract to do it."[125] Chadek used the contract on issues large and small.

A central battle (fought all over the state) was the issue of uncompensated overtime. "When I first started working [at the penitentiary], there was no such thing as getting paid for overtime," said Chadek. "In fact, it wasn't nothing to work six days a week. We still got paid for a forty-hour week....It was always time owed you—which we never got."

As Chadek read the rules and contracts, he discovered that it wasn't supposed to be that way. "That's when we started saying, 'If you want us to go downtown with inmates to a ball game, you pay for it.'" Eventually, hourly employees at Walla Walla (and everywhere in state government) were paid overtime for everything. According to Chadek, some officers at the penitentiary got thousands of dollars in back pay.[126]

Chadek's battle with Rhay over parking spaces was a smaller issue, but it typified the relationship he had with the warden. For a long time, Rhay's friends and favorites had designated parking spots next to the administration building. Everyone else had to park farther away. Since the Walla Walla summers can be blistering hot and winters arctic cold, the closer spaces were a nice perk.

Chadek told Rhay that people were complaining about the parking situation. But Rhay said it was his parking lot and he didn't need Chadek to tell him how to use it. The next day Chadek parked in Rhay's space. Rhay called him in and said, "You're in my parking place....I'd like you to move your car." Chadek left his car where it was. A little while later, Rhay called Chadek and said, "Didn't I tell you to move your car?" Chadek said, "No...you told me you'd *like* me to move it. If you tell me to move it, I'll go and move it."[127]

Chadek took Rhay to arbitration over parking spaces and won. Rhay had a notice posted on bulletin boards around the institution saying there would be no more designated parking spaces until an agreement was reached with the union. All the name signs at the assigned parking spaces, including Rhay's, came down. The next day, the union president parked in Rhay's old spot "just to prove a point. Just to be an a-hole," said Chadek.[128] Conte's prediction—that the new laws to centralize personnel decisions and create statewide collective bargaining would lead to disrespect of local leaders—didn't take long to come true in Walla Walla.

Changes were also happening on the legal front. Sometime in 1972 Don Horowitz decided his legal team at DSHS needed an attorney with knowledge of corrections.

A young lawyer by the name of John Henry Browne was working in Chicago when he read a notice at the Northwestern University placement office. The notice said the state of Washington was looking for lawyers interested in prison reform. Browne had never considered working for state government, but he was interested in prison reform.

Browne, a few years Horowitz's junior, had been active in the antiwar movement during his college years in the 1960s. When the draft board told him to report for a physical, he researched the law and discovered that the height limit for induction into the service was six-six. Browne was almost six-seven. As a result, he was classified 4-F.[129] That classification meant the person was physically unfit or otherwise unqualified to serve. Browne was definitely physically fit; he just couldn't fit into some of the tight spaces many servicemen and women found themselves in.

After this early success with the law, Browne enrolled in law school at American University in Washington, DC. Although he was accepted to other schools, he chose American University because it had more clinical programs than any other law school in the country at that time. One of those programs involved working at the Lorton Reformatory, outside of Washington, DC. While in this program, Browne and an attorney friend of his, Allen Ressler, wrote a grant to start LawCor, which Browne says was the first prison legal aid project in the country.

After law school, Browne was accepted into a Ford Foundation program at Northwestern University, where he tried his first cases in an office that represented both Jimmy Hoffa and the Black Panther Party. Ressler went to a graduate program in Kansas City, where he worked at Leavenworth Prison.

Browne's credentials appealed to Horowitz. After an interview at Northwestern, Browne was asked to come to Olympia for a second interview. "I did it as a lark, actually," said Browne. Working for the state was not what he had in mind, but he wanted to check out other employment opportunities on the West Coast and figured the State of Washington would pay his travel expenses.

"I came out and met with this guy named Horowitz. One of the first things he asked me was would I ever consider working for the state. I said no, and he said, 'You're hired!'" Browne told Horowitz he believed the prison system needed due process rules and regulations. He said he wouldn't work on death penalty cases. "I went in with a particular agenda and told them exactly what my predispositions were, and they hired me."[130]

One of the first things Browne did when he went to work for Horowitz was write a grant proposal to provide legal services to inmates in

Washington prisons. The grant was obtained, and Prison Legal Services was started. But this was no ordinary prison legal services. The first such legal services in the country had narrow mandates to counsel institutionalized clients on civil matters—divorces, property matters, and so forth. Horowitz had another idea: "My view—and in a way this was a private, personal agenda—is that the only way to really build in legal guarantees and build in ongoing change…is to build in an advocacy process which would survive any particular administration." Noting that lawyers have a great penchant for self-perpetuation, Horowitz believed that a prison legal services system that could assist inmates on a broad range of issues would build in those legal guarantees and stimulate ongoing change.[131]

If there had been experienced correctional experts in Olympia overseeing prisons, the scope of prison legal services might have been narrower. But Horowitz's "private, personal agenda" to create an advocacy system carried the day. As a result, the mandate for legal services was almost unlimited. "We were allowed to do civil rights actions, we were allowed to do class actions. We were allowed to do any kind of reform litigation that we thought was appropriate for our clients," said Richard Emery, an early director of Prison Legal Services.[132]

One of the first people hired to work for Prison Legal Services was Allen Ressler, John Henry Browne's friend from law school. Since the defendant in litigation brought by Prison Legal Services was the state of Washington, this made Ressler and Browne legal adversaries.

When reminded that Ressler was his law school buddy, Browne said, "If you're looking for some sort of juicy conspiracy that sounds bad, you're not going to find it from me."[133]

This is how Browne described the relationship between the DSHS assistant attorneys general and Prison Legal Services: "Richard Emery or Allen would call me up…and say, 'Did you know [such and such is going on]?' I'd say 'no' and check into it." If the matter could be handled internally, Browne would write a rule directing prison staff to behave in other ways. If that didn't work, he'd tell Ressler, "You better sue us on that."[134]

Emery and Ressler recall the same dynamic. Emery noted that Browne and Horowitz and other assistant attorneys general working for DSHS "came from an orientation which was very similar to the legal services orientation, and they respected the principles and ideas. But they also did their job, and they were very strong adversaries....So they would try and talk their clients [i.e. prison administrators and staff] into acting the correct way, and their clients would often perceive them as being more in our camp than in theirs—which in some cases they were, because that was what the law required them to be."[135]

Horowitz's assessment was similar. "There were times when indeed the legal decisions would push us in certain directions. But I have to say that they were directions in which we [as assistant attorneys general for DSHS] probably wanted to be pushed. And maybe we let them push us further than the decision itself would have required."[136]

This is not as unprincipled as it might seem. As Horowitz noted, "in Alabama and in some of those places, the federal courts were literally telling the administrators what to do. They were running the system." No one in Washington State wanted that. "So that was another reason we tried to get ahead of the decisions."[137]

Ressler—who in the 1970s looked like Jerry Garcia of the Grateful Dead—wasn't quite as generous as Richard Emery in his assessment of the assistant attorneys general as adversaries. "Let me tell you," he said, "Horowitz and John Henry folded on most lawsuits that we filed....In the days of Horowitz and Browne, life was a little simpler, because we could compromise each of these cases...especially the major lawsuits involving the promulgation of regulations. And they would just fold. Then we would sit down and write the regs with them."[138]

These slower and more subtle changes—in the convict culture, in the relationship between Rhay and his employees, and from local and national legal challenges—eroded Rhay's power as surely as the four reforms and the intrusions into prison operations by central office leaders unversed in correctional matters. By 1973, Bob Rhay, who at the beginning of the decade controlled almost everything in his world, controlled almost nothing.

PART 3
DESCENT
1973–1977

Inside the Chicano Club

Chapter 15

CALIFORNIA CONNECTION

D URING THE 1972 ELECTION CAMPAIGN, people in the governor's
office believed Rhay was working for their Democratic opponent, Albert Rosellini. "It was one of those times that Bob
Rhay had to go," said Governor Evans. "[Rhay] was looking ahead and
he thought Rosellini was going to win....There was a growing disen-
chantment in the administration—I think even before the election campaign started—with Bobby Rhay and his activity....There was no question from the governor's office: we had no respect at all for Rhay in those
latter years."[1]

Despite the governor's assertion that "Bob Rhay had to go," Evans
never fired Rhay. Instead, he started looking for new leaders for DSHS—
leaders who knew something about corrections. "I felt the need to have
somebody of real strength at the head of the department that was dealing with corrections," he said, "because we were running into trouble.
We had weak leadership in that area."[2]

A national search was conducted for a new DSHS secretary. The
front-runners were Charles Morris from New York and Milton Burdman from California. Evans liked them both. They had "complemen-
tary strengths," he said. Ultimately, the governor asked Morris to be secretary, for his all-around skills and strong intellect, and Burdman to be
his deputy, "because of his strong corrections background."

"I was their first choice," said Morris, and "they asked me if I would
be willing to have Milt come on as my deputy....I had never met him.
[But] Dan Evans clearly liked him a lot....My feeling was if I didn't like
Milt, he would have to leave. I wouldn't have to leave. So he was the one
taking the chance."[3]

Several months elapsed between the time Morris was offered the
job and when he could start. Morris had telephone conversations with

Burdman to discuss major issues, but Burdman ran the agency from July 1973 until Morris arrived in October.

When Morris got there, DSHS was still divided into program development, management services, and service delivery. People were scattered about rather than working together as subject matter experts in more traditional organizational units. Burdman didn't like it any more than Morris did, but he left it to Morris to make that kind of change. Morris found service delivery to be a particularly problematic area, as he later explained:

> There was this very nice group of citizens—a lot of them were friends of Dan [Evans]—who had, with [DSHS secretary] Sid Smith, developed this utterly naive and utterly idealistic notion that the Department of Social and Health Services was going to provide coordinated services through multiservice centers....Much to my horror, they had merged all the departments at the regional level....There was a regional director, and everyone worked for him....Probation people worked for him, and vocational rehabilitation, and child protective services, [and so on].... They were even trying to move the institutions under those regions. This was simply awful. No matter what kind of paper logic it had, it was clearly not working. In fact, it was really floundering.[4]

Morris quickly reorganized the agency into more traditional divisions. Like most governmental agencies, employees in each division reported up a chain of command to a division head who, in turn, reported to the secretary.

One of those new divisions was the division of adult corrections. The man selected to be the division's first director was Harold (Hal) Bradley. Like Burdman, Bradley was from California. California was a national leader in corrections in 1973, and both men were seasoned correctional administrators. For the first time in years, Bob Rhay had superiors who, in their minds if not in Rhay's, knew at least as much about corrections as he did.

Morris recalled, "We found Hal because he was sort of an enlightened conservative. He believed that [prisons] should not be repressive.... Guards should not have their way and do whatever they wanted....At the same time, he believed that prisons should be ordered, they should be safe.

The fact that freedoms are curtailed is part of the game. That's what [prisons] are there for."[5]

What Burdman and Bradley knew from their California experience wasn't Walla Walla. Images of burly men with shaggy beards walking around in swastika-decorated motorcycle jackets were not part of their experience. And it wasn't just the images that were the problem. "Milt [Burdman] didn't like Bob [Rhay] from the start," said Morris. "He knew him from before by reputation, [and] I think he'd actually met him. Bob was not viewed well in California."[6]

Rhay was on thin ice.

But Hal Bradley wasn't going to arrive until January. In his place, another administrator, on loan from the California Department of Corrections, served as interim director of adult corrections.

Rhay liked the interim director. "He was a warden's warden—probably the strongest of those that came from California. At least I thought so," said Rhay. But Rhay had no illusions about why he was there. "I saw him coming as a hatchet man," he said.[7]

Rhay was certain that Burdman wanted him fired. But "I wasn't going to stand by and be screwed by somebody that just rolled in from California," he said. "Christ almighty, I didn't just...jump off the last pumpkin wagon into town. Hell, I knew why [the interim director] was here before he got here."[8]

So when Burdman and Bradley's hatchet man came to Walla Walla, Rhay told him, "I will resist, with everything I have, any attempt you make to replace me."[9] Rhay's strong political connections made this no idle threat. In fact, during the few months the interim director was in charge, he replaced the superintendents at the other two large Washington prisons, but not Bob Rhay.

Rhay's resistance aside, he would have been hard to replace in 1973. As DSHS secretary Morris recalled, "No one felt that there was anybody to replace Rhay. I certainly wasn't ready to do that....Milt had questions about Bob. He didn't particularly like him. At the same time, he just didn't think there was anybody else inside the department strong enough to take over at Walla Walla. I think that's probably true."[10]

Furthermore, Morris contends that Bob Rhay "was undeniably one of the best crisis managers who ever lived." Whenever there were major crises, Rhay "managed them impeccably....The decision making under fire was absolutely cool. Neither Hal nor Milt nor I, when something was really coming down, [tried to] interfere. He'd keep us informed. He was punctilious about that. His decision making was cool; it was wise. He was really good when there was a crisis."[11]

But "the feeling about Bob," continued Morris, "was that he was a poor manager. The penitentiary was always run a little lackadaisically.... Everyone's strong point is their weak point...and it's what you do well that gets you into trouble. So the sort of fever chart at Walla Walla [was]... everything [is going okay]—a little slack, not run really tight—and then, BING, a major crisis. Then Bob would really shine."[12]

Though they couldn't fire or replace Bob Rhay, they wanted to undo many of the concessions he had granted the inmates. As Morris said, "The entire three years I was there, if we had a single motivating leitmotif, as it were, it would be to take back a substantial portion of that ground. [We knew] that was not something that we could do all at once; it would provoke great upheaval if you just tried to simply switch back. So we consciously used every incident that occurred [to result in] a couple millimeters' tightening of the screws."[13]

Bradley surveyed the scene at the penitentiary after he arrived in January 1974. It was clear to him that a lot of screws needed tightening.

Chapter 16

CAPITULATION

"WE HAD A BOOK we'd been operating by for years," said associate superintendent Bob Freeman. "It was an unwritten book, but we understood it."[14]

The unwritten book was made up of the rules that the inmates were to follow and the correctional officers were to enforce. With implementation of the four reforms and the concessions granted to inmates by Rhay, it became increasingly difficult for the officers to know which of these unwritten rules to enforce and which to ignore.

The rules were, in fact, supposed to be written down. A memo from headquarters in Olympia from 1965 stated that superintendents at each institution were to prepare a set of written rules and regulations that fleshed out basic guidelines for inmate conduct and discipline that the central office had developed, but the guidelines were vague. For example, one stated that "all inmates shall obey orders given them by members of the institution staff in a prompt, cooperative and courteous manner." Another said, "Inmates shall at all times behave in an orderly manner."[15]

Other guidelines from the central office were detailed, but still not very helpful. Under "personal cleanliness," for example, headquarters stated that inmates must "bathe as often as necessary, keep teeth clean, keep hair properly groomed and cut in regulation fashion...shave frequently...wash hands when needed." Guidelines like these left plenty of room for interpretation. For the most part, the only rules and regulations the officers knew at Walla Walla were the unwritten book to which Freeman referred. New officers learned the rules by listening to, or emulating, more seasoned staff. Under these circumstances, any officer could probably write an infraction on almost any inmate any day he wanted.

How an inmate could be punished was also theoretically outlined by headquarters. Discipline could run the gamut from reprimands and warnings to loss of privileges, confinement in one's cell, confinement in isolation, or adverse recommendations to the parole board. An adjustment committee made all decisions about guilt or (rarely) innocence and the type of punishment to be meted out. The associate superintendents for custody and treatment were two of the three members of the adjustment committee. Others rotated in and out as the third committee member. In theory, no inmate was to be confined in isolation for more than thirty days at a time.[16] In reality, consecutive thirty-day sentences could continue for months or even years.

By the 1970s, this kind of unfettered discretion was under attack all across the country. The hands-off policy that state and federal courts had been practicing for decades was gradually replaced by attitudes favoring examination of prison rules and discipline.

Washington wasn't the first state in the country to develop new rules and procedures for inmate discipline, but it was one of the leaders. And in some ways, the state was ahead of the courts. The people who led this effort were Don Horowitz and John Henry Browne.

One of the areas in which the state got ahead of the legal decisions was implementation of due process procedures for inmate discipline. While the scope and general content of Washington's first due process rules read remarkably like the American Correctional Association standards for inmate discipline that are in place to this day, the devil is in the details, and the details were where the regulations put members of the adjustment committee on the defensive. There were two areas in which this was particularly true: the tight time frames for moving the disciplinary hearing process forward and reaching a decision, and the introduction of lay advisors to assist inmates in disciplinary hearings. The tight time frames, coupled with automatic dismissal of charges if the time frames were not met, caused great frustration among the officers and administration. Furthermore, some of the lay advisors were disbarred lawyers who had ended up in prison. They could prepare and present cases, call and cross-examine witnesses, challenge decisions, and file appeals. The officers and administrators were ill prepared for such sophisticated maneuvering. As a result, the disciplinary hearing process was all but paralyzed.

Union president Steve Chadek described the futility of writing infractions under these circumstances. "There was a time," he said, "when you were wasting your time writing up a report. They weren't going to do anything to the guy. It could be a pretty bad write-up too…[like] catching an inmate with a shank [or] threatening with a knife or something. To me, that's serious. Chances are, if you wrote it up, nothing would happen to the inmate."[17]

Other, less serious, infractions might not even be reported. For example, if an officer saw an inmate palming a pill and went to get it from him, the inmate would immediately be surrounded by a large group of friends. "Unless you're a fool, you wouldn't jump in; not with that many inmates around," said Chadek.

Superiors would sometimes tell officers to back off. For example, according to Chadek, "if you go to your lieutenant or the captain or somebody and you say, 'Hey, I think we'd better pick up so and so. I saw him staggering down there and I wanted to check his coke and he wouldn't let me.'"

The lieutenant or captain might ask, "Was he hurting anybody?"

If he wasn't, they'd say, "Well, that's all right. Let him go."

"It was frightening, is what it was," concluded Chadek.

It wasn't just that you couldn't make a write-up stick that demoralized the correctional officer corps. The verbal abuse of staff by inmates was constant.

"When I worked Eight Wing, they knew my kids' names," said John Lambert. "They told me, 'When we get out of here we're going to fuck your daughter. We're going to tie you up and fuck her in front of you, 'cause we will get out one of these days.'" This went on all the time. "I mean continuously, all day long."[18]

In addition to being abusive, the units could be chaotic. "We didn't have the doors shut on the cells. They'd be open," said Lambert. "If we tried to close them, [the inmates would] raise hell with the administration and [the administration would] tell us to back off." And because there wasn't a gate system—that is, a system of controlled movement in which

Officers on patrol

inmates can go through a door or gate only at a certain time—a big unit like Eight Wing could have not just the four hundred inmates assigned to it, but "five hundred, six hundred inmates in there. At any given time, half of them would be drunk or loaded."[19]

The segregation unit was the worst. The inmates there would throw bottles or other blunt objects. They would fill a Dixie cup with urine or feces and throw it at an officer as he walked by. They lit fires. They flooded their cells. Things like this happened elsewhere too, but in seg it could be a daily occurrence.

Even the routine became difficult or impossible. For example, there were times when the inmates simply wouldn't go to their cells at night. John Lambert described what it was like. "From April through October we'd come to shift and [the shift commander would] say, 'Okay, you smokers, take extra cigarettes in, 'cause we're not going to get them locked up tonight. We know that.'" During the warm evenings, the inmates simply wouldn't go to their cells. They'd hang out in People's Park and "build bonfires, drink pruno [prison-made alcohol], and smoke dope....We just watched them. We'd go out amongst 'em and try to count 'em. They'd have weapons, and we'd say, 'Hey, put that stuff away, we don't want to see it.' It wasn't like twenty or thirty of us. There may be only one or two of us trying to count this big mob."[20]

In the face of the futility of writing infractions, the chaos of the living units, and the verbal (and sometimes physical) abuse the officers had to endure, many officers simply gave up. "We quit doing our jobs," said then lieutenant Robin Moses. "We allowed the inmates to run things. Besides losing control of the institution, [management] lost control of the staff."[21]

With the inmates in control, and most of the officers simply there to collect a paycheck, the physical condition of the prison deteriorated. The inmates collected huge amounts of property that they stuffed inside their cells. They hung sheets or blankets across the cell fronts so officers couldn't see inside. Because radio reception inside the cells was poor, the inmates would unwind the copper wire from a cassette tape player motor and use it to make antennas. A big, heavy nut would be tied to one end of the wire, and an inmate would throw the nut and attached wire through a pane of glass on the outside wall of the cell house. The weight of the nut would hold the wire in place. When the other end was attached to the radio, reception was greatly improved. During the day, sunlight gleamed off a giant spider web of literally hundreds of wires stretching just above head height from the cell fronts to the outside wall.

All sorts of personal clothing took the place of the blue work shirts and jeans that were required inmate attire in the past. The institution, formerly spotless, took on a beaten and dirty appearance.

The stress took its toll on many officers. Dick Morgan, who became an officer five years after his father took him on an outing with an inmate under Rhay's "Take a Lifer to Dinner" program, describes how the stress affected him. "I was not a good employee back then," he said. "There was a time [when]…I never put in a five-day work week. I called in sick. I had all the symptoms of what today is recognized as stress: diarrhea every day, not being able to sleep, and stuff like that. After five or six months of this, I got called in…and told to make a career decision: 'Either work for us or get on down the road.' I quit calling in sick, [but] that didn't improve things at work."[22]

Parley Edwards, a longtime correctional officer, described his experiences.

You ever been to a nursing home? Ever had any family in there? Sort of depressing going into a nursing home. Do you think you'd be able to work in a place like that? Well, there's some people that's meant to be correctional officers and there's some people that ain't....You're in a position where all this stress and this chaos is. Some people can handle it better than others; some can't. It's a profession—just like a nursing home.

If you work there long enough, you make friends with convicts—professional friends....There was [an inmate] named Steve McCoy. I didn't know he was holding drugs for another guy—just a hell of a nice guy to work with. Cheerful—I mean enjoyable to be around with and all that. And they killed him.[23]

Edwards paused, unable to speak. Finally he added, "And that—that sort of sets you back."

A lot of staff didn't stay. Some weren't meant to be correctional officers. Others knew what things were like in the old days, before it all changed, and couldn't take it anymore. In the middle years of the decade, staff turnover sometimes exceeded 50 percent per year. Most staff just quit, but a few—a half dozen or so, according to Edwards—killed themselves. For the rest, relationships and other aspects of life often suffered, resulting in divorce, domestic violence, drugs, and alcoholism.

There was a "great, great deal of drinking by staff," said Robin Moses. "[My wife] and I used to go down to the Elks and there'd be a table fifty people long [of correctional officers and their spouses] just night after night."[24]

Some local taverns became so annoyed with penitentiary staff that they banned them from the premises. This happened one time when more than a dozen officers were promoted in rank and the new sergeants decided to hold a bash for all the officers. They each chipped in something like $200, took over a bar, and scheduled the event so that officers from all three shifts could come—free drinks and food for everyone. By the time the last shift arrived, fights between officers and other patrons had spilled out into the street and the cops were called. Perhaps it was "professional courtesy" that no officers were arrested that night—but that was the final prison event at that watering hole.

Chapter 17

HARVEY

I N JANUARY 1974, shortly after he took over the job as director of the division of adult corrections, Hal Bradley made a surprise visit to the penitentiary. He knew Walla Walla by reputation and through staff briefings. But when he saw firsthand how out of control the penitentiary actually was, it was clear to him that Bob Rhay needed better help, including a new associate superintendent for custody. No one in headquarters wanted another Bill Macklin, but they did want someone stronger than Rhay's current associate for custody, Art Crowley.

When asked to describe Crowley's character, a prisoner who had been a death row inmate until the U.S. Supreme Court invalidated most death penalty convictions in 1972 whistled through his teeth. "Genuine human being," he said. "That job didn't fit his personality....He was more of a humanitarian than that job dictated he be."[25] One staff member put it this way: "You couldn't ask for a nicer person."[26]

Nice tributes, perhaps, but not the characteristics usually associated with the head of custody at a maximum security prison. Furthermore, the job took its toll on Crowley. "It ruined his health," agreed Rhay and his associate superintendent for treatment, Bob Freeman.

The man selected to replace Crowley was Jim Harvey.

"Hal told me that he had had his eye on Harvey for a long time and that moving him up was a very important thing," recalled DSHS secretary Charlie Morris. "The California guys were trained under Earl Warren,[27] and they had this very orderly sort of textbook school of public administration approach to government....I know that [Hal] spent a lot of time thinking about...layers of succession five, ten years down the road. He kept records and personnel files and so forth....So a guy like Harvey would not have been coming out of the blue."[28]

In fact, "Hal was sort of grooming him with the hope of his being [Rhay's] replacement. He viewed Jim as an enlightened guy, one whom he could trust....He was the guy that if there was anybody Hal could manage Bob through, it would be Jim."[29]

Managing Bob through someone else was a tall order. Nobody really managed Rhay. As one Olympia administrator put it, "Bob Rhay felt that he owned the penitentiary. He had married the former warden's daughter. He was a hot-shot fly boy from World War II....He wasn't even a bomber pilot. He was a fighter pilot. 'I'm in charge here. I shoot my own guns. I run this thing, and nobody else.'"[30] Nevertheless, Bradley thought Harvey might pull it off.

Barbara Miller, the first paralegal for Prison Services, had known Harvey from his days at the state's newest prison in Shelton, Washington. In the beginning she thought Harvey's by-the-book, no-nonsense approach might work. "There needed to be some lines drawn in the sand," she said, "and people needed to respect those lines—not only from the standpoint of inmates killing inmates, but also in terms of some of the things that occurred at the hands of the officers."[31] Reducing violence on both sides of the bars would be a difficult challenge.

Harvey understood the challenge. "I went in with my eyes open," he said. "Staff were pretty much in little groups....They weren't all pulling together....They wanted someone that could take the institution and bring the staff together and sort of rebuild discipline and control back in the prison....[I] knew the prison from previous experience. I knew a lot of the staff....I knew all those things—that's one of the reasons I went back."[32]

It was also a good promotion and the surest way to become a superintendent. Harvey was not without ambition, and Bradley's confidence in him must have been gratifying.

A few weeks after he took the associate superintendent job, Harvey got a late evening phone call at his new home, a small state-provided house next to the prison. The officers were refusing to take their shift. After Harvey arrived on the scene, union president Steve Chadek told him the night shift officers wanted two more people added to the shift because of vacancies from staff shortages and men calling in sick. The workplace wasn't safe, said Chadek.[33]

After discussing the situation with Rhay, Harvey decided to use overtime to provide additional officers. That solved the immediate problem, but Harvey laid out the bigger picture in a memo to Rhay:

> At the present time we are down fifteen Correctional Officer positions. These officers are needed to provide coverage in the areas where most of the incidents take place. Many requests are coming from the inmate population that supervision be provided so their present programs can continue. They are [also] requesting closer supervision in the cellblock areas to prevent the assaults and thievery that is continually happening....[Additional] personnel in the custody department will surely boost the morale of both the Institutional personnel and the inmate population.[34]

Amid strike threats by the union, as well as the promise of a sympathy strike by the inmates if the officers walked out, headquarters authorized Rhay to fill six of the fifteen vacancies and to use overtime as needed to maintain minimum staffing levels. Rhay delegated the authority to determine when a shift was undermanned to Harvey and the captain who reported to him. Both men were instructed to accumulate officer overtime whenever needed.

But Harvey didn't think this was enough. The earliest surviving memo from Harvey directly to Hal Bradley is dated October 21, 1974, two months after Harvey arrived at the penitentiary. There is no indication that a copy went to Rhay.

Harvey's memo was detailed and specific. He referred to a visit by Bradley when the two had conducted a review of the staffing needs of various penitentiary buildings and shifts. "We cannot provide the needed coverage and supervision for the areas we covered in the post-audit during your visit," he wrote. "The cellblocks are much too large for two officers and a sergeant to supervise during the hours when the activities are taking place." Harvey cited a laundry list of incidents that had occurred over a four week period that could be traced to insufficient staff:

- In late September, a cell was burned out and three staff had to be taken to the hospital for treatment.
- Ten days later, three officers were stabbed. One officer was put on extended sick leave and another was scheduled for surgery.

- The next week, an officer working alone in the telephone room was assaulted.
- Four days later, an inmate was fire bombed in his locked cell, receiving first and second degree burns.
- Two days after that, an inmate was raped in Eight Wing.

The most serious incident occurred the following day, on October 19. Some inmates started a fire in the segregation unit that caused so much smoke that the entire tier had to be evacuated. After the inmates were taken outdoors to the segregation yard, they forced the lock on the fenced-in enclosure and disappeared into the prison's general population. Off-duty officers were called in, and the local police department and the state patrol were placed on alert.

Harvey told Bradley, "These incidents could have been prevented or reduced considerably if we had had adequate staff to carry out our regularly scheduled programs and to provide the supervision that is absolutely essential. [Furthermore,] we have approximately sixty correctional officers on duty [who] are not properly trained. They receive three to five days training and are then placed on shift because we need them so desperately."[35]

At the end of the memo, Harvey requested an additional fourteen correctional officers and four more sergeants. These staff were needed, he explained, to provide three officers in the large cellblocks during waking hours, an additional officer in segregation and admissions, and needed sergeant coverage in various areas of the prison at various times of day.[36]

This is the kind of detail that Bradley needed to make a strong case for additional staff—first within the agency, then to the governor, and finally before the legislature. It was a long process, but eight months later, when the next fiscal year rolled around, twenty additional positions were funded for Walla Walla.

So it was Harvey, not Rhay, to whom corrections director Hal Bradley turned. As Secretary Morris recalled, "If Hal told me that he wanted to do something and that he and Harvey had worked it out, that was sort of the imprimatur. It was going to work. Harvey," said Morris, "was a very influential person in terms of Walla Walla policy as far as Hal was concerned—because Hal did not trust Bob...and he did trust Jim."[37]

But if Bradley's plan was to manage Rhay through Harvey, it didn't work. If anything, it appears that the process—if not the plan—became to marginalize Rhay and manage the penitentiary through Harvey.

Chapter 18

LINES IN THE SAND

WITH THE CHANGE OF ADMINISTRATION in Olympia and the addition of Harvey at Walla Walla, the plan was to incrementally take back many of the concessions given to the inmates since 1971. Everyone agreed—it had to be a gradual process, because a swift transition could trigger a riot.

The first attempt to increase administrative control was to reduce the number of inmates not locked up at night.

Most large prisons have some inmates out of their cells at night. These might include early kitchen workers preparing the morning meal, cleaners assigned to parts of the prison best cleaned when not in use, laundry workers assigned to the night shift, and so forth. The procedure used to keep track of inmates not locked in their cells, and the word used to describe those so situated, is the "out-count."

When Harvey arrived in August 1974, there were often scores of inmates on out-count every night. And these weren't just inmates assigned to night jobs. Every RGC officer, every club head, and many club officers were often out of their cells until as late as five o'clock in the morning. For a long time the RGC office was open twenty-four hours a day. Allegedly this was because the workload of these leaders was so substantial that they couldn't get everything done without working late into the night. In reality, as one of the captains had discovered, most of the leaders were watching TV, playing cards, getting high, and generally having a good time.

The precipitating event for reducing the number of out-counts occurred in September 1974, a month after Harvey arrived. The officers were threatening to strike because there were too few staff to supervise the out-count inmates. In response to the officers' threat, Rhay attempted to reduce the number of inmates, and the hours, for the out-count.

The issue was discussed at an early October 1974 "rap session" between the RGC leaders, B. J. Rhay, associate superintendents Freeman and

Harvey, and others. According to the prison newspaper, Rhay said, "I want the RGC to have all the latitude it needs to function properly, but I cannot imagine why we need all these people up until 5:00 a.m."[38]

When the RGC president and others continued to insist they needed the time to get their work done, Rhay and the others weren't convinced. "I do not know why I'm going along with you, honest to Pete, I don't," said Rhay in his inimitable style, "but I'm here to cooperate....I would like to settle this situation...once and for all and never have to discuss it again."[39]

After negotiating, Rhay agreed that all RGC leaders, club officers, and a reporter for the prison newspaper could stay out until five in the morning, provided that a list was submitted to the shift lieutenant by two o'clock every afternoon and that "they are remaining out during these hours for the purpose of conducting business."

Needless to say, since the precipitating circumstance was insufficient staff to supervise the out-count inmates, staff still couldn't supervise them. The inmates could do what they wanted until someone caught them violating the requirement to only conduct business. And since the RGC and club doors were locked (with inmates having the only keys), there was generally ample time to get down to business before an officer got in. The issue would not be settled for long, let alone "once and for all" as Rhay had hoped.

But Rhay was still the boss, and if he struck a compromise with the inmates that undermined the intent of a new policy or practice, there was nothing Harvey could do. And it wasn't just Harvey who couldn't sway Rhay; neither could corrections director Bradley. "I've seen [Bob Rhay] stand up tooth and nail with Hal Bradley—nose-to-nose in his office—and argue back and forth," said Harvey. "I told [Rhay], 'How in the name of God are you ever going to survive when you talk, and threaten, and refuse to obey a director as you're doing?'"[40]

By November 1974, three months after Harvey arrived, it was clear that tensions were on the rise in the penitentiary. The use of protective custody was growing. Protective custody, or PC, is provided to inmates who can't make it in general population. Receiving a death threat, being victim of a rape, having a reputation for being a snitch, or just overwhelming fear can cause a man to check into PC. There he's isolated from the rest of the population. In the '70s, PC in Walla Walla was essentially voluntary segregation. There was little freedom of movement and very little to do. Correctional professionals know: when PC grows, something is wrong in the prison.

Harvey knew one place where things were wrong: the B.P.F.U. (Black Prisoners Forum Unlimited) clubhouse. While the early activities of the B.P.F.U. were generally benign, and even helpful, by the middle of the decade the B.P.F.U. clubhouse was the site of some of the most debased and self-destructive behavior that occurred in the prison during the 1970s. When Harvey arrived, the club's meeting place was carved into a warren of little rooms. There were shooting galleries, gambling tables, and rooms for homosexual activity. And not all the sex was consensual. Some of the more predatory blacks would pick a younger, weaker inmate as he arrived at the penitentiary and claim him as their own. Some of these inmates were made to dance naked atop a table and then be sold in a single night to six, eight, or ten men for their sexual pleasure. "I'd rather be dead," one such youth said to the associate superintendent. And some of them acted out the thought. "They went in there and hung themselves...or took an overdose," said Harvey.[41]

A few days after Christmas 1974, the simmering tensions boiled over.

Rhay and his top administrative staff were meeting with the RGC and club heads. Members of the Citizens Advisory Council were also present. The inmates had a particularly long list of demands, ending with the threat that if certain demands were not met, "the Resident Government Council shall see to the total destruction of the Washington State Penitentiary."[42]

This inflammatory language did not sit well with the prison administrators or members of the Citizens Advisory Council. The same was true for many of the demands, fourteen of which were about associate superintendent Harvey. Among them was insistence on removal of "all security gates constructed since the day that Harvey was hired" and a demand for Harvey's removal.[43]

Usually these meetings between administrators and inmate leaders took place in the visiting room, a secure space just outside the prison wall. But at the request of the RGC, this one was held in the education building, inside the prison. Harvey remembers telling Rhay, "Why... are we having it up here?...Things could happen and we'd lose control real fast." He remembers Rhay saying, "We have to give in to them once in a while."[44]

But Harvey had intelligence that trouble was afoot.

Harvey told the shift lieutenant, "I have a bad feeling. I want you to be on the alert....I want your people to be on the alert. If you see anything whatsoever that don't look right—if you get the uneasy feeling too—let me know."

During the meeting, the shift lieutenant came to the door and motioned for Harvey. When Harvey joined him, the message wasn't good. "Jim, something's coming down....I can't get ahold of Eight Wing. I sent some officers down there and they haven't returned yet.... Something's wrong."

Harvey told Rhay, "There's something going on....We better get out of here [and] we better get out right now." Rhay immediately canceled the meeting. "The inmates tried to argue him out of it," Harvey recalled, "[but] Rhay said, 'No, we're leaving.'"[45]

The shift lieutenant had instructed officers to lock the gates on both sides of Central Control, thus creating a secure corridor for Rhay and others to exit the institution and enter the old administration building. As they left, they could see hundreds of inmates jammed up against the gates.

Everything was coordinated. The inmates took over Eight Wing and locked the wing officers in the shower room. Two inmates took over the hospital and held the nurses at knifepoint.

What happened next depends on who is telling the story. When asked if it would surprise him to learn that Rhay plays a more prominent role when he's telling the story, Harvey chuckled. "It wouldn't surprise me....He was the superintendent."[46]

As Rhay and the others left, Harvey and the shift lieutenant could see inmates throwing drugs and whatever else they could find out a window of the third floor of the hospital. Other inmates were scooping up the loot and disappearing down the breezeway. Rhay yelled for Harvey to join him.

Rhay probably made the big decisions—such as mustering the SWAT team and rescuing the nurses first. In Harvey's telling, Rhay directed the first part of the operation from the superintendent's conference room just outside the institution. In Rhay's telling, he was in the thick of things from the very beginning. In any event, the SWAT team assembled at the main gate. They went through the yard under One Tower and into the hospital.

"We took it floor by floor," said Harvey. "[When] we got to the third floor we looked into the nurses' station—it's all enclosed in glass—and [an inmate] had one nurse by the throat. He had a large knife in his hand. The other inmate was standing around. He was shouting and screaming. The sergeant looked at me and said, 'What shall we do?' I said, 'Smash that window and let's get to her right now.'"[47]

The officers came in from two directions. They simultaneously broke the glass on one side of the nurses' station and broke through the top of a Dutch door on the other. As the glass shattered, the inmate with the knife began stabbing. One nurse was hit four times in the arm. The other was stabbed once in the shoulder. The officers subdued the inmates, handcuffed them, and took them to Big Red. The nurses were taken to the local hospital, where one was treated and released. The other was released the next day. Both quickly resigned their prison jobs.

With the two inmates locked up in Big Red, the officers turned their attention to Eight Wing. In separate interviews, Rhay and Harvey both claim they told the inmate spokesman in Eight Wing that if the hostage officers weren't released unharmed, they were going to come in shooting. Furthermore, they'd shoot the leaders first. It doesn't really matter who made the threat—it worked. Within minutes the hostages were walking up the tier escorted by the inmate leaders. According to Rhay, one of the hostages—a sergeant who was very unpopular with the inmates—said, "Thank God you came when you did. They had me in [the shower] and they were going to fuck me."[48]

By six in the evening, three hours after it started, the crisis was over. The prison was locked down. Because some inmates were instrumental in ending the hostage taking in Eight Wing, the lockdown was brief.

Whatever his role, Rhay got the credit in Olympia. This was one of the events that led DSHS secretary Charlie Morris to conclude that Bob Rhay "was undeniably one of the best crisis managers who ever lived." In a letter to Rhay and copied to the governor, Morris wrote, "I want to commend you and express appreciation for your virtually flawless handling of last week's disturbance. Your coolness and decisiveness under great pressure undoubtedly saved lives and prevented much worse from occurring. Your performance continues to be a credit to the state."[49]

But the trouble continued. Two days later, on New Year's Day, more hostages were taken. One of the morning shift sergeants told Harvey what happened in a memo.

> At approximately 0620, after searching the Valve Room and the back of [segregation], Sergeant Talbot and I received word there might be trouble in the kitchen....Upon arriving at the south door to the kitchen, the grill door, which should have been locked, was open. No staff were in sight. Several inmates were seated in the chow hall and when I asked "Where is everybody?" one of the residents motioned us to the grill area. As we proceeded thru the drop door we observed [an inmate] coming our way with at least three knives, two small carving knives (approximately 8" long) in his left hand and a large butcher knife (approximately 20" long) in his right hand.[50]

Other inmates were attempting to control the inmate who was brandishing the knives. They circled him at a safe distance, and after a few minutes they talked him into retreating to the bakery area. A short time later, one of the inmates came out of the bakery and handed five knives and some staff keys to the officers.

Six staff—civilian cooks and correctional officers—were locked in a walk-in cooler and the head cook's office. When released, they said their keys had been taken at knifepoint.

Within hours, eight officers quit.

Like a contagion, the hostage taking continued. Eleven days into January 1975, two inmates held four staff at knifepoint in the prison hospital. They were looking for drugs. RGC members talked them down and turned the inmates over to the administration. No one was injured.

More officers quit. The union drew up a strike plan.

By early March, Rhay had had enough. In a letter to a DSHS assistant attorney general, he wrote, "We have [recently] had four incidents concerning RGC members who have been infracted for serious infractions....I am in need of an opinion concerning my rights as a superintendent...to act on removing a member of the RGC whom I feel is not a creditable, trustworthy member."[51]

Before the assistant attorney general could respond, Hal Bradley wrote to Rhay and sent a copy to the assistant AG. "Let me remind both of you that if, in the best judgment of the superintendent, the failure of the RGC to recall a member represents a threat to the good order or safety of the institution, then the superintendent may simply abolish the RGC."[52] Not long after Bradley wrote his letter, Rhay did exactly that.

A few weeks later, something occurred far outside the prison that would ultimately have ramifications inside. In late May 1975, a group calling themselves the George Jackson Brigade planted a bomb in the division of adult corrections headquarters building in Olympia. The weekend explosion claimed no casualties, but a hole was blown through the concrete floor two doors from Hal Bradley's office. Damage was estimated at $100,000.

An anonymous caller contacted a Seattle newspaper with instructions to look for a document in a telephone booth. Among other things, the lengthy communiqué from the brigade demanded the removal of a penitentiary doctor, nurse, and Harvey. The brigade also wanted reinstatement of the recently disbanded Resident Government Council.

At the time, hardly anyone had heard of the George Jackson Brigade. The group was named after the author of *Soledad Brother*, who was killed trying to escape from a California prison in 1971. The bombing of the adult corrections headquarters raised the brigade's profile, as did their subsequent attempts to finance their revolutionary agenda through criminal activity.

"It was shortly after the George Jackson Brigade became known to the public and to the correctional system [that] they put a contract on Bob Rhay and me," said Harvey. "I had a twenty thousand dollar contract on myself. I don't remember how much Bob Rhay had placed on him."[53]

A year later, one of the leaders of the George Jackson Brigade, who had been involved in a shootout during an attempted bank robbery, was convicted on two counts of assault with intent to kill police officers. The brigade would no longer have to rely on secondhand reports of conditions at the penitentiary—one of their leaders, with his radical agenda and bomb-making skills, was going to Walla Walla.

According to Harvey, "after [he] came…the most notorious people in the penitentiary became part of that brigade."[54] The brigade also continued to have active members on the outside who were not finished making headlines.

Meanwhile—probably during or soon after Harvey's first year at Walla Walla—the method for assigning inmates to cells was changed. Until then, inmates could basically live wherever they wanted. As one inmate put it, "If you got people that you want to live in a four-man house with…and they're livin' in all different areas…[the assignment lieutenant] would say, 'Just give me the names.' You gave it to him and it was done."[55]

This created problems. The prison had an entrenched status hierarchy, and some cells were "owned" by higher-status inmates—or at least, longer-serving ones. If you were assigned to one of these cells, or chose to live there, you were charged rent.

Typically, an inmate would fix up a cell with various amenities and then charge others for the privilege of living there. Even before Harvey arrived, rule enforcement was so lax that many inmates could make thousands of dollars on various legal or illegal activities, buy whatever they wanted, and keep virtually unlimited personal property in their cells. Some of that money was spent on improving the value of their real estate.

An inmate who owned three cells described one of them: "I spent like three thousand dollars fixing up my cell—putting tile on the floor and I got curtains. I even bought my own toilet.…I was getting a carton of cigarettes a week [for it]. Cartons of cigarettes, understand—they can do a lot of things."[56]

Another inmate "landlord" said he owned three cells in Six and Eight Wing. One "was so nice I could rent it out for a hundred fifty dollars a month. It had TV and everything, wall to wall carpeting, shelves."[57]

A change of policy and a new assignment lieutenant put a damper on the cell rental business. In the November 1975 issue of *Voice of Prison*, an inmate wrote a blurb titled "Recession": "Custody is causing a recession in the real estate market. They are placing people in any cell they want, that's how. News is that it is being done with that in mind, to deflate the value of real estate."[58]

Toward the end of 1975, Bob Freeman retired as associate superintendent for treatment. His replacement, Jim Cummins, a former Catholic priest who drank a lot, was liked by everyone. But Cummins was never strong—certainly not strong enough to stand up to Harvey. With little opposition, Harvey quickly usurped Cummins's authority. By the end of 1975, sixteen months after he arrived, reasserting control of the prison was squarely on Harvey's shoulders.

Chapter 19

PARALLEL TRACKS

FOLLOWING THE TURMOIL of the 1960s, the world outside the prison continued to change. Mothers, fathers, and grandparents joined the young in the antiwar movement. Pot became something other than a cooking utensil. The sexual revolution flourished. Facing impeachment, Nixon resigned as president. The Vietnam War came to its ignominious end.

The face of corrections was changing too.

In 1974, a graph of the inmate population at Walla Walla over the previous ten years would have shown ups and downs, but the overall trend was clear: the population was falling fast. In ten years, the number of inmates at the penitentiary plummeted from nearly eighteen hundred to less than nine hundred. By 1974, there were vacant beds throughout the prison. The big cells that had housed four men at the beginning of the decade now housed two. A new institution for men and the slow expansion of work release accounted for some of the decline in numbers at Walla Walla. But this was a statewide (and nationwide) phenomenon. By 1974, there were 20 percent fewer inmates in Washington prisons than ten years before.

In the middle of this sharp decline, Rhay went to Europe and returned with tales of mini-prisons—institutions with a hundred people, sometimes fewer. "One hundred prisoners is considered a big institution," wrote Rhay, "and the administrators of these prisons follow a general pattern of breaking their populations into smaller units."[59] Rhay thought this small size made treatment programs more effective in Europe than in the states.

On the national scene, the President's Commission on Law Enforcement and Criminal Justice concluded that "when the relatively few dangerous convicted offenders are weeded out for secure confinement, the rest can be handled at far less cost, and no great risk, in community programs."[60]

A few months after Rhay wrote about his impressions of European prisons, Governor Evans began singing the praises of mini-prisons. The future of corrections, said Evans, "should be smaller, community-based treatment centers, serving maybe two hundred instead of this mass warehousing." Smaller treatment centers wouldn't save money in the short run, but "we're more interested in saving lives and reducing the recidivism rate," said Evans.[61] In the meantime, the old prisons were both deteriorating and no longer in step with modern correctional practices. The penitentiary, Evans said, should go.

In October 1971, a month after the prison riot in Attica, New York, claimed forty-three lives, the second RGC took up the call. Under the leadership of inmates Gordy Graham and Johnnie Harris, they researched, planned, and invited outside experts. Within a few months of Evans's speech, the RGC held a day-long seminar titled "A Search for the Prison of Tomorrow." News media and agency personnel from around the state were invited. Audio tapes were made for state legislators. The inmates even made a plan and model of a prototype for a one-hundred-bed community-based treatment center. Rhay praised the plan and the RGC.[62]

A few days later, at a speaking engagement in Walla Walla, Rhay said, "It may make me unpopular with the legislature, but the days of the old territorial prison [are numbered], the old walled enclosure is on its way out."[63]

Evans continued to argue for an end to large, old prisons. At the National Conference of Chief Justices in August 1972 he said, "So often prisoners are just warehoused in [these old facilities] where they learn more crime....Crime is a problem of the communities. Answers must come from communities....Massive state prisons should be torn down and community treatment centers for inmates built in their place."[64]

By December 1972, the capital budget for the Department of Social and Health Services reflected these sentiments. "We will not need three adult male institutions like we have now sometime within the next five to ten years," said Secretary Smith. "In that case, we would probably phase out the penitentiary." As a result, the agency would not ask for

Maintenance suffered—showers in Eight Wing

any major improvements at the penitentiary or "anything that would last much beyond five years."[65]

Although a bill was introduced in the 1973 legislative session to phase out both the penitentiary and the state's other old prison at Monroe, nothing came of it. But the mindset remained for years: the penitentiary was a dinosaur, old and decrepit, out of touch with the needs of a modern world. Why spend a dime on it?

Another factor, far removed from the issues of prisons and reform, undoubtedly reinforced this unwillingness to invest in Walla Walla. For many years Boeing drove the economy of not just Seattle, but the state. The sixties were hot for Boeing—first with an expansion of commercial aviation and later with the buildup of the Vietnam War. The Puget Sound economy was bustling, and the state coffers were full. Then, at a pace that staggered personal and institutional fortunes, the aviation market collapsed. Beginning in 1970, Boeing began a layoff that would ultimately eliminate 100,000 workers. By 1972 there were whole neighborhoods in Seattle where almost every house was for sale and many abandoned to foreclosure. A billboard near the airport read, "Will the last person leaving Seattle—Turn out the lights."

As a result, there was precious little money in the state's till. The oldest institution in Washington, with its ancient infrastructure and worn-out buildings, was left to decay. The penitentiary's physical plant deficiencies were yet another factor that contributed to the chaos at Walla Walla. Until money was found, those deficiencies would only get worse.

Meanwhile, the mini-prison concept retained its currency. Six months after Hal Bradley became the first director of the division of adult corrections, Secretary Morris named the runner-up for Bradley's job as head of a task force to study Washington State's criminal justice system. His name was Douglas Vinzant.[66] Among other things, Vinzant's task force was told to consider small community-based correctional facilities.

Vinzant appears to have been something of a Renaissance man. According to the newspaper article introducing him, not only was he a warden and correctional expert, he was an ordained Methodist minister, "a master electrician, first-class welder and carpenter, an oil painter and [he] breeds and trains horses and bird dogs."[67]

Vinzant was selected for the Washington State task force in May 1974. Before that, he had been warden at Walpole Penitentiary in Massachusetts for less than nine months. But it was a critical nine months, according to Charlie Morris: "Walpole was in total chaos when Doug took it over last year and he really cleaned the place up fast."[68] On the other hand, maybe Morris didn't get the complete story about what Vinzant did, or didn't do, at Walpole.

The real chaos at Walpole was over before Vinzant became warden. The previous spring, the correctional officers literally walked off the job and abandoned the prison. For three months, the inmates ran the penitentiary, with nonuniformed cadet officers operating door controls and outside observers from the community monitoring the prison twenty-four hours a day. By the time Vinzant arrived, state troopers and the department of corrections had regained control of the prison and locked the institution down. This was the situation Vinzant inherited.[69] Perhaps he didn't make matters worse, but Walpole continued to be a corrupt and brutal prison long after Vinzant's departure.[70]

While Morris's endorsement of the man may have been a little over the top, there's no denying that Vinzant was well-read, knowledgeable, and articulate about current trends in corrections. On top of that, he was a charming Southern gentleman. According to Morris, "he loved to play the Mississippi thing." He'd toss off idioms foreign to Northwestern ears. A phrase like "Just because kittens are born in the oven don't make 'em biscuits" might be part of his testimony at a legislative hearing. "You can tell them anything if you've got a heavy Southern accent," Vinzant once told Morris.[71] Morris thought he was a great testifier. The legislators ate it up.

Vinzant performed well as director of the Governor's Task Force on Corrections. Meetings were held around the state, and the task force ended up recommending mini-prisons. While Vinzant's strength was in his ideas, this one wasn't terribly original. As Morris put it, "I don't think the answers that Doug came up with were any great surprise. There was a shared model that we all had in mind, and the task force essentially filled out that model."[72]

When the task force was done, Morris liked the report so much that he made Vinzant head of the DSHS Bureau of Juvenile Rehabilitation. Vinzant would stick around.

Of course, falling prison populations never led to the penitentiary's closing. One day in the summer of 1974, just before Harvey arrived as associate superintendent for custody, adult corrections director Hal Bradley told Secretary Morris, "We have a temporary pickup in population."

The pickup wasn't temporary. With nearly 150,000 young men returning from Vietnam and the beginning of the war on drugs, prison populations began to rise around the country. In Washington State, the rise began in July 1974.

"I never forgot that day," said Morris, "because that was a…complete sea change. From that day on populations rose."[73] Throughout Harvey's tenure as associate superintendent, and for several years thereafter, the prison population continued to grow. By the time Harvey left in 1977, there were six hundred more prisoners than when he arrived. For the penitentiary, six hundred more inmates is the difference between having two men in every 120-square-foot cell and having four. This return to crowding only added to the growing tensions in the prison.

Chapter 20

THE THIRD FLOOR

B Y THE MID-'70s there were few places in the prison where Rhay had much control other than the perimeter wall. Thanks to his friend, prison psychologist Dr. William Hunter, the mental health program on the third floor of the hospital was an exception. The fear factor survived in this small corner of the prison.

"You had to be pretty bad to get up there because there wasn't very many slots," explained associate superintendent Freeman. "That was [Hunter's] base of operation. He had the absolute worst people."[74]

Dick Morgan, a man with an excellent memory and a gift for story-telling, had been working at the penitentiary less than four months when a lieutenant told him to go up to the third floor of the hospital and keep an eye on things. Morgan recalled this unusual assignment, including what he and others said at the time. "Custody wasn't allowed up there," explained Morgan. "That was kind of an island that you just did not go to. You took inmates up to them, handed them through the gate, and then you weren't allowed on the floor."[75]

Morgan asked the lieutenant what he should do on the third floor. The lieutenant told him: "look for swollen jaws, black eyes, bruises, anything that says something's going wrong in there."

The real reason he was assigned there, according to Morgan, was because "too many people had hung themselves with their hands tied behind their back up on the third floor....A lot of people died up there, but everybody just rolled their eyes. And the inmates—if you wanted to get an inmate to [panic]—all you had to do was tell them you're taking them to the third floor—because it was the solid belief that if they were going to the third floor, they had a good chance of dying."

Morgan found two kinds of inmates in the mental health program: prior patients Dr. Hunter had "cured" and inmates who were currently "in treatment." Civilian attendants carried the keys, but opened and closed the doors on the orders of the "cured" inmates. Morgan made a tour and looked into each cell. "Everybody except for this goon squad [of prior patients] had been beat up. None of them would talk with me. They would actually cower in the back of the cell and say, 'Get away from me. I can't talk to you.'"

"Something's not right there," Morgan told the lieutenant.

The next day Morgan got the same assignment. As he arrived, he heard screaming from the back of the wing. Gardie Saylors, a severely mentally ill inmate, was standing at rigid attention inside the cell (probably in a drug-induced stupor from too much antipsychotic medication). Three inmates, all members of the goon squad Hunter left in charge, were standing by the bars. One was reaching inside and cutting Saylors's face with his fingernails. "You'd better get me away from him because I'm going to kill him," screamed Saylors's attacker. Morgan separated the men and got Saylors protected. Eventually all the men were locked up.

While Morgan was locking the men up, one of the inmates told him, "Don't go near Snook. He's going to try to kill you." Donald Snook was mad at Morgan for locking up the man who attacked Saylors, the inmate explained. A little while later, Morgan heard noise from Snook's cell. When he went to investigate, Snook said, "I've got some information for you."

"So spit it out," said Morgan.

"Come here," said Snook.

"I'm not getting any closer than this, Snook. What have you got to tell me?"

Snook had torn up his guitar and had a guitar string strung tight between two Bic pens. "Come here, you son of a bitch!" raged Snook. "I'm going to cut your fucking head off, you punk!"

Morgan thought it was time to talk to his lieutenant. He got on the phone, but it was a different lieutenant this time.

"Morgan, where are you at?" asked the lieutenant.

"I'm on the third floor."

"And there are medical supervisors up there, right?"

"Well, yeah." Morgan thought to himself, "There's a guy that's just a complete lump of coal."

"And these are patients, are they not?" continued the lieutenant.

"Yeah."

"And they're under a doctor's care, aren't they, Morgan?"

"Yeah."

"Then it's none of our goddamned business," said the lieutenant as he hung up.

What do I do now? thought Morgan.

A little while later, a sergeant working on one of the lower floors took Gardie Saylors downstairs for a phone call from his attorney. Something happened while Saylors was out of Morgan's sight, and the captain called Morgan.

"Tell me, Officer Morgan, what are you doing on the third floor?" asked the captain.

"I was assigned here," replied Morgan.

"And what were you told to do?"

"Well, I was supposed to keep an eye on things and make sure that nothing happens to the inmates."

"That's right, Officer Morgan," said the captain. "So why in the hell have I got Gardie Saylors standing in front of me bleeding all over my desk?"

Morgan went ballistic. He yelled at the captain and named the lieutenant who told him to forget about it. As he hung up, he was pretty sure his career as an officer was over. You don't yell at the captain.

The captain called again. "I'm sorry, Morgan. I didn't understand the situation. I want you to come to my office just as soon as you're relieved." When Morgan reported to the captain, he was told to write everything up. As he wrote his report, another officer sat watching him, all the while shaking his head.

"I was mad," recalled Morgan. "I [thought I] must be doing something stupid. And boy, was I. How was I to know that [the lieutenant who had told me to ignore the situation] was related to B. J.?"[76]

Even the captain got in trouble for standing up for Morgan. In what can only be described as retaliation, Morgan was assigned to Eight Wing—"which was purgatory as far as jobs went."

There were many complaints about the penitentiary's mental health program. After receiving a letter from a legal services lawyer, DSHS secretary Charlie Morris decided to go to Walla Walla to see for himself. He wrote about this experience in his book, *A Time of Passion: America 1960–1980*. While he was there, Morris sat down with a group of ten inmates in the mental health program. Much to his surprise the inmates didn't curse or interrupt. In fact, in Morris's words, "they were the most orderly and polite group of inmates I'd ever met."[77]

The inmates told Morris that the program helped them learn self-control. This was accomplished through an elaborate set of rules accompanied by a system of punishments devised and imposed by the inmates who had been "cured" by Hunter's program. These inmates were, of course, the goon squad Morgan saw in action.

The punishment for a first transgression was trivial: "Loss of smoking privileges for an hour perhaps—but became progressively stiffer and finally truly draconian." The ultimate punishment, he was told, was confinement in a cell in the dark while strapped to a cot and wearing nothing but a diaper.

"The essential principle," Morris concluded, "was that the mutinous group member never won....Eventually, for the sake of a respite, [the non-cooperative inmate] would decide to *pretend* to comply. At that point he was hooked. After a relatively short period of complying with the rules, he invariably internalized them."[78]

In 1975 an independent review of the third floor was conducted by the National Commission for the Protection of Human Subjects of Biomedical and Behavioral Research. Commission members had already visited several prisons by the time they reached Walla Walla, and they were impressed with Hunter's program and inmates with whom they spoke. They clearly saw it as an effective behavior modification program. However, despite generally favorable comments, one commission member noted that "while I would give [Hunter] all the credit in the world for what he was accomplishing, I wanted to make it perfectly clear to him that I did not regard it as original—that Mao had worked it out long before him and had made it work very effectively with our prisoners of war during the Korean Affair."[79]

The same commission member noted that he had a difficult time separating what Hunter was doing from what Hunter said was the cause of the inmates' mental problems.[80] Underlying Hunter's operation was a theory that can only be called unorthodox.

Hunter believed that because many criminals were raised in single-parent homes by their mothers, they never had an appropriate male role model. He told a reporter from the Walla Walla newspaper, "these boys all got too much of a female orientation to life...and in order to cover up that secret...they act tough."[81]

"What all these so-called tough guys out there are doing," continued Hunter, "is advertising to all the world, 'I'm not really man enough to carry my weight out on the street.' Everyone is hiding that secret and they've got a lot of people fooled." For example, "a lot of these so-called tough bikers have real problems with their male identities, and a lot of them are just out-and-out homosexuals."

Whenever a new patient arrived on the third floor, Hunter would tell him, "I'm going to teach you one lesson—and that's a lesson a father should have taught you when you were [a child:]...you don't do as you damn please." Furthermore, "when they get out of line here, we make it very plain nobody is going to put up with their damn foolishness."[82]

Hunter used to tell DSHS attorney John Henry Browne that his program was "regression therapy" in which inmates were reduced to the role of infant and then retrained, with Dr. Hunter cast as the father figure. Browne didn't buy Hunter's theory. "I saw people chained to beds with no clothes on—just vinyl mattresses—with feces all over them. It was the worst I've ever seen." And then, "there were these inmate Gestapo guys—Dr. Hunter's goon squad. They had...hypos full of medicine. There were rumors that they had their own enforcement program and that they were somehow tied in with the bad guys in the prison and that people would get up there and get tortured. Half of that's probably not true, but the remaining half was awful."[83]

Richard Emery, a former director of Washington's Prison Legal Services, described Hunter's program as "a complete nightmarish torture chamber."[84]

When told that B. J. Rhay still defended the program decades later, Emery said, "Of course—because it does have that sort of stupid kernel of truth in it about the father figure and all that crap. The thing they forgot about is that fathers' relationships with sons work only because of the enormous amount of love involved—[something] which Hunter didn't have to offer."

Legal Services tried to make a case to close Hunter's program. "We'd always known what was going on up there, but nobody would come forward and give us the information," explained Legal Services attorney Allen Ressler.[85] Everyone was too scared. An inmate by the name of Michael Brookshire finally agreed to testify. An affidavit filed in Walla Walla Superior Court told Brookshire's story.[86]

Late in October 1974, Brookshire was transferred to the Washington State Penitentiary and immediately placed in Dr. Hunter's program on the third floor. Three days later, after he refused to have his hair cut, Brookshire was put in a double-locked, double-door isolation cell furnished with only a hard mattress, sink, and toilet. He remained there for the next ninety-eight days. His only clothing during this time was a pair of boxer shorts. His only hygienic items were a toothbrush and toothpowder. Despite requests, he was denied exercise periods, reading material, written or telephonic communication, access to legal counsel, or permission to see visitors. Once, when he realized that a legal services attorney was on the floor, Brookshire shouted out for attention. For this he was given a shot of Thorazine, a powerful antipsychotic.

Brookshire finally agreed to have his hair cut and he was released from isolation. Six days later, after refusing to report on the activities of other penitentiary inmates, he was placed in isolation again.

Seventeen days later Brookshire swallowed a pencil and made numerous cuts on his body so that he would be transferred to a medical floor in the hospital where he hoped to secure legal help.

When the prisoner attendants discovered Brookshire, they scrubbed his cuts with a bristle brush and rubbing alcohol before taking him to the first floor of the hospital where some of the cuts were stitched. Afterwards, he was handcuffed and put back in his isolation cell wearing nothing but a football helmet secured by a wire chin strap. After Brookshire pried off the helmet, he was chained to a bed, where he remained naked for approximately nine days, covered with a sheet. During this time, prisoner attendants "showered" Brookshire by pouring a bucket of water on him and replacing the sheet on his still wet body.

After almost four weeks, Brookshire was unchained and let out of his cell. Six days later it started all over again.

Eventually, Brookshire was able to talk with Prison Legal Services. With the affidavit in hand, "we filed a lawsuit and [the state] folded.... They just closed the place up and transferred everybody," said Ressler.[87]

Brookshire was transferred to segregation. Donald Snook was there as well—different cell, same tier. Somehow Brookshire got too close to Snook, and Snook killed him. Brookshire "didn't die right away. He hung on for like a week," recalled Allen Ressler. "There was a bill that came to the state in the amount of twelve, fifteen thousand dollars. Dr. Hunter sent it to me, saying I was responsible...because I had been the one responsible for closing down the program."

Ressler continued, "I sent his letter and my response to the newspaper." When the reporter interviewed him, Ressler called Hunter a nut. "I thought I was going to get sued on that one," chuckled Ressler. When informed that Hunter died many years ago, Ressler warmed to the subject: "Well, fuck, he was a nut," he boomed.[88]

Chapter 21

The Goon Squad

J IM HARVEY SAID THAT when he arrived in August 1974, probably 95 percent of the correctional officers had stopped even pretending to do the job for which they were hired. While most officers did nothing, a few took matters into their own hands. For some, it was a game; for others, a vendetta.

The inmates understood the situation. "We were so much in control of the prison [that] a lot of guards didn't have an opportunity to really do much with us," explained one inmate. "The only thing they had to do was keep down the violence, bust somebody if they could.... When help was needed, that's when they were called. I can't even really remember them walkin' around too much." For the most part, "they were kinda like out of the way."[89]

From the inmates' perspective, there were basically three kinds of officers. First, a large group was there just for the paycheck. They wanted to make it through the day, go home, and forget about it. They were the ones who, according to both staff and the inmates, did little or nothing. The second group was a small number of "professionals"— career correctional officers who actually did their job. They wanted to stop trouble, not start it. They would bust a man if he deserved it, but they never hated inmates. Finally, "you had guards who needed to have a reputation," said an inmate. "When they put that uniform on, they became Superman—and they were the shitheads. They're the ones that caused all the problems and had all the hatred thing going."[90]

A "good" officer, in the eyes of the inmates, was simply fair. Not fair were the guards turned Superman who "caused all the problems." When the inmates didn't call them "shitheads," they called them "the goon squad"—the universal term for bullying thugs.

To staff, the goon squad was the "utility crew," or later, "Search and Escort" (S&E). The utility crew was a group of four to seven officers who didn't have fixed posts—they moved around. They did shakedowns and impromptu searches, rooftop checks, basement checks, and other kinds of security checks. They ran the pill line and did the out-counts. But above all, they responded to emergencies.

To the inmates, the man who personified the utility crew—that is, the goon squad—was Hartford.

Jim Hartford came to the penitentiary in October 1975, a little more than a year after Harvey took over as associate superintendent for custody. Hartford had been in college on a Law Enforcement Education Program (LEEP) grant. After he dropped out and went to work on the county road crew, he started getting notices from the government saying he owed them money. The best way to cancel the debt was to work two years in a field related to law enforcement. "So I figured I'd just work two years at the penitentiary and get that off my back and then go back to working on the survey crew or whatever."[91] It didn't really work out that way.

A skydiver, Hartford had made hundreds of jumps by the time he started work at the penitentiary. He rode motorcycles, loved to shoot handguns, and liked to fight. When he was interviewed by the local paper in 1977, his apartment was decorated with fighting knives, swords, and bayonets mounted on black felt. "I like excitement....I liked excitement before I ever heard the word macho," he said.[92]

Hartford went to work at the penitentiary and found excitement. "The thing I enjoyed most and felt that I excelled at was working S&E, Search and Escort," he said. "That's where the fun was."

Hartford's idea of fun was somewhat unusual. He liked to do cell searches and stop inmates on the breezeway to look for contraband. The most common contraband was drugs, but it wasn't just drugs that were found. There were "good weapons, well-made, edged weapons," he said. "Of course there were zip guns; there were firearms—factory firearms smuggled inside—ammunition and explosives....It was just a wide open place."[93]

"[Fighting was] the way you ran business," he explained. "If you could get the inmate to run, [he] was fair game. I chased inmates all over that place—foot races and tackles, wrestling matches, getting cuffs on....That was fun, chasing people and fighting them. It really was. It was pitting your skills against [theirs]."

Sometimes a fleeing inmate would run into the sanctuary of their club and Hartford would have a locked door slammed in his face. While this made him mad, he and other members of Search and Escort had ways to circumvent locked clubhouse doors. For example, sometimes at night they would take off their uniform hat, put on inmate coat, and charge in behind an inmate entering a club before the door could be closed and locked. Hartford described one incident when he and another officer used this trick to get into the Bikers' Club where there was a half pound of marijuana being broken up.

"It was just [this other guy] and me and the whole bike shop," he explained. Hartford grabbed the bag of marijuana and one of the bikers said, "You ain't taking the dope." Hartford begged to differ. He and the other officer stood their ground and finally the president of the Bikers' Club gave the nod allowing them to leave. "He could just as easily have given the nod to take the dope back and to have us stabbed or beat up. There were enough of them. They could have just physically taken it."[94]

Hartford was good at what he did, and the inmates hated him for it—most of them, at least. One inmate voiced an opinion that was shared by many: "He was a piece of shit." On the other hand, no one at the penitentiary had as many informants or gathered as much intelligence as Jim Hartford. He could gain a man's confidence in minutes and protected those who helped him. While many inmates hated him, others trusted and confided in him.

Knowledge of where to look, what to look for, and who to closely watch often came from snitches. While there are many reasons for inmates to give staff information, some did it for money. They weren't paid in actual dollars, because real money—called "white money" by the convicts—was contraband in prison. Of course, there was plenty of white money in the prison, just like every other kind of contraband. But the "legal tender" in the penitentiary was scrip that could be used to buy various items in the inmate store.

"I'll be honest with you," said associate superintendent Harvey. "We'd search an inmate's cell or [an inmate] on the sidewalk...[and if] we got an enormous amount of scrip, we kept it because [a large quantity of scrip] was considered contraband." There were times when Harvey had thousands of dollars of scrip that he would use to pay informants. In this way, he got information about drugs, murders, and corrupt staff. "I bought information on two guns that were in the Lifers' Club," said Harvey, "a .38 and a .45. [My informant] told me exactly where they were at and how many rounds of ammunition....We tore that club completely apart. We smashed walls in....I personally have the .38 now because it was given to me by Bob Rhay and by the director of prisons, who was Hal Bradley at that time."[95]

The inmates knew that people like Harvey and Hartford would bust them if they could. "It was a game," said Hartford. "The inmates took it as a game....[And] if anybody could bust them, it'd be me or guys that I was running with."[96]

But it wasn't always a game. Throughout the decade, whenever anything particularly egregious happened, the inmates blamed it on the goon squad. Even Harvey acknowledged that staff brutality and other serious misconduct was going on while he was there.

> There was a lot of good staff at Walla Walla at that time—a lot of good staff. There was some bad [too]. The bad ones were the ones who were bringing in the drugs. The bad ones were the ones that were causing the inmates to act out more than they would have if the person had been halfway decent. They were abusive to them. They were doing things that were not allowed: cuffing 'em up and then beating the hell out of them; putting them in segregation and depriving them of everything you could possibly think of. They caused a lot of their own problems. The inmates didn't cause all of them. The staff caused a lot.[97]

While Harvey believed that most abusive acts by staff were caused by frustration, he knew there were other reasons. "Some of it was because you put certain people in a uniform and they let the privilege of that authority go to their head. And when they're not controlled by some supervisory staff person, they just go crazy with it. That's what they were doing: depriving the inmates of privileges that they are entitled to; depriving them of rights that they have—like going to religious services, having a good meal served to them....Especially in Big Red. They did things down there that was completely out of line."

Then, presumably referring to incidents such as staff smuggling drugs or officers cuffing inmates and then beating the hell out of them, he added: "I'm talking about when I was over there from '74 to '77. [The officers] were doing things…that were actually criminal."[98]

Chapter 22

POWER SHIFT

WHEN RHAY ABOLISHED the Resident Government Council
in April 1975, it was quickly replaced by a weaker Resident Council. The transformation of the RGC into the RC
simply continued the RGC's downward spiral to irrelevance that had
started years before. The power vacuum left behind was filled by the
three major clubs: Lifers with Hope, the Black Prisoners Forum Unlimited, and the Bikers' Club.

Each of the major clubs had legitimate activities, but as the flow
of drugs into the penitentiary increased, the money, and therefore the
power, became inextricably linked with the drug trade. By 1975, heroin
was big business. Tens of thousands of dollars exchanged hands inside
the prison each month. And while scrip could be used to buy drugs, for
the most part real money, white money, was used—money that was contraband like the drugs it could buy. Big money brought big trouble. A
small debt could cost you your life.

As the drug trade became the central business of the prison, the
power of the B.P.F.U. rested on Cadillac Brown's heroin pipeline. The
bikers' power came from a contract they had with Cadillac for the distribution and control of heroin sales inside the prison. The bikers were
the monitors, enforcers, and debt collectors. The lifers had the power
of numbers. They were the largest group in the penitentiary, and their
membership included leaders from the other major clubs. Whenever
there was an important decision to be made, the lifers had a say.

Increasingly, the important decisions involved management of
what might be called the "business climate." Anything that provoked
a lockdown was bad for business—especially the drug trade. Under a
lockdown, sellers couldn't supply customers; the money stopped flowing, and the junkies went into withdrawal. Maintaining sales required

maintaining at least a semblance of order within the prison. The inmates called it "keeping the lid on."

As long as the lid was on, marijuana was everywhere. It was smoked openly and often. Most staff tolerated it—some, of course, used it. Unlike the uppers and the homemade booze (known in every joint as "pruno"), marijuana kept the inmates mellow. One inmate said that Rhay once sat next to him while he was enjoying himself in the yard. Being sociable, he offered the superintendent a toke. "Hey, Mr. Rhay, want some?" Declining, Rhay responded, "Is everything all right around here?…That's all I wanna know. You guys just stay outta trouble."[99]

Marijuana was brought in by visitors and staff on the take. It came through the mail. It was smuggled in through every means that men with too much time on their hands could think of. And the price was cheap. The clubs often had major suppliers and large distribution networks, but no one had a corner on the marijuana market. For the most part, an individual could get his own stash, even do some dealing, and not get into serious trouble with the big boys.

It was a different story with heroin. There was a lot of it, plenty of users, and lots of money. Once hooked, whether on the streets or in prison, a junkie will do almost anything to keep getting it. The more that's used, the more that's needed for the same high. It's a market that grows by itself. Most of the inmates interviewed said that at its height, 40 to 65 percent of the population was using heroin. The spread between the high and low percentage probably reflected the people you hung with—users or nonusers. Whatever the number, they weren't all long-term junkies; but even at the lower percentage, that's three to four hundred users.

Heavy drug use was no secret. A former president of the B.P.F.U. said, "There were people shooting dope, and all the cops would do is walk by you—like they didn't see nothing.…At any given time—like in the evening—you see people on the side of the building or sitting on corners, sitting up against the fence or whatever, and you see 'em there puking—enjoying their heroin high. You'd see people sitting there with a needle stuck in their arm."[100]

The needle stuck in the arm was usually a homemade syringe, which the inmates called a "binkie." The syringe would include an actual hypodermic needle that was either smuggled in or stolen from the prison hospital. But the binkie itself was homemade. The easiest way to make one involved the hypodermic needle plus two additional parts: a Bic pen from which the ink cartridge and pen tip had been removed, and the end of the rubber dispenser from a large institutional milk carton—preferably the sealed end that is cut to activate the carton. The empty pen worked like a funnel with the hypodermic needle inserted at the pen tip end and the sealed rubber tube attached to the other end.

"A good doper likes to play with it," explained Jim Hartford. "With a binkie, you can sit there and pump it in and out. Whereas with a hypodermic needle, it's difficult to pull the plunger—push it in and pull it out and play with it that way."[101]

One inmate, who was apparently a good doper, said, "The heroin was a kicker, man. When I was there, we were getting the Mexican brown powder—which was real good. We was also getting the China white, which was like ten times better than Mexican brown. We was getting some salt and pepper—Canadian dope....I'd say eighty-five, ninety percent of the time it was Grade-A dope....For a twenty-dollar paper, you were good to go for a week. It wasn't expensive, 'cause there was so much of it."[102]

According to the inmates, while marijuana and other drugs came from everywhere, the main smugglers of heroin were a few prison staff. And the quantities were indeed staggering. One former inmate leader said, "Staff would bring it in—eighteen, nineteen pieces. That's eighteen or nineteen ounces—that's what a 'piece' means."[103] The same inmate claimed he personally made as much as $10,000 a month in the heroin trade. When another longtime convict was asked whether one man could have made that much money in such a short time, he gave a one-word answer: "Easy."

Payment "was an honor thing," said one inmate.

> If you came up to buy dope—you knew who had the dope—you'd go say, "Hey, I want a twenty-dollar paper" or something. "Well, when can you pay me?" "Soon as I get scrip this week...." Come payday, you go up and tell the guy, "Man, I don't know what happened to my money—but I got another order." He says, "Okay, we'll wait a week." You wait

a week—go up and pay the guy or [the debt] is doubled....If you kept putting it off, sooner or later you were gonna get nailed.[104]

It was the bike shop that did most of the "nailing." Most of the bikers lived on A Tier in Eight Wing, where Dick Morgan was an officer. "I was actually put on notice," said Morgan. "I remember when the bikers would come through Eight Wing and tell us...'You're going to see a lot of black eyes today and some busted hands. It's debt collection week.' We saw people come in [to the wing] limping and moaning and groaning. There'd be a lot of guys in one day."[105]

The bikers weren't just collecting debts. For a while, "the bikers were taxing dope sales," said Jim Hartford. If an inmate had marijuana to sell, he could sell it as long as he gave some of the profits to the Bikers' Club. "If you didn't," explained Hartford, "that was untaxed dope, and you ran the risk of getting fucked up, killed, or getting your hands put in the bike shop vise." The bike shop vise routine was especially brutal. If someone was slow on paying dope debts, or not paying their taxes, they would be taken to the bike shop, where the bikers would "stick their hands in the vise and just smash their hands—break all the bones in [both] hands."[106]

Everyone knew what was going on. There were pictures of mangled hands but not of the violence itself. And since inmates who valued their lives didn't snitch on their oppressors, no one was ever charged.

But the biker vise wasn't the final sanction. "Guys who couldn't pay for it were only allowed so many excuses, and then they lost their life," said one inmate. "There was one kid there got stabbed something like twenty-five times—over like fifteen bucks or something."[107]

Steve McCoy, an inmate kitchen worker and contributor to the prison newspaper, discovered the hard way how unauthorized selling of dope could get you killed.

In March 1976 one of the bikers saw McCoy selling smack, then watched him for several days. "I knew McCoy didn't have that kind of money to be running around selling two, three hundred dollars of heroin a day," said the biker. "We had the contract to deal the dope Cadillac [brought in]. Something happened—maybe we didn't make all our payment [to Cadillac] that month, and he tried to give the drugs to somebody else to deal, and I found out about it. So I go to the president [of the Bikers' Club]. I tell the president, 'McCoy got the bike shop dope.'"[108]

The two men agreed that McCoy should be told to give the dope back to Cadillac. "So I go to McCoy and I said, 'That's the bike shop's dope. Come on—let's you and me go give it to Cadillac—take it up with him and the president of the bike shop....If you don't do this, I'll see you in the morning, man."[109] McCoy didn't cooperate.

The men met the next morning, and the biker killed McCoy. For twenty-five years, the biker claimed it was self-defense. Finally he came clean and confessed to the parole board sometime around 2002. Despite the confession, he was still in prison when interviewed in 2010. This is what he said during the interview: "Morning [McCoy] come out. He looked at me and I'm looking at him. He's with three bodyguards....I seen him, so I started walking up on him, and all three are pulling knives on me. The rest is history. I pulled out an eighteen-inch sword. They say I cut his heart in half....It was a knife fight. It wasn't no self-defense."[110]

Why the bike shop was allowed to continue these practices is an unanswered question. Perhaps it was indifference, maybe fear or corruption. In all likelihood, however, it was need. No one was controlling the inside of the prison except the strongest clubs. They could keep the lid on.

The bikers were particularly adept at controlling situations. In a way, they were a somewhat disciplined group. They stuck together and followed their own agenda. Dick Morgan described one way the bikers would assert their unity, discipline, and independence:

> Nine o'clock at night was always the high drama of the evening. Everybody else would lock up....The bikers would not. They would stand out on the tier, and you'd have seventeen cells open. As wing sergeant, I would go down on the tier by myself, and I'd find the president. I'd go up to [him] and...say, "What are we doing here? Are we locking up tonight, or are we going to rock and roll?" And he'd go, "Oh, Morgan, is it nine?" I'd say, "Yeah, it's nine o'clock. It's time to lock up...." The president would snap his fingers, and guys would pull into seventeen cells, and all seventeen [doors] would clang together all at once.[111]

This unity was helpful when the bikers wanted to keep the lid on. Robin Moses, a lieutenant at the time, described how the bikers sometimes "saved our butts." During particularly dangerous times, bikers would stand shoulder to shoulder with correctional officers. One of those times was following the incident when inmates took over the hospital and Eight Wing. Coming off lockdown, "every place you saw an officer, there was a biker standing with him," said Moses.[112]

The Bikers' Club continued as a major power center within the prison for several more years. Some broken bones, bruises, and an inmate killed every now and then was the price of maintaining a semblance of order and avoiding total chaos.

Chapter 23

ABDICATION

B Y 1976, B. J. RHAY HAD ALMOST NO SUPPORT. Rhay's bosses in
Olympia didn't trust him. Terse memos between Rhay and corrections director Hal Bradley showed exasperation by both parties. In January, Bradley wrote to Rhay about a remark Rhay made to a
reporter: "Frankly, Bobby, I am tired of having things blamed on Olympia...when in fact they depend on decisions which you can and must
make."[113] Rhay replied the next day: "I, too, am getting tired of this
kind of thing and if you will just point me in the right direction, I
will be damn glad to do it."[114] Meanwhile, all correspondence to Bradley on important matters—like the discovery of firearms in the Lifers
with Hope club, inmates smashing windows and setting multiple fires
in Eight Wing, or locking the institution down—was from Harvey.

Rhay was senior warden in the United States, but shunned by his
peers. His professional reputation was in tatters. Correctional leaders
from around the country read the news and talked among themselves.
They didn't like what they read and heard. "I went from [being] probably one of the most popular persons—the head of the West Central
Wardens [Association]—to where people were pointing at me from [the
American Correctional Association]. A very uncomfortable situation,"
said Rhay. "Pretty soon you hole up and do your thing."[115]

By 1976 Bob Rhay's "thing" wasn't his work or his home life. By then
most of his children were grown and on their own. Relations with his
wife, whom he divorced a few years later, were strained.

Increasingly, Bob Rhay simply wasn't there. "B. J. was always going
hunting with the guys, going fishing with the guys, going horseback riding with the guys," said Prison Legal Services paralegal Barbara Miller.[116]

Jim Harvey saw it the same way. "I think Bob Rhay took advantage
of me because he would go out pheasant hunting or take off and go on
a military training [detail]," said Harvey. "If there was any problem,

he didn't want to be at the institution....That's what a lot of the staff realized too....They told me, 'If anything ever happens, you're the one who's going to take the fall.'"[117]

Even the inmates noticed it. According to one long-term inmate, toward the end of his tenure as warden, "Mr. Rhay didn't know what he wanted to do—whether he wanted to run for political office, whether he wanted to be warden, or whatever. He was gone a lot of the time."[118]

Rhay had announced he would retire in January 1977 when his retirement benefits maxed out. Rhay was a short-termer with little satis-faction in his job. He started looking for something to do.

At first, Rhay decided to run for political office. The Democratic state senator who had represented the Walla Walla area for years was retiring. Leading Democrats from various parts of the state encouraged Rhay to run. The election would be the following November, and if Rhay was successful, he'd be sworn in right after he retired in January 1977. It would be great timing.

It didn't work out that way. It wasn't just with his peers that Rhay's reputation had slipped. It was a little late to single out Conte for all that had gone wrong at the penitentiary over the last six years. In the brief campaigning that took place before the July filing period, Rhay was blasted for his handling of the prison. "I was beat to death with that 'loss of control' thing,"[119] said Rhay. When a strong Republican announced she would file for the position, Rhay had second thoughts. On the last day of filing, Rhay decided he wouldn't run.

Rhay's growing lack of interest, along with his eagerness to dele-gate, bothered staff who knew him well. The plant manager, who had attended Rhay's staff meetings for years, put it this way: "It used to kind of gripe me because I wanted him to come right out and say, 'Hey! This is it.' You know, his old dynamite punch like he used to. But he'd tell [us], 'You guys handle it. You make the decisions.' So we did."[120]

By 1976, Jim Harvey was the one making most of the decisions. In January, when the U.S. attorney, the DEA, and the FBI wanted to bring agents into the penitentiary to investigate Cadillac Brown's heroin ring, they were told to work with Harvey, not Rhay. "They didn't want Mr. Rhay to know about it," said Harvey.[121]

That same month, Harvey began to issue a flurry of "General Orders" designed to increase custody's control over the prison. In some weeks there was a new General Order every day. Over the next twelve months he issued thirty-four. The unwritten rule book that Freeman said was thrown out in 1971 was finally being replaced with something concrete.

The first few General Orders were benign, but this slow start was followed by more intrusive ones. For example, an order dealing with locking cell doors and restricting access to a cellblock to those who lived there, was designed "to stop the continuing murders, rapes, and assaults, which are OCCURRING FREQUENTLY IN THE CELLBLOCK AREAS" (emphasis in original).[122]

In March 1976, two months after Harvey began issuing his General Orders, an incident occurred that allowed Harvey to implement various physical changes to the prison that he had discussed with headquarters since at least the previous September. The incident involved a relatively small group of blacks who staged a loud, but peaceful, protest in front of Central Control. The inmates were ordered to disperse, and by midafternoon the entire prison was on lockdown.

The real reason for the lockdown—and most certainly for its duration—was Harvey's desire to make physical changes to the prison. The changes included altering some of the circulation patterns inside the walls and eliminating blind spots by removing covers over prison walkways.

Rhay was clearly out of the loop. In fact, Bradley had informed Rhay of the plan in a memo the previous October: "All staff consulted recommended that the roofing be removed from the walkways to provide proper safety and security for the residents and the institution. I agree with the recommendations, and if you are in agreement and can accomplish the task within your authorized staff and budget, you are authorized to make the appropriate revisions to the walkways."[123] While not a direct order, the intent was clear: your staff wants this done, your boss wants this done, and unless you come up with a good reason not to do it, you had better get it done. The lockdown provided the perfect opportunity.

The worst blind spot in the prison was known to convicts and staff alike as "Blood Alley." Blood Alley was a high-traffic area that led to

Blood Alley—hospital on the right; Central Control, B.P.F.U. and Four/Five wing on the left; auditorium in the distance

Four, Five, and Six Wings, the prison auditorium, the side door of the hospital, and the B.P.F.U. clubhouse. It was a covered walkway with buildings on one side and chain link fence on the other. Officers couldn't see anything from the towers or wall, and a hump in the middle of the more than two-hundred-yard-long walkway made it impossible for an officer standing at one end to see what was happening at the other.

Blood Alley had earned its name. According to penitentiary incident reports, in one twelve-month period Blood Alley was the scene of one murder by stabbing, four knife assaults, two strong-arm robberies, and twenty-one other assaults.[124] Since not all incidents were known to staff, much less their locations, it was likely that the official reports under-counted the number of serious incidents in Blood Alley.

Not only did prison maintenance staff remove the cover over Blood Alley, the walkway was closed to inmate traffic. Staff also substantially dismantled the second and third floors of the B.P.F.U. clubhouse, and they installed electric gates to regulate inmate traffic on the south side of the prison from Big Red to the hospital. The latter change made it impossible for inmates to congregate in front of Central Control. Staff also relocated access to the auditorium and cellblocks Four, Five, and Six to the north side of the institution—directly under two towers with good visibility of inmate movement through the area.

Finally, because protective custody (PC) had outgrown its location in the admissions building and was causing crowding in segregation, various programs were moved out of Five Wing and into admissions so that all of Five Wing could be used for PC.

A lengthy progress report on the lockdown and changes made to the institution was sent to Bradley by Harvey. There is no indication that even a copy went to Rhay.

Harvey was on a roll. In April 1976 he announced that the penitentiary would hire female correctional officers. The union objected strongly and considered filing a lawsuit. They were sure that women correctional officers would be at risk inside the walls. More importantly—in their minds at least—they were sure that women couldn't do the job that men did.[125] But Harvey had a different idea.

Many of the drugs entering the prison came through the visiting room, and it was generally inmate wives and girlfriends doing the packing. Harvey issued a General Order requiring all civilian guests and sponsors to submit to a body frisk whenever they entered the institution. If female visitors were going to be frisked, female correctional officers were needed to do the job. If hubby was getting high after every visit, the search could be very thorough. Some women—even young girls—were taken into the women's restroom and frisked in their underwear. If suspicions were sufficiently high, a nurse would be called from the hospital to do oral, vaginal, and anal searches.

To the inmates, things had taken a bad turn. This is how one put it: "In [Rhay's] absence Harvey would do certain things—create situations—and cause a lot of turmoil and chaos....Whatever he could do to sabotage [inmate government and the clubs] and create chaos and havoc—he did that."[126]

It wasn't just the inmates who saw it this way. To everyone in Prison Legal Services, Harvey was the problem. Paralegal Barbara Miller put it this way: "I don't know what happened to Jim, but in the process he kicked sand on the lines. He took all of his face from that gung-ho 'We are right, they are wrong' kind of thing. [Maybe] it was the war with the [really violent inmates]. I don't know what it was, but I know that there was a point at which you couldn't find that [better] side of him very often, and I quit trying."[127]

For Harvey, the work was nonstop. "That three years was a lifetime," he said. "There was not a free moment at all—twenty-four hours a day. My phone was ringing at night. Something was [always] happening. Someone was getting stabbed, someone was being murdered." In the same breath, Harvey said that stress never bothered him. "I don't know. Maybe I'm just a different type of person....Some people get ulcers or have breakdowns. I seemed to thrive on that activity."[128]

Some people respond to stress by buckling down and plowing ahead—no matter what the consequences. They don't feel the stress unless they stop working. Harvey seemed to be one of those people. But there's a downside to constant work under stressful conditions: mistakes creep in, judgment gets clouded, action replaces thought.

Perhaps Harvey's words, twenty years after the fact, provide some insight into how he reacted to the situations he inherited. One of those situations was the dismantling of the second and third floors of the B.P.F.U.: "That was a den of iniquity in there. There was homosexual activity. There was gambling....It was sickening the things that were going on in there....I take pleasure in smashing that place up and eliminating the abuse some of the inmates had to take....I'm a disciplinarian. I admit it. I take pleasure in it."[129]

Harvey continued to make the decisions, even usurping the authority of the associate superintendent for treatment and engaging in direct supervision of staff in all areas of the prison. As Harvey spread himself thinner, his effectiveness waned, and headquarters began to notice.

Chapter 24

B. J. Rhay's Final Chapter

I N November 1976, as the months ticked away to Rhay's retirement, Dixy Lee Ray became the first Democrat elected governor of the State of Washington in twelve years. Among other things, the governor-elect had campaigned on the idea of removing adult corrections from the Department of Social and Health Services. Democratic legislators—including good friends of B. J. Rhay—promised to introduce a bill in the next legislative session to create a separate department of corrections.

In the days after the election, Rhay got a phone call from Albert Rosellini, the former Democratic governor defeated by Evans in 1972. Rhay recalled the conversation. "I'm calling for the new governor," said Rosellini. "She doesn't want to handle Walla Walla the first thing she gets there, and she wants you to stay on....Bob, I think it will be the directorship for you."[130]

Rhay met with the governor-elect when she attended the Apple Cup, the annual end-of-season football game between the University of Washington and Washington State University. According to Rhay, not only did the governor-elect confirm that she had asked Rosellini to call him, she told him, "Don't worry, the California bandits will be gone. Burdman and Bradley are going to be leaving."[131] Rhay's old nemeses were on their way out.

In light of this new information, Rhay announced that he would postpone his retirement and stay on as superintendent, at least until the following summer. Furthermore, if a new department of corrections was created, he wanted the job. "The department of corrections would be the most comfortable possibility for me," he said in an interview with the local newspaper.[132]

When Governor Ray was sworn in, she named her old friend, psychiatrist Harlan McNutt, to be secretary of DSHS. For a while at least,

McNutt kept Burdman as his deputy secretary, and Bradley as director of the division of adult corrections.

Rosellini's tempting speculation aside, other moves were afoot. Both the governor and Dr. McNutt recognized that the penitentiary was out of control and that Rhay was part of the problem. "There were terrible problems with [Rhay]," said McNutt. "My idea was to get him out of there as fast as I possibly could [in order] to get the thing onto a different course."[133]

More terrible things would happen before Rhay left.

It was April 5, 1977. Two inmates were on trial in Walla Walla Superior Court for stabbing, and almost killing, a biker who had killed a popular inmate. The trial was nearly over, and officers Hartford and Chadek had escorted the defendants to court for the last time. The jury would get the case later that afternoon.

Hartford went to the courthouse law library for a break. The defendants had been there about forty minutes earlier, conferring with their lawyer, and the room had been locked during the noon recess. Now it was empty, and Hartford could relax. He used his key and let himself in. As he sat down, he saw a blue disposable lighter under the table. His lucky day—he was a smoker, and maybe the lighter still worked. He reached for it and picked it up.

Hartford tested the lighter. "Well, it worked. It worked real good," said Hartford. "You could have lit several cigarettes off that thing if you'd been real quick....Even then I didn't realize what had happened or what I'd done. [There was] a terribly loud noise, but there was no pain initially. I didn't feel anything at all."[134]

Chadek was at the door when Hartford clicked the lighter and set off the explosion. With blood splattered on his uniform, Chadek stumbled into the hall. Not understanding what had happened, he yelled, "My God, he's shot himself."[135]

Hartford jumped up. For an instant, the thought raced through his mind: "It's a gunfight! They're escaping from the courtroom!" Then he saw his right hand, and the pain began.

Laboratory analysis of the residue from the explosion by the Bureau of Alcohol, Tobacco, and Firearms determined that the lighter had been packed with match heads. When Hartford tested the flint, the bomb blast was heard throughout the building. People dived for cover and barricaded themselves in their offices. Within seconds, a police officer entered the courtroom. "We're evacuating the building," he cried. The judge banged his gavel and ordered a recess. The jurors scurried into the jury room and huddled under a table. The defendants, cuffed and shackled, were returned to Big Red. Hartford, accompanied by Chadek, was rushed by ambulance to the local hospital.

The two inmates arrived at Big Red before the news of Hartford's injury reached the segregation unit. They weren't expected so soon, and the lieutenant was surprised to see them. According to one of the inmates, the lieutenant asked why they were back so soon, and the other inmate described what happened. "And [the segregation officers] just went nuts," claimed the inmate. "We went straight to A Tier and got our ass kicked for three hours."[136]

It should come as no surprise that one can't always take a convict at his word—particularly with allegations of this kind. Neither the inmates' attorney at the trial nor the county's deputy prosecuting attorney recalls any indication that either man was bruised and battered when they were returned to court later that day.[137] Furthermore, as noted by the county's attorney, it is almost certain they would have complained loud and long at the trial if they had been beaten between court sessions. While it's unlikely the defendants were beaten that afternoon, even Harvey acknowledged that this kind of thing happened, particularly in segregation.

The trial resumed late in the day. The jury wasted no time in reaching a verdict. The two men were convicted of first degree assault seven hours after the bomb went off.

Hartford lost three fingers and part of his thumb that day. Later, doctors removed the middle bone in his right hand to allow a better grip between the stub of a thumb and his remaining little finger.

According to Hartford, another inmate who had testified at the trial earlier in the week had made the bomb in the hope of creating a diversion in order to escape. When that didn't work, the inmates on trial got the bomb and tossed it out simply to create mayhem. While no one believed the bomb was intended specifically for Hartford, because of his reputation, a lot of inmates were pleased he was the one to pick it up. When Hartford returned to work three months later, inmates some-times held up a hand in grotesque contortion, taunting him with the nickname "Claw."

Although nothing was ever proven, the obvious connection was to the defendants and therefore back to Big Red. A shakedown of the unit was ordered. In the days following Hartford's injury, contraband was found and many of the prisoners in segregation—not just the two prime suspects—were roughed up. The extent of abuse can't be verified, but the record shows that the lieutenant in charge was reprimanded for unauthorized use of Mace.[138]

According to one of the defendants, the use of Mace that week "was the least of it." According to him, prisoners were chained to the bars and beaten.[139]

The last day of the trial was a Tuesday. According to a lengthy report by a Resident Council officer, over the next few days "there was much yelling from seg for the aid of the population....The club heads requested emergency meetings with the Resident Council. Two such meetings were held and...Mr. Rhay and Mr. Harvey were called at least twice, but the Council was put off twice by them."[140]

With no response from the administration, the club heads and Resi-dent Council called for a strike. A strike always meant a lockdown, and since officers don't issue snacks and supplies to inmates locked in their cells, hundreds of inmates descended on the inmate store. On Sunday afternoon, a small diversionary fire was set in the chapel, and the inmates broke into the inmate store and stripped it bare. Most of the inmates simply grabbed some loot and calmly walked to their cells. By early eve-ning, the entire institution was on lockdown. Because it occurred on Easter Sunday, it became known as the Easter riot.

Around eight o'clock in the evening, Harvey gave the okay for the eleven members of the Resident Council to leave their cells and go to the RC office, where they would meet with the superintendent.[141] Rhay's insistence that night that "I'm the one you have to deal with, baby,"[142] proved a false prophecy. After the meeting, as the inmates were escorted to their cells, an officer overheard some of the leaders say that "they were going to the governor and that no one would talk to Rhay or Harvey."[143]

The resulting lockdown lasted forty-six days—the longest in the prison's history up to that time. A full-scale shakedown of the entire institution found tons of contraband and unsanctioned property.

During the strike, the inmate leaders kept their promise not to talk with Rhay or Harvey. They wrote to the governor. The inmates were under lockdown of their own choice, and "further negotiations with the prison administration would be futile," the letter said.[144]

A few weeks into the lockdown, a "select committee" was appointed by Governor Ray to dig deeper into the prison's problems. McNutt, Burdman, and Bradley—who had already met once with inmate leaders—were joined by three others: Sam Kelly, who was a special assistant to the president of the University of Washington; the president of the Washington State Council on Crime and Delinquency; and a superior court judge.

Simultaneously, adult corrections headquarters in Olympia dispatched a senior staffer to Walla Walla to conduct an internal review of penitentiary operations. The review concluded that associate superintendent for custody Jim Harvey was "unable to limit his managerial activities...[and had] extended himself to the point of ineffectiveness."[145]

On Monday, May 2, five days after this report was written, the governor's select committee met with inmate leaders. Inside the prison, rumors started flying. The inmates wanted Rhay and Harvey removed.

It's not known whether the select committee members read the report that characterized Harvey as "overextended" and "ineffective," but the next day committee member Sam Kelly told the press that "there needs to be a radical change in the staff, at least where the associate warden is concerned."[146]

Kelly minced no words in a lengthy letter to Secretary McNutt. "It is obvious to me after reviewing the information and digesting a number of other items, including phone calls and letters, that the largest problem at Walla Walla is its associate superintendent for custody. To say that he has been heavy-handed is, in my view, an understatement!...I recommend that James Harvey, Associate Superintendent for Custody, be relieved forthwith from his assignment."[147]

The officers were furious. "These people came over here two times to listen to a bunch of mealy-mouthed convicts and didn't come once to talk to the staff. We aren't the ones who burned the chapel!" steamed the union vice president as he spoke to a local newspaper reporter.[148] Union president Steve Chadek said the union wouldn't strike if Harvey or Rhay were removed—"We'd just leave with them....Our jobs just wouldn't be worth sticking around here if things were that way."[149]

Rhay assured the officers that neither he nor Harvey was in danger of being fired.[150] The announcement came the next day. Harvey wasn't being fired—he was being transferred.

The prepared statement from the office of Secretary McNutt said Harvey had requested a transfer to the Corrections Center, outside the town of Shelton, about a year ago. Now, because of a vacancy, "Mr. Harvey's request has been granted and he will return to Shelton in due course." Of course, this move is "independent of the current situation," the press release said.[151]

The inmates were jubilant. They had won. They were still locked in their cells, and much personal property had been destroyed in the shakedown, but they had won.

Despite skepticism that Harvey's transfer was "independent of the current situation," Harvey *had* told Bradley the prior year that he wanted to return to Shelton if there wasn't a chance of becoming penitentiary superintendent. In the middle of the lockdown at the penitentiary, the opportunity unexpectedly presented itself. Tragically, the associate superintendent for custody at Shelton had attempted suicide. He was placed on extended sick leave with the plan to grant medical retirement a few months later.[152] The position was open.

"It was right after that that I put in [a formal request] for a transfer," said Harvey. "I had my home and my property [there], and I wanted to come back to Shelton....I told [Hal Bradley] that I'd like to stay until the lockdown was over....I didn't want to be chased off the hill, so to speak."[153] But the position couldn't be held open indefinitely, and Harvey transferred just before the lockdown ended.

The man who said he wasn't affected by stress had finally had enough. "Jim was heartbroken when he left here," said one longtime officer. "He was absolutely at the bottom of strength and morale and everything. They had broken him."[154]

Toward the end of May 1977, forty-four days after the Easter riot, Rhay announced that the lockdown would end at seven o'clock the next morning. Officers were ordered to let inmate cooks out to prepare the morning meal. The officers refused, and Rhay suspended them. The next morning, 129 prison employees walked off the job in a wildcat strike. The lockdown continued, and state troopers could be seen manning the towers and walls in place of the striking correctional officers.

But the union hadn't sanctioned the strike, and those who walked off were in danger of losing their jobs. Rhay and the union leaders negotiated: no action would be taken against the striking employees, the suspended officers would be reinstated, and there would be a "controlled" end to the lockdown. Forty-six days after it started, the lockdown ended. The inmates would eat something other than TV dinners that day.

"We're confused," said Walla Walla area legislators. First they were told that Rhay was getting pressure from Olympia to end the lockdown. Now, said one representative, "the message we are getting...is that they (the prison staff) don't have confidence in Mr. Rhay."[155]

Behind the scenes, momentum was gathering. After the lockdown was over, an assistant director for the division of adult corrections conducted an internal investigation of Rhay's activities. He discovered that Rhay "had the plant maintenance people install some wrought iron fencing at his mother's house. And there was a state-tagged, state-owned, color TV in her house."[156] Another corrections employee, who had read the now vanished file, recalled more. There was state-owned property in Rhay's hunting cabin as well.[157] None of this was made public. Instead, according to Rhay, "McNutt gave me a letter reprimanding me for having taken a couple of inmates on the weekend up to my cabin in the mountains and building a chimney....They mentioned some bricks too."[158]

The bricks were from an old penitentiary building torn down in the 1960s. Rhay said the contractor was supposed to salvage the bricks, but instead put them in the institution's dump. He and other prison staff hauled bricks away using their own trucks. Rhay believed Steve Chadek told McNutt that Rhay had stolen the bricks. If so, it was more than a little hypocritical. As Chadek once said, "There used to be a saying up at the penitentiary: if you didn't have a pickup, you weren't getting your share."[159]

Rhay got the news on a Friday—he too was being transferred. Dr. McNutt, Hal Bradley, and McNutt's personal assistant flew to Walla Walla on the state patrol airplane. Although never publicly acknowledged, at least parts of the internal investigation were presumably shared with Rhay.

The final details were worked out at a meeting at the Seattle-Tacoma airport on Sunday. Rhay would be transferred to Olympia to head up the mini-prison project just approved by the legislature.

The press conference took place on Monday. The new warden, Douglas Vinzant—former Methodist minister, one-time superintendent at Walpole, and author of the state's mini-prison plan—talked about the changes he would make. Standing next to him in the front-page photo, Rhay's "Can't this just be over?" expression made him look like a grounded teenager being lectured by a disappointed parent.[160]

Four days later, the governor vetoed the appropriation for the mini-prisons.[161] Rhay, who had been the longest serving warden in the United States until his transfer to Olympia, had a job with nothing to do.

The governor, true to her word that the "the California bandits will be gone," fired Burdman and asked for Bradley's resignation, effective the following November.[162]

Rhay collected a few paychecks and then did what he said he had always wanted to do—he became Commissioner of Corrections in another state.[163]

PART 4
NADIR
1977–1978

Bikers in the Big Yard

Site Plan: 1978–1979

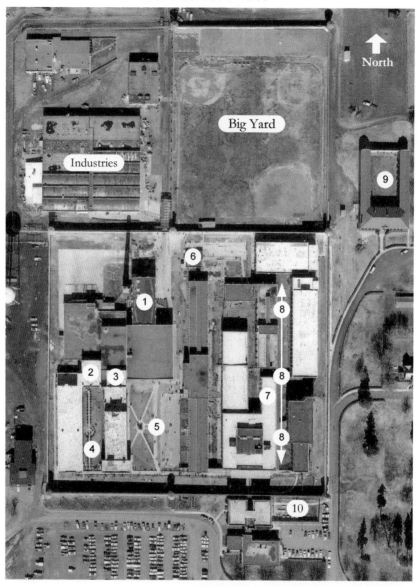

North

Big Yard

Industries

KEY

1. Bikers' Club and RGC
2. Lifers' Club
3. Chicano Club
4. Lifers' Park
5. People's Park
6. Inmate Store
7. B.P.F.U. Club
8. Blood Alley
9. Women's Prison (vacant)
10. Outdoor Visiting

Chapter 25

VINZANT

I N JUNE 1977, WHEN B. J. RHAY was suddenly moved to a dead-end job in Olympia, the newly appointed secretary of Department of Social and Health Services, Harlan McNutt, didn't have time to do a nationwide search to replace Rhay as penitentiary superintendent. He quickly asked Douglas Vinzant—then head of the agency's Bureau of Juvenile Rehabilitation and a brilliant, likable, smooth-talking Southern gentleman—to take the job. "In those days, I had to go with what I had," said McNutt. "Vinzant was there....He was well recommended, and he was the best man I had."[1]

When Vinzant walked into the superintendent's office at the penitentiary for the first time, the prevailing assumption was that he was a seasoned correctional administrator. In fact, other than his recent experience with juveniles in Washington State, it appears that Vinzant's entire experience in corrections had consisted of three senior administrative jobs, each lasting less than a year. The first was a stint as assistant superintendent of a juvenile correctional facility in Mississippi in 1969–70. After getting his master's degree and working on a doctorate at the University of Southern California, he spent eleven months as superintendent of Concord prison and ten months as superintendent of Walpole prison, both in Massachusetts. He apparently always started at, or near, the top, and it appears he never worked a day at any other prison job. As B. J. Rhay might have said, "He had never walked the line." As others did say, Vinzant was good at selling himself.

While surprised to be asked, Vinzant believed that assistant secretary Milton Burdman recommended him for the job because, according to Vinzant, "he knew about my adult corrections experience in Massachusetts with some pretty tough prisons. He was pretty confident that I could handle what was there."[2]

Vinzant was certainly confident. When interviewed, he said, "You're talking to somebody who had taken over two prisons that were in about as bad a shape as you can get 'em. When I went to Concord it had been in a riot and lockdown. Then when I went to Walpole, it had been in constant eruption. So Walla Walla was a very low-key emergency in my repertoire of experience....It was not what I considered to be a mean institution. It was a very bunglesome dinosaur, but it wasn't mean."

Then, using the kind of language that made him a hit with legislators, Vinzant described what he considered a mean institution. "When I walked into Walpole or Concord prison on some days, you could just feel the air crackle with tension. I mean it was so tight, if somebody coughed, you'd look for the wall to crumble, just like an eggshell."

But there was no crackling air or crumbling walls at the bunglesome dinosaur in Vinzant's eye. "I never felt that kind of tension and energy in Walla Walla. What I felt in Walla Walla was a group of people [i.e., the inmates] who had basically been disregarded as being worth considering as human beings. They had been manipulated. They had been disappointed. They had not been dealt with on top of the table in a broad sense. There were favorites. There was a very, very apparent con structure."[3]

In terms of danger, and certainly corruption, Walpole in the mid-1970s probably was worse than Walla Walla. But Walla Walla, with three times as many inmates and an ancient infrastructure compared to the much newer Walpole prison, had issues. When Vinzant took over at Walla Walla, an officer had recently been maimed; there had been a coordinated action by the inmates, including the Easter riot that forced out Harvey and Rhay; and the institution had just come off the longest lockdown in its history.

In June 1977 almost no one working at the penitentiary had known any superintendent other than B. J. Rhay. Everyone was curious about Vinzant. Furthermore, because Vinzant came with baggage from his mini-prison planning days, there was concern about what he might do. The baggage was from comments Vinzant had made at a public hearing three years earlier, which included, "If people can't make a living anywhere else but in a prison, they shouldn't be handling human beings." He also said it was hard to find good officers because of the dangers of working in a maximum security prison.[4] When union president Steve Chadek read these remarks in the Walla Walla paper, he said they were offensive. "I take it as calling us a bunch of bums," said Chadek.[5]

While he didn't directly call them bums, Vinzant's assessment of the penitentiary when he arrived suggests he had little confidence in the staff he inherited.

> I think the big problem in Walla Walla [was] that you had an old insti-tution [that] was put in Walla Walla because that was the furthest point from civilization that they could find in the state of Washington that they could place it. It was manned by local people. You had a super-intendent who had married a former warden's daughter....You had a staff that had not been supported well from a professional standpoint, but that had been treated more like family....[For example,] you had [staff taking] guns...from the armory to deer hunt with....You had peo-ple who'd grown up in Walla Walla, they'd married people from Walla Walla, they knew people from Walla Walla. All of that group became an inner group. You had a few people that were add-ons, but the core there was always the people who had been there....So you just had a whole bunch of this incestuousness that is common in a small, isolated town—and that's what Walla Walla [was].[6]

Given this situation, when asked to whom he turned for support, Vinzant said, "I think anytime you take on a position like that—or at least the way I do it—is to say to myself, if it came down to this, will you run this thing by yourself? Given that I was young and had lived through two or three of those decisions in my life, I decided, yeah."[7]

Of course, Vinzant didn't have to run *everything* by himself at an eighteen-hundred-bed maximum security prison; he did have staff. But he wasn't getting much support from the correctional officers, most of whom were simply marking time, collecting paychecks, and trying to get home in one piece at the end of their shift. Nor did he get much support from his senior staff—the associate superintendents, captains, lieutenants, and key administrative personnel. They all probably gave Vinzant the benefit of the doubt at first, but quickly discovered he had little time for them. After Vinzant promised frequent and open commu-nications at a kickoff meeting with them, "that's about the last meeting we had," said then lieutenant and law liaison officer Robin Moses.[8] In fact, although the archive record is full of minutes from superintendent staff meetings from the years before and after Vinzant, the only minutes that have survived from Vinzant's tenure are those from this initial meeting a few days after he arrived in Walla Walla.

Despite Vinzant's stated willingness to run the penitentiary by himself, there was one man he knew he wanted as his associate superintendent for custody. Nicholas Genakos—or "Nick the Greek," as Walla Walla staff called him—had been Vinzant's associate superintendent during his months at Walpole. When Vinzant came to Washington, Genakos was promoted to superintendent at Concord, where he served for several years before being fired by the Massachusetts Commissioner of Corrections.[9]

When interviewed, Vinzant expressed ignorance of Genakos's firing, but it seems likely he knew his former colleague was available. Whatever Vinzant knew or didn't know about Genakos's employment situation, he knew that Genakos was someone with whom he could work, someone who understood what he was trying to do and how they would make it happen.

Two characters less alike are hard to imagine. Vinzant was smooth, charming, and well read. He could talk about almost anything in an intelligent way. He was entertaining and had a droll sense of humor. Genakos was rough-cut, blunt, and sometimes came across as not too bright. Some people liked him; others detested him. It was Rhay and Macklin all over again—but with a twist. It was never said of Macklin, but even some of those who liked Genakos sometimes wondered whether he was on the wrong side of the bars.

Both Vinzant and Genakos brought experiences from Massachusetts that were foreign to those who worked at the penitentiary. Robin Moses experienced the gulf between Genakos's expectations and the reality of Washington State on what must have been one of Genakos's first days in Walla Walla. Moses, in his capacity as law liaison officer, was called into the associate superintendent's office. Moses recalled both sides of the conversation.[10]

Genakos asked, "You have contacts with the state patrol?"

When Moses said he did, Genakos said, "Get me tickets to the Pendleton Roundup."

"Excuse me?" replied a puzzled Moses.

In a louder voice, Genakos again asked Moses whether he had contacts with the state patrol. When Moses once again assured him that he did, Genakos said in measured tones, "Well, I want tickets to the Pendleton Roundup."

Moses finally got it. "There are two things," he replied. "One, [the Pendleton Roundup is in] Oregon, and another, the state patrol isn't going to get you tickets to anything."

"Oh, really?" marveled Genakos. "That's amazing. You know, back [in Massachusetts], whenever the state patrol wanted to have a party or something, we used to empty out one of the [prison] camps and they'd use the mess hall and the food and everything, and they'd do reciprocal things like that."

"It don't work that way in Washington State," said Moses. "Trust me."

Not long after this exchange, Genakos called Moses into his office again. This time Genakos asked Moses to arrange a meeting between the superintendent and local law and justice officials. Moses called the sheriff, police chief, county prosecutor, and others and set up the meeting. Now it was Vinzant's turn to demonstrate his ignorance of local mores. Moses described what happened:

> We went [to the meeting] and within the first five minutes, [Vinzant] had alienated every single person in the room by out-front telling them that what went on at the institution was his responsibility and his business and not theirs and to stay out of it....My mouth fell clear to the floor. Afterward the phone calls started coming into my office. "What are you doing bringing that jerk down here?!" Boy, they were mad....
> They thought it was going to be a get-to-know-each-other, how-can-we-cooperate [sort of thing]. He had no intention of cooperating.[11]

In contrast, union president Steve Chadek seems to have hit it off quickly with Vinzant. "His first day as superintendent, I went up and knocked on his door," said Chadek. "I told the secretary, 'Can I talk with the superintendent?'"[12]

Vinzant overheard Chadek and invited him in. As he sat down, Chadek said, "I've got something I've got to tell you...We—meaning management and staff—have had some bad words in the past…[But] we'll back you one hundred percent as long as we don't get any bullshit from you. We don't want any bullshit, and we won't give any bullshit."[13]

According to Chadek, Vinzant leaned back in his chair, put his feet up on the desk, and said, "You know, you're the kind of guy I like to talk to." Chadek ended his recollection by holding up his right hand showing a crossed index and middle finger. "From that day on, him and me were like that."[14]

Within a few months, Vinzant took on even more responsibility. DSHS Secretary McNutt served as enabler-in-chief.

Hal Bradley was scheduled to leave as director of the division of adult corrections on November 1, 1977, and Secretary McNutt had more than three months to do a national search for Bradley's replacement. Despite having ample time, there is no record that McNutt looked very far. He offered the job to Vinzant.

Vinzant accepted the job as director on the condition that he continue as penitentiary superintendent at the same time. Vinzant said there were two reasons he took the director job. First, he respected Dr. McNutt and the way he tried to run the department. The second reason was perhaps more telling. Given Governor Ray's temperament, he said, "I had no idea who she might have appointed director that I would have had to work for."[15]

Vinzant kept the job as superintendent because under a new leader "we're going to lose whatever little ground we've made.…Just from a stability factor, you don't whipsaw an institution and build stability," he said.

While he wore two hats for much of his tenure in Washington adult corrections, Vinzant clearly enjoyed being superintendent more than being director. "I always said that when I was superintendent and I spent a dollar's worth of energy, I probably got fifty, sixty cents' worth of work done," said Vinzant. "When I spent a dollar's worth of energy as a director, I might have got a dime's worth of work done. At the institutional level, you're really dealing with the problems of corrections. When you're at the director level, you're simply babysitting politicians and the agenda of the governor rather than the agenda of corrections."[16]

Chapter 26

PRISON MANAGEMENT

I N HIS POSTGRADUATE WORK at the University of Southern California, Vinzant studied under one of the foremost correctional experts in the United States at the time, Richard McGee. When Vinzant talked about correctional theory or prison best practices, he came across as thoughtful and authoritative.

How he managed the penitentiary was another matter. No one anticipated the chasm between Vinzant's ideas and his actions.

"One of the ways to run a prison for a long time is to develop relationships with lead cons," said Vinzant. The downside of this approach, he explained, is that it enhances the power of the leaders, because anyone who wants something from the warden is better off talking to a man who talks to the warden rather than talking to his social worker.

"From what I've seen at other institutions, and what I saw [at Walla Walla], it was apparent that [the inmate council leaders] were the boss cons," said Vinzant. "They represented groups within the prison....If you wanted to control the prison, you dealt with those people." This is the style of prison management that Vinzant believed he inherited, but "that's not the way I run a prison," he said.[17]

Despite Vinzant's assertion that he did not run a prison by dealing with the inmate leaders, that's exactly what he did. While meetings with staff were rare, meetings with inmate leaders were common. According to Robin Moses, these meetings happened all the time, often in the middle of the night. Vinzant and associate superintendent Genakos "had no working hours," said Moses. "It might be midnight or four o'clock in the morning...and they'd bring the [Resident Council] out and they'd talk to them." Vinzant and Genakos would give them answers and make decisions. Moses and others would find out about them the next day, often from the inmates themselves.[18]

With frequent meetings between the superintendent and inmate leaders, Vinzant's and Genakos's expectations were well understood by the inmates. According to the man who was president of Lifers with Hope during Vinzant's tenure as superintendent, "if you didn't have a body to explain to the prosecutor, if you didn't have to call the police from downtown, if you didn't have an escape, they kind of let you run the show the way you wanted."[19]

Vinzant opened avenues for inmates to run the show the way they wanted in both traditional and creative ways. On the traditional side, he doubled enrollment in education and presided over the largest graduating class of inmates who received GEDs, high school diplomas, and two- and four-year college degrees the penitentiary had ever seen. Other approaches harnessed the entrepreneurial spirit of individuals and groups. Shops were set up on the breezeways to sell ice cream cones, slushies, clothing, and other items. Men did woodworking and leatherwork, and they made musical instruments and other objects using sharp cutting tools and even bench grinders that they kept in their cells.

Contrary to state law regarding inmate furloughs, Vinzant gave approval for members of a program known as the Lifers' Construction Crew to leave the institution to winterize the homes of needy people in Walla Walla. He moved the manufacturing functions of the bike shop into the industries area, and he encouraged the Bikers' Club to expand their business by allowing individual bikers to go into the community to visit bike shows, acquire parts, and promote their motorcycle restoration and customization business. He allowed inmate artisans to set up booths at the mall to sell their wares. Some furloughs were for hours, some for days.

The penitentiary was a permissive place prior to Vinzant's arrival, but under Vinzant it was wide open. While he created and encouraged activity, the favorite activity for most of the inmates was having a good time. Almost everything was tolerated.

The president of the B.P.F.U. during Vinzant's tenure described it this way:

> It was a prison though it wasn't; it was like you're on the streets and you weren't....There was no such thing as a [restricted list] as far as clothing and anything else you had. There was no such thing as hourly gates. It

"The girls would come in from Whitman College…some of the fellas too."

was just open movement from breakfast all the way clean up till lockup. We'd be out—the entire prison—running around, hanging out…in the mornings all the way through the evening.…The girls would come in from Whitman College and be hanging out—some of the fellas too— be hanging out with us all day. We'd be lounging, laying around in the grass, playing music.…It was pretty much, do what you wanna do— just don't let me see you killing nobody or beating nobody up or don't let me see you trying to escape.…As long as you did your time, they didn't care.[20]

Another inmate said that if you were a convict and you "caught a case" during this time, you wanted to go to Walla Walla "because it was *the* place…to be."[21]

The idea of keeping inmates busy was to keep them out of trouble. That didn't always work. Sometimes more direct action was required.

One pillar of Vinzant's management style was his belief that convicts respect unflinching power, and his primary mean of projecting such power was with a shotgun.

Before and after Vinzant, no one inside Washington's prisons was armed. It's not that there were no guns or even the rare use of deadly force—the armories were well stocked, the staff well trained, and under certain circumstances, tower officers with high-power rifles had orders to shoot to kill. But the idea of bringing a firearm inside the security perimeter of a prison was something contemplated only under the most extreme circumstances. Even less-than-lethal weapons (like Mace) were kept under lock and key. Except for perimeter security, blatant intimidation through the threat or open display of deadly force was not part of the repertoire of Washington corrections.

Douglas Vinzant, on the other hand, had no hesitation about bringing guns inside the prison. A few examples illustrate the point.

In Washington, a bus called "the chain" moves inmates from one institution to another. Most of the time, operation of the chain is routine: transporting newly convicted felons from the reception center to their assigned institutions or moving a few prisoners between facilities. At one point during Vinzant's tenure as superintendent, a chain was sent to Walla Walla that was not routine. A busload of inmates described as "unmanageable" by staff at the reformatory (the other large, old prison in Washington) was sent to the penitentiary where, it was hoped, the penitentiary staff would have better luck.

Because of the nature of the arriving inmates, a larger than usual contingent of officers was ready to assist in escorting the prisoners from the bus to their cells. In case of trouble, all the officers had riot batons at the ready. Vinzant arrived cradling a shotgun. "You're going to put your clubs up," he told the officers. "'We don't need 'em.'"[22]

"I stepped on the bus with a shotgun," said Vinzant. Then he politely asked the inmates, "Will you please file off of this bus into those cells?" It worked. The inmates moved without incident. Furthermore, according to Vinzant, "within two weeks, all of those people were in...general population, and they had been in segregation units at the reformatory, [where] they were branded as people you couldn't handle."[23]

On another occasion, there was a rumor that there would be some sort of violent confrontation in the dining hall. Vinzant called in the club heads and other inmate leaders. According to Vinzant, this is what he said: "You go back and tell your people that in the balcony over the dining hall, Mr. Genakos, and whatever officers he needs, will be standing there with shotguns, and you can have any kind of riot you want.

I will be on the ground floor walking around among you. If somebody wants to say something to me, they can say it directly. But we're going to serve supper at...the regular time...and we won't have a long riot."[24]

Vinzant's faith in shotguns superseded all other means of control. Robin Moses, in addition to being the law liaison officer, was the gas man during Vinzant's tenure. The gas man was trained to use tear gas and other chemicals during a riot or other major incident.

According to Moses, Vinzant told him that he was "absolutely, positively, restricted on using tear gas." If there was a threatening confrontation that might normally call for the use of gas, Vinzant told Moses that "we would shoot the first four or five in the front line, and then we'd go from there."[25]

Vinzant's unusual management style extended to staff as well. While not adept at using staff or keeping them informed, Vinzant understood the value of loyal subordinates. Usually that kind of support either comes with the territory or is earned over time. It appears that Vinzant's primary way to obtain loyalty was to buy it.

By the time Vinzant arrived at Walla Walla, the merit system for hiring and promoting state employees was well established in Washington. Except for high-ranking "exempt" positions, promotions were governed by rules, procedures, and tests that determined who was eligible to be hired or promoted and in what order they were to be considered. Whoever was making the decision would consult a register of candidates and then interview the three people with the best test scores. The prescribed process was detailed in the Washington Administrative Code, or WAC. Like statutes and case law, the administrative code is considered primary and binding law on the citizens of the state.

Doug Vinzant either didn't know or didn't care about the WAC—at least as far as it pertained to things he wanted to do. The employees he liked got promoted.

Robin Moses was someone Vinzant liked.

"I got promoted to captain because I stopped an escape," said Moses. Recalling the event, and both sides of several conversations, he described what happened.[26]

It was one of those lazy afternoons...when we didn't have a heck of a lot going. We had a Toastmasters meeting [for inmates] out front in the visiting room. We used to send a couple of inmates out there early to clean up and make coffee....This was just something that we always did.

I was sitting there and I got a call, and they said those two guys were gone. They found bars cut out [in the visiting room] and they were gone. I thought, Why me? This was such a good day....

We didn't have SWAT teams and riot squads and all the stuff they had later...I had myself and [a few officers]....I grabbed [one] and said, "We've got a couple of escapees. I don't know where they are. Get a car. Take this [other] officer and a shotgun and start patrolling around the local neighborhood or something."

While Moses contemplated what to do next, the visiting desk officer came to him accompanied by a visitor and said, "Moses, this woman wants to talk with you." Moses told them to go away.

Moses called the county sheriff's office, the Walla Walla police department, and Genakos to tell them of the escape.

The visiting officer returned and said, "This woman really needs to talk to you." Moses said he didn't have time, but the officer persisted: "I think you should listen to what she has to say." Moses relented.

"I was sitting down there waiting for my visit," said the woman, "and these two guys dressed in suits came in the front door of the administration building, and they used this pay phone and called a taxi to take them to the airport."

Moses didn't know what to think. It seemed unbelievable that two inmates would cut the bars out, then calmly walk into the administration building and call a cab. He thanked the woman, and she left. As Moses pondered his next move, he thought, "I can't let this go." He called the police and said, "Believe this or not, I think they're in a taxi on the way to the airport."

A few minutes later, the police saw a taxi on the freeway, pulled it over with shotguns showing, and got the inmates.

Shortly after Moses learned the inmates had been apprehended, Genakos came around the corner and shouted, "Well, what are you doing? What are you doing about this?"

"Nothing," said Moses.

"What?" Genakos yelled.

"Oh, I got 'em. They were in a taxi on the way to the airport."

The next thing he knew, Moses was promoted to captain.[27]

At an institution like Walla Walla in the 1970s, there were only one or two captains, so Moses's promotion was unusual. But there was always a need for a lot of sergeants, and promotion to sergeant was one of the ways Vinzant rewarded those he considered loyal. He would simply announce that so-and-so was now a sergeant, and the next day a new favorite arrived at work with stripes on his shoulder. Vinzant got some loyalty out of such actions, but he also angered others who were trying to make sergeant the legitimate way.

The loyalty test, if that's what to call it, cut both ways. If you questioned what was going on, you didn't have a chance. Dick Morgan found this out when he interviewed with Genakos for promotion.

"My motivation for getting promoted," said Morgan, was "to get out of a work detail....I could see that it was either get out of Eight Wing or get out of corrections. It was just wearing me down...So I took the sergeant's test...and ranked number three in the state."[28]

"I had no false confidence that Genakos was ever going to promote me," continued Morgan. "I'd been a pretty vocal opponent to anything he wanted to do. So I was going in there just to look him in the eye." Morgan was in uniform when he appeared before Genakos, but it wasn't entirely regulation. His belt sported a large brass buckle that an inmate had made for him. It said "R. L. Morgan, Agitator" on it.

"Genakos called me on the belt buckle," said Morgan. "He said, 'Where'd you get that?' I said, 'An inmate made it for me.' 'Probably made out of some keys too,'" said Genakos. Morgan didn't say so at the time, but chuckling at the recollection, he acknowledged, "Well, that much brass, it probably was."[29]

Summing up Vinzant's management style, Bob Tropp, deputy director of the division of adult corrections during Vinzant's tenure, said, "There almost wasn't any management. He just...followed his intuition and did what he felt like doing. The idea of calling a person a manager who felt he could comfortably fill the role of both director and penitentiary warden simultaneously [is incredible]....Geographically, these positions are over three hundred miles apart. If you had no other problem, you've got that one. They're both hands-on jobs requiring a good fifty, sixty hours a week of your presence....He was at the penitentiary—over the weekend and generally clear through Wednesday evening, if not Thursday morning—and he would come over to Olympia...sign a few papers, mend a few fences, see some people, attend a meeting or two, go over to DSHS headquarters. And then he'd go back.

"This [was] not management. . . ," said Tropp. "This [was] a man just flying by the seat of his pants doing what was comfortable for him.... There was no way he could explain [what he was doing] to anybody else, because it wouldn't stand the light of day."[30]

Chapter 27

RULES TO LIVE BY

B Y THE TIME VINZANT ARRIVED, the old convict code had few teeth. New leaders were in control, and their agendas did not always comport with every facet of the convict code. The strong dominated the weak and the wannabes reinforced the culture. Personal property was no longer safe. Older, vulnerable men were sometimes victimized by those with greater strength and fewer scruples. Small wrongs brought disproportionate responses. The leaders led, the followers followed, and the victims suffered.

Groups divided along racial and ethnic lines, with the largest and most ruthless sometimes vying for supremacy. Each group had its own leaders and members of high status, low status, and others somewhere in the middle. During times of stability, leaders from the different groups would cooperate to maintain what passed for order. During the Vinzant era, all the leaders wanted to keep the good times rolling. "Don't rock the boat" was the mantra by which they lived.

If the boat was rocked, as it sometimes was, the leaders often acted before the administration's hand was forced. One time when Vinzant was superintendent, two convicts—one white and one black—were robbing older men of their scrip. The convicts called them "breezeway bandits." Before the administration could step in, the presidents of the B.P.F.U. and Lifers with Hope got together with the head of the Bikers' Club to develop a message meant to discourage these, and potential other, breezeway bandits from engaging in such activities.

But what passed for honor behind the walls was a severe morality. As the president of the B.P.F.U. explained, "The only way people learned back then was if an example was set."[31] So it was decided that the lifers and B.P.F.U. would each set an example—the lifers with the white guy and the B.P.F.U. with the black.

"We'll handle [our guy]," said the president of Lifers with Hope. "Make sure you handle [yours]." "Ain't no problem—it's handled," agreed the president of the B.P.F.U.[32]

The B.P.F.U. president assembled his "cadre," a group of ten men who would do whatever he told them. He called the black man into his office and said, "You know, man, I told my cadre to take care of you." The cadre took the bandit to a back room and broke his leg and one of his arms. "He ain't going to be robbin' nobody for a while," said the B.P.F.U. president.

According to the head of the B.P.F.U., the lifers also broke the white man's bones. "Broke his knuckles with a ball peen hammer—hit him in the head a few times....Beat him almost senseless. He survived it, but at least he did learn."

Of course, not everyone was a leader or enjoyed the extra privileges of the "upper structure," as the convicts called those with highest status. At the bottom of the hierarchy were the punks, snitches, and sex offenders.

Punks were weak inmates. They were almost always smaller and physically weaker than the buff convicts who ruled their lives, and they were also mentally weaker. They lacked the toughness and ruthlessness necessary for self-preservation in a hostile environment like the Walla Walla penitentiary of the 1970s.

Sometimes a punk would attach himself, more or less voluntarily, to a stronger convict in exchange for protection. Sometimes a man was punked through force and intimidation. Some had good protectors; other punks could be cruelly abused.

While the primary image of a punk is that of sex slave, a punk is not a queen. The latter was often prized and pampered and kept for sex alone. By Vinzant's time, the penitentiary's queens wore makeup, skirts, and blouses. Some were gay; some were opportunists. On the streets, the inmates who used queens or punks were generally straight. But this was prison, and the strong took what they could get.

In contrast, a punk was generally despised and could be a slave in everything he did. A punk served his master: get this, get that; do this, do that. A common practice was to use a punk as a safe. He'd store drugs in his rectum and retrieve them on his master's command. As property, a punk could be sold or traded for other things of value.

The snitch was both despised and in danger of his life. Considering the risks of ratting on his peers, there were a surprising number of snitches. From superintendent to ambitious officer, many staff had informants of their own. Sometimes one hundred men or more might be interviewed using the same questions just to hide the identity of the one man known to have something important to say. A careless remark or action could—and did—get some informants killed.

Because a snitch was among the lowest of the low, it was dangerous for any convict to talk with an officer. A common practice was to stand far apart and shout the words that needed to be exchanged. This way there was no misunderstanding the content of the communication. Leaders who met with prison administrators never went alone. Witnesses were needed to preserve the leader's credibility.

The motivations for informing were many. Sometimes it was done for favors. While Jim Harvey paid informants with scrip confiscated from other inmates, a consistently good informant might get transferred to minimum security or be recommended for parole. Sometimes an informant knew where to find a gun and felt safer having it out of certain hands. Some informants ratted on rival drug dealers just to improve their market share. Idle convicts have all day, every day, to work the system. False accusations could hobble a foe—at least for a while.

The final group occupying the lower tiers of the inmate hierarchy was sex offenders. For most convicts, sex offenders were a subspecies worthy of contempt—a special circle in hell was reserved for child molesters. Knowing this, a sex offender rarely revealed his true crime. But when inmates worked as clerks in the Classification and Parole office, they had access to everyone's file, so there were ample opportunities to read an inmate's record and pass the information on.

When the practice of having inmate clerks handle sensitive information was stopped, the convicts still had their ways. As a former con boss said, "we didn't have to check paperwork to find out whether you was a good guy or a bad guy." When a new inmate came in with a past unknown, they'd spend time with him and run "little scenarios" on him—maybe put him with a guy who'd pretend he was a child molester and watch for a reaction. "If [he] got off on that, that's telling us that [he's] a sex offender. [If he was,] we'd take [him] somewhere and have [him] beat up or something."[33]

But not all sex offenders were created equal. Sometimes it was possible for a sex offender—as long as he wasn't a serial rapist or child molester—to avoid being a pariah. The B.P.F.U. president during the Vinzant era explained that whenever a new inmate arrived at the penitentiary, somebody eventually asked, "What are you in for?" There would be a negative reaction if the man said "rape." But sometimes the new inmate would explain, "Yeah, man, I caught a charge....But realistically, man, I did it and I didn't do it. I was high....I don't know what happened. I just know I'm here." An admission like this, said the B.P.F.U. president, could make a difference. "If you could tell somebody and be honest about what you just said and your feelings—and you're showin' 'em throughout doing time you ain't runnin' around rapin' nobody and you ain't playin' nobody for their store or manhandling people—people learn to respect you, they pull you in....Your case don't mean nothin' to 'em no more, because you're walkin' and talkin' a different life."[34]

Those of lowest status—child molesters, known snitches, and the very weak and scared—checked into protective custody at the first opportunity.

Between the "upper structure" and the dregs of prison society lived the majority of the prison population. Some were followers—wannabes who reinforced the prison culture by validating those on top and joining in the abuse of those at the bottom. Others tried to lie low and just do their time. The latter were the survivors who flew below the horizon.

According to one convict, if a person came to Walla Walla and didn't get caught up in the drug culture, "as long as [he] maintained respect, didn't owe nobody [money he] couldn't pay..., didn't mess with nobody's punk—[he] had no problems at Walla Walla."[35] Their numbers are not known, but during these years certainly many hundreds of inmates did their best to simply get by and get out.

Not only these quiet survivors, but almost every man took care to avoid the private beefs of others. But staying uninvolved could take its toll. Sometimes a convict had to step over or around a dead body, stop

Quiet survivors passing the time

his ears to cries for help, or ignore the bloody hands of perpetrators as they fled the scene of a crime. It wasn't callousness; it was self-preservation. Being witness to a murder was danger enough. Assisting a dying man meant you were on his side, and that meant you might be killed as well. For the worst of the worst, there wasn't much humanity to lose, but feigned indifference to the suffering of others diminished each man every time he turned away. The former B.P.F.U. president described what it was like:

> You walk through Blood Alley and you see somebody on the ground bleedin' to death, and they're reachin' up at you askin' you to help 'em. That helpin' hand might cost you your life, so the best thing you could do is turn your head and walk....
>
> "Man, hey, I'm sorry, man, but your beef's not my beef....I'm sorry, but there's nothin' I can do, man. I see you, but I don't."
>
> And you gotta keep on walkin'. Because if you don't, somebody is watching—believe that—somebody is watching, and somebody is gonna say, "You were there and you helped him."[36]

There were many ways a man might be killed or hurt in the penitentiary, but the most common way was with a knife. "I don't like talking about this," said the B.P.F.U. president, "but I guess it's all right." Having a shank—wood, plastic, or metal—was "nothing" according to him. Some shanks, he explained, were made with breakaway handle so that you could stab somebody and break off the handle by bending it sideways. That way, he said, "they're internally bleeding—there's nothing escaping....They ain't gonna make it [anywhere] before they bleed to death. All that blood inside 'em starts coming out of their mouth and nose."[37]

Staff and inmates were also hurt or killed by bombs. Knowledge of how to make bombs may have been aided by members of the George Jackson Brigade incarcerated in the penitentiary, but there were other avenues for learning such skills.

"Back then there was no such thing as a limit to anything," explained the former B.P.F.U. president. "There was no 'You can't have this kind of magazine or that,' so a lot of people was ordering...*Soldier of Fortune* [magazine]—and *Soldier of Fortune* would tell you exactly how to make zip guns, pipe bombs, this, that, and the other." So bomb-making instruction from the George Jackson Brigade wasn't actually necessary.

"My brother...was kind of a jack of all trades, and he was a hellacious one at makin' bombs," continued the B.P.F.U. president. "That guy, he'd sit there and peel hundreds and hundreds of match heads and put 'em in a Noxzema jar....He would put a fuse or a wick down in there....He'd light it and set that baby down somewhere, and next thing you hear 'kaboom'—because it's gotta explode." The bomb that took off Hartford's fingers was made in a similar way.

The inmates also made something they called a shoe-can bomb. It was made out of a partly filled can of shoe polish. When it exploded, it would shoot out gobs of flaming shoe polish like a miniature napalm bomb.

Another trick was to use a syringe to inject fuel—either gasoline or naphtha—into a light bulb. When someone flipped the switch, the light would explode, spewing broken glass and flames. "That was one way you could fry somebody," said the former B.P.F.U. president. "[There was] nothin' lightweight about none of that. And people did it because they had the means of doing it."[38]

The Washington State Penitentiary was a dangerous place in the 1970s, but not as dangerous as the wildest stories. One inmate claimed there were thirty-two murders in one year—a number that bears no relationship to reality. Another said that "everybody wanted to go there—until it got to be the number one most dangerous penitentiary in the States."[39] This last opinion was common, sometimes expressed like it was a badge of honor to have lived and survived in such a place.

There were bad days, weeks, months, and years at the penitentiary in Walla Walla in the 1970s, but it was far from the worst prison in the country during those years. Using the somewhat crude metric of murders, Walla Walla was like a slow burn in comparison to the incendiary riots at Attica and New Mexico, which more or less bracketed the penitentiary's most troubled decade. Forty-three people died in one day at Attica prison in 1971; thirty-three at the New Mexico State Penitentiary in 1981. Between those years, there were twenty-nine murders at Walla Walla reported in the *Walla Walla Union-Bulletin*.

"That's it?" said the man who had been president of Lifers with Hope when Vinzant was superintendent. "I thought more than that." When informed that these were murders reported in the local newspaper, he immediately understood the discrepancy. "Oh, 'cause there were 'suicides' that weren't officially murders," he said.[40]

There is no way to know how many deaths reported as suicide or accidental overdose were "assisted." The former leader of Lifers with Hope isn't saying, and even he probably doesn't know for sure. Similarly, there is no way to know how many stabbings, beatings, broken bones, rapes, mutilations, and humiliations occurred during those years. But the hundreds of men who crowded into the deprivations of protective custody knew one thing for certain: the penitentiary was a dangerous place.

A seventy-year-old man who had spent most of his life in prison, and who was still locked up at the time of his interview in 2010, was moved to tears as the old days were discussed. "To be honest with you," he said, "this is dredgin' up some old memories that I'd buried. A lotta things I've seen my convict friends do, I'm not proud of....A lot of unguided people—I won't say 'innocent'—lost their lives in Walla Walla or got hurt real bad for some real stupid things."

"You know what the old saying used to be?" he asked. "It's the principle." He repeated the word, making it sound like he was spitting out a foul taste. "Principle!" Then, his voice falling almost to a whisper, he said, "It's a hard row, man. I lost a lot."[41]

Chapter 28

THE WASTEBASKET CAPER

E VERYONE AT THE PENITENTIARY knew Vinzant liked to use shotguns in certain situations. One day in February 1978, so did
everyone in Olympia.

"To meet this man, you wouldn't think he had judgment as poor as
this. You really wouldn't," said Vinzant's deputy director, Bob Tropp.
"But he just did some of the damnedest things you ever heard of." An
incident in February 1978, eight months after Vinzant became superintendent, led Tropp and others in headquarters to conclude that "Vinzant
was doing things that were increasingly neurotic."[42]

According to Steve Chadek, then the union president and armory
officer, the incident began with a telephone call from the superintendent. Chadek recalled both sides of the conversation.[43]

"Chadek, do you have any of those plastic shotgun shells?" asked
Vinzant.

Chadek said he did and offered to bring them to the superintendent.
Vinzant said he'd get them himself.

Chadek asked Vinzant what he intended to do with the plastic shells
and Vinzant told him, "Don't worry about what I'm going to do, just
tell me where the shells are at."

Chadek had a guess about what Vinzant was going to do, so he cautioned the superintendent: "If you're going to put those [plastic shells]
with some double ought [a type of buckshot ammunition used in a
shotgun], remember to put the double ought in first and the plastic in
last."

Later that day an order was given, presumably through Central Control, to bring two inmate leaders, one white and one black, to the superintendent's conference room. John Lambert, one of the officers who
escorted the inmates, recalled what he saw and heard.

The superintendent's conference room was outside the walls, so the inmates were first shackled. When they arrived at their destination, associate superintendent Genakos told the officers to take the shackles off.

Lambert thought, "Unchain them? Here? You gotta be shitting me!"[44]

Lambert recalled Genakos repeating himself: "Unchain these guys—and don't come in here if you hear a shot."

"Say what? Would you repeat that?"

"You don't come in here."

Lambert wasn't armed, so he stationed another officer with a gun at the back door of the conference room. According to Lambert, after about fifteen to twenty minutes, the quiet was shattered by a shotgun blast. The officer with the gun ran to the main door of the conference room just as Genakos walked out.

"Get your ass outta here," said Genakos. "I told you I didn't want you up here with that gun."

"I was just doing my job," explained the officer.

"You guys go back [inside the prison] and go to work," said Genakos. "I'm giving you a direct order. Get everybody outta here."[45]

Lambert and the other officer left, leaving the two—possibly dead—inmates in the conference room with the superintendent.

Before the story hit the newspapers, it was water cooler gossip and speculation throughout much of DSHS and the state capital. While the superintendent at Walla Walla was conferring with two inmates in his conference room, a shotgun had gone off, blasting a hole in a wastebasket sitting on the table between the two inmates, and peppering the far wall.

It was an accident, said the prison spokesman. The gun was on safety, and it must have malfunctioned. The armory officer was asked to check the gun to determine what had gone wrong. At least that's how it was reported in the Walla Walla paper the next day.[46]

Steve Chadek, in his capacity as the armory officer, met with the newspaper reporter. The gun had misfired before, he said. After this second misfiring, he took the gun apart, and in his official report, he said he found a broken compression spring. "The three-quarter-inch spring had broken in two pieces, jammed the safety lever and caused the firing pin to be open." So, according to Chadek, "any time you'd pump the bolt forward the gun would go off."[47]

When Vinzant was asked about this incident, he said, "The reason [the two inmates] were brought out there was to discuss a situation where they had been identified by another inmate as the two inmates who had raped him."[48]

"The rest of it was simply as it was reported," said Vinzant. "It was an accidental firing. I had the shotgun, and when it was examined by the armorer...he said that there was...some fault in the firing mechanism....It was reported to [DSHS secretary] Dr. McNutt as an accidental firing."

But why was the wastebasket on the table? "I don't know," said Vinzant. "I guess it was set there by people who were cleaning up or something. I really don't know. The gun was lying on the table...until I picked it up. That was the way it happened. Nobody got hurt."[49]

What actually happened is somewhat more complicated. Referring to his written report and what he said to the newspaper reporter, Chadek said, "I flat-assed lied."

The true story according to Chadek was that Vinzant loaded the gun wrong. He put the plastic shells in first and the double ought last. Which meant when he injected the first shell, it was double ought buck.

Perhaps it happened that way, but Vinzant was an expert with shotguns. Maybe that's why some people believe it was Chadek who loaded the shotgun the wrong way. In any event, when Vinzant pulled the trigger, the double ought flew down the table between the heads of the two inmates, through the wastebasket, and into the far wall.

When Chadek returned to work, Vinzant called him into his office and told him what had happened. "Gol dang it," said Chadek. "I told you how to load that gun."

"Aw, I done it wrong," said Vinzant. "What can you do to help me?"

Chadek helped by making up the story reported in the newspaper.

There are no credible first-hand accounts of what happened in the conference room, but there are second- and third-hand reports from what one of the inmates in the room reportedly told at least one staff member and some inmates. According to these stories, Vinzant had the two inmates brought to the conference room, where he said an inmate had fingered them as those who had beat and raped him. So far, this jibes with Vinzant's account.

Vinzant reportedly told the inmates something to the effect that he wasn't going to tolerate that kind of thing in his prison. One inmate, a black, wondered what was going on. How could he and a white man be in the same lineup on a rape charge? They didn't even associate with the same people. Puzzled, the black inmate made some smart-ass remark. This apparently irritated Vinzant, and it was then that he blasted the wastebasket off the table. The blast was so close to the inmates that the shotgun shell wadding got caught in the black inmate's beard and hair. The other inmate reportedly dived under the table.

After the shot, the inmates acquired a newfound cooperative attitude, and discussion resumed. At some point, the black suggested they take a lie detector test to prove their innocence. He looked at the other inmate and said, "Won't we?" The other responded, "I will about *this*." Reportedly, Vinzant agreed to their proposal, and they were subsequently tested and cleared of the charge.

It's difficult to find staff from this period who say anything positive about Vinzant, but those who commented on this issue seemed certain that Vinzant wouldn't have intentionally fired off a live round between the heads of two inmates. That's probably true. Furthermore, it would make no sense to fire a warning shot with double ought and have plastic shot as backup. But not all the inmates were so sure. "He didn't make no mistake," said one inmate. "He was showing he's the boss."[50] That may be true, at least the "showing he's the boss" part. The wastebasket on the table suggests forethought. At close range, even if the wastebasket had been hit by plastic shot, the blast would have gotten everyone's attention.

Firing a shotgun between the heads of inmates was an outlier for Vinzant, but pulling inmates into special meetings was common. The president of Lifers with Hope had such meetings himself. He put it this way: "Periodically, we were our own worst enemies with respect to how far we would let things deteriorate before we would do something about it ourselves. And that's what [those meetings with Vinzant were] all about. It had gotten to that point where [the administration] couldn't look away any longer, and they were pulling people up and saying, 'Look, this has got to stop.'"[51]

Chapter 29

SPRING CLEANING

IN THE SPRING OF 1978, as the days were getting warmer, so were the correctional officers. Anger over how Vinzant and Genakos ran the prison was turning from a simmer to a boil. In less than nine months, Vinzant had alienated most of his staff and caused leaders in Olympia to seriously question his judgment and stability.

It wasn't just that Vinzant and Genakos paid little or no attention to most of the staff. It wasn't that they seemed to prefer the company of inmates over that of correctional officers. It wasn't even how they circumvented the state personnel system by promoting their favorites over those who had applied for promotion and done well on the state exams. By the spring of 1978, there was a growing consensus among the prison staff that Vinzant and Genakos were bending the rules beyond all recognition.

The situation was so bad that officer after officer said both men were crooks. An inmate con boss, who called Vinzant and Genakos "cool as all outdoors," agreed. In a tone that sounded a lot like admiration, he said, "They was gangsters, man. They was corrupt."[52]

Most of the stories involve Genakos. Even Vinzant hinted that Genakos sometimes strayed from the straight and narrow. "He's a good man," said Vinzant. "He's as loyal to me as a man can be and a good friend. But the thing he could not quite control was the tendency to play a little bit of a game." Then, referring to Genakos's dismissal as superintendent of Concord prison, Vinzant said, "That's probably what got him in trouble with [the Commissioner of Corrections in Massachusetts], and that could have gotten him in some other trouble [too]."[53]

Among the games that Genakos was alleged to have played was selling furloughs—hours or days away from the prison, usually without supervision. A weekend furlough was said to cost $600.

Steve Chadek claimed to have witnessed the front end of one such transaction while he was helping Genakos with some paperwork. According to Chadek, when an inmate asked Genakos why his requests for a furlough were never granted, Genakos replied, "Well, you never paid me nothing."

The inmate, who was an accomplished artist, didn't have any money, but he did have a large painting that Genakos admired. According to Chadek, the inmate offered the painting in exchange for a weekend furlough. Genakos told the inmate he would think about it. Chadek checked the next weekend, and both the inmate and painting were gone.[54]

When inmates were asked whether furloughs could be bought during the Vinzant era, the answers were noncommittal. Several said, "I heard that, too." Another replied, "That's possible."

In another incident, officer John Lambert was at one of the Bikers' Club banquets when Genakos handed him a check for about $900. It was made out to Genakos and signed by the Bikers' Club president. Genakos had a plausible explanation. He told Lambert he'd loaned the money to the bikers for food and other things for the banquet, and they were just paying him back. After hearing the explanation, Lambert told Genakos, "Listen, you're the boss. I don't want to hear it, nor do I want my fingerprints on that stuff."[55]

Other incidents made officers believe that the cooperative attitude of some inmates toward the administration must have involved some kind of quid pro quo.

Robin Moses, for example, believed that Vinzant "bought the Bikers' Club" when he moved part of their operation to the industries area, made them part of correctional industries, gave them at least a five-figure budget, and allowed various bikers numerous furloughs in connection with their business. Moses said Vinzant was "buying himself an army" through the benefits he gave the bikers.[56]

For the bikers, the advantage of having a budget and the ability to go to motorcycle shops near and far, or to brother bikers on the street, was not just that they could buy parts for their choppers. They could buy other things as well. During Vinzant's time at Walla Walla, "that's how the main drugs came in—through the bikes—through the frames," said a former B.P.F.U. president. Harley Sportsters were the best, he explained. On most bikes the gas tank and frame are separate parts, but not on the Sportster—the entire frame and gas tank come as a unit. It had lots of room for packing contraband. "Cannabinol and heroin and everything else used to come in hollow tubes like that—in the frames."[57]

Unusual treatment of specific inmates was also viewed as suspicious by some officers. John Lambert recalled an incident involving a particularly dangerous inmate and a missing kitchen knife. While Lambert was working the gate at Central Control, Genakos said the inmate was coming and told Lambert, "Don't shake him down."

When Lambert asked why the inmate shouldn't be searched, Genakos told him the inmate was bringing the missing butcher knife to him.

Lambert thought this was crazy. This inmate had tried to kill staff with a knife in the past. He told Genakos, "I'm not going to open the damn door....You run the keys....I'm not doing that crazy shit." Lambert handed the keys to Genakos and left.

Genakos let the inmate into the control room, and the inmate gave him the knife. Through the glass, Lambert could see them talking. "They were just like they were best buddies," he said. To Lambert, the only explanation for such behavior was that Genakos was buying off the inmate.[58]

It doesn't really matter whether such stories are true, because most staff believed they were. It was with this mindset that groups of correctional officers began to hold meetings, some small and quiet, others loud and boisterous. By the spring of 1978 those most involved decided that Vinzant and Genakos had to go, as well as union president Steve Chadek, now seen as a company-owned man. In the union election, two months after the shotgun blasted a hole in the superintendent's wastebasket and Chadek spun his tale about a broken firing mechanism, Parley Edwards was elected union president.

Parley Edwards was not complicated. A handsome, conscientious man, he spent decades working in Washington prisons, never rising above the rank of correctional officer—the entry-level custody position. He had little formal education, but he did have old-fashioned, down-home values: you're as good as your word; right is right and wrong is wrong.

To Edwards, there were no two ways about it: Vinzant and Genakos were about as wrong as anybody could be. The last years of Rhay had been bad enough, but Vinzant and Genakos were simply too much to bear. Edwards was loud, he was insistent, and after defeating Chadek in the April election, he was the voice of the union.

The election of Edwards was not the only change that spring.

The day after the union election, Governor Dixy Lee Ray fired her longtime friend, Harlan McNutt, from his job as secretary of the Department of Social and Health Services.[59] Jerry Thomas, McNutt's deputy secretary, took over until a permanent replacement could be named.

At the penitentiary, a new associate superintendent, Larry Kincheloe, was added to Vinzant's administrative team.

Kincheloe came to Washington State as an advisor to the Army National Guard after nearly fifteen years as a commissioned officer in the army and three tours of infantry duty in Vietnam. In his spare time, he enrolled as a graduate student in sociology at Pacific Lutheran University, where he became interested in corrections through some of the courses he took. By coincidence, Kincheloe lived directly across the street from where Vinzant stayed when he was in Olympia. After learning who Vinzant was, Kincheloe discussed ideas for his master's thesis with his knowledgeable neighbor. He even cited Vinzant as a source in his writing.

Kincheloe obviously made a good impression on Vinzant. As a graduate student without any experience in corrections whatsoever, Kincheloe was hired by Vinzant at the rank of associate superintendent. The plan was that Kincheloe would go to Walla Walla for three or four months to learn something about corrections, then work for Vinzant in central office. Because of the level at which Kincheloe was hired, this appointment didn't violate civil service rules, but it was consistent with how Vinzant selected and promoted employees.

Less than a month later, Governor Ray visited the penitentiary. She was not predisposed to like what she saw. "She really didn't like corrections," said John Shaughnessey, the division's assistant director for management at the time. "She didn't want to have anything to do with it. I know she told [various high-ranking officials] a time or two, 'Just keep the lid on the damn thing.'"[60]

Acting DSHS secretary Jerry Thomas accompanied the governor on the state patrol airplane and on the tour. "The purpose of the visit…was not just to see the penitentiary," said Thomas. "If my memory is correct, we had a town hall meeting in Walla Walla that night."[61] The penitentiary tour was on the agenda earlier in the day.

After the tour, the governor was upbeat in her public comments. She was "impressed at the changes and improvements at the penitentiary," the reporter wrote.[62] Privately, she was appalled. "She did not like what she thought were pretty slovenly conditions at the institution. She also felt that there was far too much leniency," said Jerry Thompson, the man named permanent secretary of DSHS a few weeks later. Furthermore, "the governor did not like Doug Vinzant at all."[63]

Thompson explained, "[The governor] and I shared a view with regard to Vinzant. He never seemed to answer a question—at least to me he never did….You got these big, long answers, and you never got anything out of him. I didn't like that. I always thought that he was looking at me—and maybe he should have—as someone who didn't know the first thing about an institution, and he was just going to kind of finesse this guy out of the way. I think he approached the governor in exactly the same…way. That's probably the wrong thing to do with Governor Ray."[64]

There is no record of what the governor said to Vinzant during her visit. But it's probably not a coincidence that the next day, Vinzant told the local paper that he would name a successor to serve as superintendent within thirty to forty-five days.[65] Vinzant's commuting days were about to end—he would return to Olympia as full-time director of adult corrections.

Before that would happen, however, yet another incident took place to reinforce Jerry Thompson's resolve that Vinzant had to go.

Chapter 30

THE MAS BANQUET

W HO WAS MORE OUT OF TOUCH WITH REALITY: violent revolutionaries who planned an assault on the penitentiary to free their friends, or those who sought to prevent it from happening by setting up an ambush where women and children might die?

"One of my informants was giving us information relative to an escape plan involving a group out of Seattle," said Jim Hartford, the officer whose hand had been blown apart the previous year. "[Another officer] and I flew to Seattle to meet with Seattle [police] intelligence and an FBI agent. They had an informant of their own that was giving similar information that there was an escape plan plotted for the institution."[66]

After their meeting with law enforcement in Seattle, Hartford and the other officer returned and briefed Vinzant and Genakos. Members of the George Jackson Brigade, he informed them, were planning to make an assault on the institution and spring three of their followers sometime early in July.

A banquet for Men Against Sexism (MAS) was scheduled for Saturday, July 1, 1978. MAS was the gay rights group in the prison, and their banquet was to be held in the new visiting room. Vinzant had moved visiting from the west side of the old administration building to the east side, and created an outdoor visiting area. But many staff thought the location of the outdoor area was crazy, because it was *outside* the walls. Nothing but a single chain link fence with an obscuring mesh separated the men and their visitors from the free world. This fact had not escaped the attention of the inmates or members of the George Jackson Brigade who were still on the streets.

Officer Dick Morgan was working Eight Wing the day before the scheduled banquet. After a stifling week, a cooling trend had set in,

Outdoor visiting (at arrow)—1978

and the wing was somewhat comfortable. But something wasn't quite right.

One of the leaders of the George Jackson Brigade, the man who had been arrested after the adult corrections headquarters building in Olympia was bombed, lived on the unit. A self-proclaimed revolutionary anarchist, he was good at stirring things up. But on this day, "he was behaving himself real well. We couldn't figure out what was going on," said Morgan.[67]

Morgan went to the lock box to close some cell doors. As he raised the handle, he realized somebody had smeared feces on it. "Aw! I've got this shit all over my hand," he recalled saying. "I just sat there and steamed....It ain't right for an officer to have to clean this off."[68]

Morgan starting going through his list of who might be available to clean the handle. There was an inmate living in the unit who had been released from segregation on a behavior contract. Most officers thought these contracts were phony as hell, but one condition they all contained was the stipulation to follow all orders given by an officer.

Morgan knew "it would be a cold day in hell before you could get an inmate to clean shit off a handle....So I thought [it was] a win-win situation. Number one, I figured [the inmate] would refuse, and then I'd get to lock him up for refusing to obey his contract. Or, number two, he'd do it and get in a lot of trouble with his peers for kowtowing to an officer's order to clean shit off of a lock box handle. I thought it was a really neat plan."

"So I went down to [the inmate's cell] and said, 'There's shit on my lock box. I want you to clean it up.'" To Morgan's surprise, "he hopped right to it."

Morgan remembers thinking, "Oh, this ain't right." This inmate, he recalled, "wanted to be out [of segregation] so bad that he would even clean shit when told by an officer. I even talked it over with the other guys."[69]

Both the inmate who cleaned the lock box and the strangely quiet revolutionary anarchist planned to go to the MAS banquet the next day.

According to Jim Hartford, the George Jackson Brigade members on the outside had weapons, police uniforms, and camping equipment purchased from a major supplier of outdoor gear in Seattle. They had brand new tents, parkas, sleeping bags, freeze-dried food, and camp stoves. There was another van—a rental van—hidden in the bushes across the state line in Oregon, stuffed with additional camping supplies.[70]

Inside the prison, one of the brigade followers had a large radio—a "boom box," as they were called then—that had been hollowed out. A small transistor radio was installed so it could still play music. Hidden inside was a loaded handgun and pipe bombs. The bombs would be used to either blow a hole in the fence around the outdoor visiting area, create a diversion, or just cause mayhem.

The inmates had even written a statement that was to be released after they escaped. The *Black Dragon Communiqué*, as they called it, "was a combination declaration of war and an apology to the inmate population," explained Hartford. An apology was offered because they knew there'd be reprisals and a security clampdown after the escape. It was a declaration of war because the communiqué said it was their intent to wage guerilla war from the Blue Mountains in southeast Washington and northeast Oregon.

It was an ambitious plan.

But Vinzant had a plan of his own. Upon learning of the plot, he decided that they would ambush the Brigade members when they assaulted the institution, stop the escape, and catch all the bad guys. He had the perfect man to make it happen: associate superintendent Larry Kincheloe, the infantry vet from the Vietnam War, knew how to stage an ambush.

"We set up an L-shaped ambush," said Kincheloe. Everyone had assigned stations; everyone had assigned targets. A sniper was on the wall to cover the parking lot. One man was on the third floor of the administration building with a Thompson submachine gun. State patrol officers were also stationed there. Another submachine gun and additional men with rifles were hidden in the bushes near the superintendent's residence. Everyone had a clear line of fire to the outside visiting area. A bullet-resistant polycarbonate shield was installed to protect the Tower One officer from errant crossfire or shots from brigade members. Vinzant had a Ruger .44. Hartford carried a snubnose .38. There were guns everywhere.

Meanwhile, back in Olympia, one day before the assault on the penitentiary was supposed to happen, Gerald Thompson was sworn in as the new secretary for DSHS.

> I was introduced to the media at about two thirty on Friday. I went back to the office, and I had an urgent call from [the chief] of the state patrol....ATF had picked up from [an informant] down in the Pioneer Square area [in Seattle] that there was going to be some sort of attempted breakout or major disturbance associated with this family picnic [at the penitentiary]....The FBI was also involved in it. [The state patrol chief] and the guy from ATF...said this was a real thing....Talk about being in over your head—it was [my] first hour in the office.[71]

The state patrol "had already moved a small detachment over to Walla Walla in anticipation of this thing," said Thompson. The chief of the state patrol, the ATF, the FBI, and Thompson's assistant secretary all recommended that the prison be locked down. "But Vinzant wanted to tough it out," said Thompson. "He was going to somehow contain this thing."[72]

It could have been a bloodbath. Women and children would be present. Guns would be fired, bombs would go off. Fortunately, "we overruled him and we locked down," said Thompson.

Other parts of the plot—the gun and bombs in the boom box; the uniforms, camping gear, and rental car hidden over the state line—all turned out to be true.

"I didn't know anything at the time about prison administration," said Thompson, "but I knew something about *administration*. [I thought to myself], boy, this Vinzant guy is some kind of character if he wants to just let this rip….I remember the next day getting some feedback on what had happened, what they'd found, and what might have occurred. I just couldn't believe it….I recall the next day just being terrified."[73]

Two weeks later, Genakos was named superintendent and Vinzant returned full-time to Olympia. Behind the scenes, Secretary Thompson and his senior aides began planning to replace both Vinzant and Genakos in an orderly way. Unfortunately, as so often happened in Walla Walla in those days, there was nothing orderly about what happened next.

Chapter 31

"A LITTLE GUARD"

LIEUTENANT ROGER SANDERS WAS once hospitalized after being stabbed by an inmate. The injury was severe enough to require weeks on disability leave, and when he returned to work he was assigned light duty. Light duty can mean a number of things; for Sanders it meant little direct contact with inmates. That's why he was working the night shift in Central Control when an officer brought in a suspicious piece of iron pipe in the early morning hours of August 11, 1978.

The pipe had been found in the plenum of a suspended ceiling in the education building during a routine search. It was about four inches long with caps on both ends. In the center was a small pinhole.[74]

In 1978 the penitentiary offered little training and nothing in writing about how to handle a bomb. Supposedly, if a suspected bomb was found, the protocol was to leave it untouched, call the lieutenant on duty, and wait for the bomb squad.[75] The lieutenant on duty that night was Roger Sanders, and if there actually was established protocol, no one seemed to know it. Certainly no one followed it.

After retrieving the device from its hiding place, one of the officers put it in his rear pocket. He then took it to Central Control where he passed it to a sergeant through a security slot.

As if putting a possible bomb in your back pocket and handing it through the security slot to Central Control wasn't bad enough, what happened next was difficult for prison staff to accept. Even fifteen years after the fact, there were still people who insisted that "Roger Sanders was one of the most cautious people who worked [at the penitentiary]."[76] A review of the facts suggests a different appraisal. The following description is taken from the investigative report presented to the superintendent a few days later.[77]

The sergeant took the object from the security slot and passed it across the room. As he did so he cautioned Sanders to "either get rid of it or take care of it." When Sanders inspected the device he noticed a small amount of powder coming out of a pinhole in the approximate center of the pipe. He then placed a portion of the powder in an ash-tray and attempted to set it on fire. Nothing happened. Next, Sanders removed one of the end caps from the device. The sergeant again cautioned Sanders. Another officer, becoming concerned for his safety, left the area.

Sanders replaced the first end cap. He removed the other end cap and some grayish power spilled out. As he tightly screwed the second end cap back onto the pipe, the device detonated.

The report also noted that paper wadding was found just inside the end caps. It's possible that the paper had been repeatedly soaked in urine to concentrate enough urea to make a detonating device. When Sanders tightened the end cap, the friction created by metal on metal either ignited the "grayish powder" that had spilled out of the end, or the urea, or both. However it happened, the bomb exploded in his hands.

Sanders wasn't killed instantly, but his guts were splattered everywhere. Witnesses said the room smelled like onions, and when they looked up they could see the jagged ends of Sanders' severed fingers stuck in the ceiling tiles.[78]

The next morning, with Sanders in critical condition at the hospital, union president Parley Edwards stormed into the superintendent's office. The union's number one issue was nonnegotiable: the current lockdown—started in the early hours of Friday morning shortly after the bomb exploded—would not end until the union's safety demands were met. Otherwise, the officers would walk.

Back in Olympia, the bomb blast was the last straw for the DSHS leadership. Sometime on Friday, assistant secretary Gerry Thomas picked up the phone and invited Bob Tropp, Vinzant's deputy director, to join him for a drink after work at the Oyster House, a popular Olympia watering hole across the street from the division of adult corrections offices. While they were there, Thomas told Tropp that Vinzant was going to be fired and asked Tropp if he would serve as acting director until a permanent director could be found. Tropp said yes.[79]

On Saturday, Genakos agreed to the union demands. There would be a thorough search of the institution and grounds, including a search with drug- and bomb-sniffing dogs. A view-obstructing canopy over an entrance to the dining hall would be removed. All of the bike shop—not just their manufacturing operations—would be moved to the industries area. New fencing would be installed to improve views and help control inmate movement.[80]

With Vinzant's replacement identified, Thomas called Vinzant the following Monday. John Shaughnessy, the business manager for the division, was in the room when Vinzant received the call. According to Shaughnessy, "It was very much a one-sided conversation, with Thomas doing all the talking and Doug doing all the listening. I think at the end of it [Vinzant] said, 'I understand.'" Shaughnessy's recollection was that Vinzant then called his wife and said, "Well, mama, I just got fired."[81]

When Vinzant came to Secretary Thompson's office the next day, he showed up with a letter of resignation. Thompson told the press that the decision to fire Vinzant was made the previous day and that Bob Tropp was now the acting director. Vinzant said he resigned. While these conflicting versions of events caused confusion in the press about Vinzant's departure, there was nothing confusing about Vinzant's subsequent remarks. Speaking of Gerald Thompson, the boyish-looking thirty-six-year-old secretary of DSHS, Vinzant said, "It just demonstrates the naiveté of the man sitting in the secretary's chair. It's unfair for some youngster to say the whole system is going to hell, because it's not."[82] In several interviews, Vinzant included Governor Ray in his parting shots: "I was being asked to deal with the fantasies of a nice little old lady and a nice young chap who is getting into something he really doesn't know anything about."[83] Referring to the bomb blast in the control room, he told one reporter, "Sooner or later a big inmate is going to hurt a little guard or find a way to hurt somebody, so I just don't think you can run a system that has no problems or incidents."[84]

Genakos was also speaking to the press, although in more measured tones. He said he would continue as superintendent despite Vinzant's departure. But Bob Tropp knew he didn't want Genakos. "Not just because he was Vinzant's selection—that would not have been sufficient," said Tropp. "I would have left Genakos there if I had any confidence that he could do the job. But I didn't think he could." While Tropp claimed not to remember any of the "questionable" stories about Genakos, "I had pretty substantial reason to think that this was not our kind of man."[85]

To find someone quickly, Tropp had to look within the department. But there were few people to choose from.

Jim Spalding was then associate superintendent for custody at Monroe, the state's other large and aging prison. Tropp asked Spalding to come to Olympia, where he met with Tropp, Thompson, and Thomas. The meeting took place at Thomas's house after work.[86]

"There was a big salesman job that went on," recalled Spalding. Initially Spalding said he didn't want the job, but they kept sweetening the deal. "They gave me the option of selecting my own staff and [told me] I could pretty much have my own way," said Spalding. "They made their good pitch, and finally I agreed."[87] One condition Spalding stipulated was that a thorough safety review of the prison be conducted by an expert on prison design and security.

Secretary Thompson, who knew next to nothing about adult corrections at the time, was pleased. "When I met Jim, I remember thinking, 'This is the guy.' He even looked the part. He was young and fairly articulate, strong looking, aggressive. He looked like a guy who could run a prison."[88]

It was a week into the lockdown. Genakos, presumably unaware that his replacement had been identified, proposed that nine inmate kitchen workers be released to help prepare the food and deliver the meals to the cellblocks. Despite the small number of inmates, Parley Edwards was furious. He considered this a breach of the agreement to continue the lockdown until all the safety improvements were completed. Referring to the bomb in Central Control, he told the press, "The blood's hardly dried on the floor…and the administration wants to turn [the inmates] loose."[89] To another reporter, Edwards said, "We've been negotiating in good faith with the administration. Now they've stabbed us in the back. If they want war, they've got war."[90]

Over the weekend, Genakos agreed to keep the kitchen workers locked in their cells, and the threatened walkout by the correctional officers was averted.[91]

Sometime around Monday, August 21, Bob Tropp visited Genakos, and they came to a mutual agreement that Genakos would resign. Jim Spalding moved into one of the cottages behind the superintendent's residence in the shadow of the penitentiary walls.[92]

Genakos rented a storage locker and filled it with possessions he couldn't fit in his car—plus some state furniture and equipment from the superintendent's residence. He told the site manager he'd give a forwarding address after he reached the East Coast.[93]

On Tuesday, August 22, 1978, Genakos resigned, packed up his Lincoln, and drove away.[94]

Someone reported there was state-owned property in Genakos's storage locker, and the items were recovered. Charges were considered, but when Genakos told the county prosecutor it must have been a mistake, that ended the matter.[95] A display of prison contraband items—shanks, zip guns, keister tubes, and so on—kept behind glass in the superintendent's conference room disappeared at the same time, however, never to be seen again.

Chapter 32

POST MORTEM

EVER SINCE THE EARLY '70s, when an inmate on furlough from the penitentiary had murdered a state trooper, statute and administrative regulations restricted who could leave the institution and the circumstances under which a leave could be granted. For higher custody inmates—which meant almost everyone confined behind the prison walls—furloughs were supposed to be limited to situations such as attending the funeral of an immediate family member, going to the bedside of a seriously ill family member, going to court, or receiving medical care not available at the prison.

It was common knowledge at the penitentiary and in headquarters that these rules had been routinely violated during Vinzant's tenure. However, since Vinzant was director as well as superintendent, no one thought they could do anything about it. Furthermore, under some circumstances the director could waive certain restrictions, so when a furlough was signed by Vinzant it was not always clear that the law had been violated. It was another matter when a furlough was signed by Genakos and there wasn't a waiver signed by the director.

With Vinzant gone, headquarters decided to conduct an investigation of furloughs authorized by Vinzant and Genakos.

In the days before computerized records, furlough authorizations were written by hand on preprinted forms, so the investigation examined forms for a single month. July 1978 was selected, since Vinzant was superintendent for the first part of the month and Genakos for the remainder. The investigator identified 197 furloughs during July. Of course, some approved leaves were for legitimate reasons recognized in statute. For example, there were thirty-one trips to outside health care providers, four trips to attend funerals, and two trips to attend court proceedings. But there were also thirty-six trips to go shopping, eight trips to play music or give speeches, and numerous trips to attend community functions. Individual bikers made trips to pick up motorcycle parts. Several inmates were authorized to work in a fireworks stand. The investigator called these furloughs "illegal."[96]

Financial audits were also ordered. One audit discovered that an inmate group called Seven Arts was given a $4,000 grant and that the Washington State Penitentiary Motorcycle Association (that is, the Bikers' Club) received $10,000. Both grants came from funds earmarked for correctional industries. While there were no written agreements, a newspaper article said the grants were supposed to help expand the businesses run by these organizations and be repaid out of profits.[97] The audit determined that Seven Arts overspent its grant by nearly $2,500 and the bikers overspent theirs by more than $9,000. None of the money was ever repaid. The person conducting the audit was told by members of the Bikers' Club and Seven Arts that Vinzant did not want formal written agreements regarding these transactions.[98]

Another review identified improper use of the Inmate Welfare Fund. State law required that the money be used for the benefit of inmates in general. Instead, some of the Inmate Welfare Fund money was given to specific groups. Some was repaid, some not.[99]

An audit also determined that capital funds appropriated for specific purposes identified in law were used by Vinzant for other purposes. In the local newspaper, Vinzant said he was going to spend $1 million on security improvements at the penitentiary "unless somebody stops me."[100] In July 1978, somebody stopped him. A guard station and some fencing he had constructed with inmate labor were torn down.

Another investigation found that for more than half a year, ten bikers were paid twenty dollars a month to attend a school that the investigator could not verify even existed. Furthermore, over objections by the penitentiary business manager, the money to pay the bikers came from the same account used to pay the wages of officers. Documents authorizing these payments bore the initials of both Vinzant and Genakos.[101]

There was no investigation, or at least no surviving documentation of an investigation, into allegations that furloughs were sold for cash or other considerations.

Summing up Vinzant's tenure as superintendent and director, Bob Tropp said, "Part of [what happened] may have reflected his approach to how you run a prison—by being very liberal. Part of it was like brib-ery. It was like a payoff. 'Hey, you guys got a good thing going here. You keep it cool, and I'll take care of you. I'll give you your good times.' That was my perception of what was happening. And we had to take [the prison] back."[102]

PART 5
WAR
1978–1981

Overlooking the Big Yard

Chapter 33

DYSFUNCTION

UGUST 1978 SAW THE ARRIVAL OF a new superintendent in Walla
Walla. Everywhere he looked there were problems. It wasn't just
the inmates who wouldn't follow orders; neither would the staff.
Where to begin?

The union was flying high. Their goal of ridding the penitentiary of
Vinzant and Genakos had been realized. But it wasn't just the flush feeling of success that emboldened them. Many union members believed
that only they knew how to restore order to the prison. In their minds,
what was needed was a crackdown in which force was met with force
and violence with violence. Many of the old-timers—including union
president Parley Edwards—had seen that approach work in the days of
super custody, and they knew no other way. Any superior who suggested
otherwise was simply wrong.

The frustration, anger, and rebellion of the loudest leaders among
the officers infected many of the new recruits—always a large group
because of high staff turnover. It was also a group that included young
officers who were easily led. The minimum qualifications for the job
were a high school diploma and no criminal record. The pay was poor,
working conditions awful, training minimal, and an officer always stood
the chance of getting injured or killed. While there were certainly excep-
tions, in 1978 prison jobs in general, and penitentiary jobs in particular,
did not always attract the best recruits.

Many officers—both new and old—ignored orders they didn't like.
Worse still, rogue elements among the officers were taking matters into
their own hands. It certainly didn't start with Genakos, but it was common knowledge that in the last weeks he was associate superintendent,
Genakos slugged two inmates who had their hands cuffed behind their
backs. If it didn't apply to the associate superintendent, the old notion
that "it's cowardly to strike a shackled man" certainly didn't apply to

anyone else. Not only were the inmates out of control, so were the officers.

This was the chaotic situation that Jim Spalding inherited when he took over as superintendent on August 22, 1978.

Spalding wasn't new to the penitentiary. He started his career there. The son of a former captain of the guards at the state prison in Deer Lodge, Montana, Jim had talents that were quickly recognized. During his first year at the penitentiary he took the sergeant's exam, and after eleven months on the job he was ranked number one in the state on the sergeant register. As much as he liked Jim, Bob Rhay wasn't going to promote anyone with so little experience, so it was another year or so before Spalding made sergeant.

Sergeant Spalding then took the lieutenant's exam and came out on top. Although Spalding was still young and not terribly experienced, Rhay promoted him again. Lieutenant Spalding quickly took the captain's exam and, true to form, was ranked number one in the state. Soon, Captain Spalding was supervising lieutenants much older than himself. As he put it, "I don't think there was a one of them that didn't have twenty-five years on me."[1]

In 1973, when the hatchet man for incoming adult corrections director Hal Bradley fired all the superintendents except Rhay, Spalding was promoted to associate superintendent for custody at the state's second largest prison in Monroe, Washington. From the western side of the state, he watched the penitentiary at Walla Walla spiral out of control. Four and a half years later, at the age of thirty-seven, he took over the largest and most troubled prison in the state. Although acting director of adult corrections Bob Tropp believed Spalding was the best man available, he still had concerns. "I felt he had legitimacy," said Tropp, "but he didn't have a lot of experience. I didn't know how well he'd do."[2]

Spalding held his first staff meeting the day he became superintendent. He said his administration would be one of teamwork and openness and that there would be regular staff meetings. He also promised to complete the security improvements the union had demanded after the bomb exploded in Central Control. The next day he held his first press conference. He said that his approach to inmates would be based on the guidelines established in the Washington Administrative

Code. Operating policies would be tightened, but inmates would still be afforded opportunities for work and training.[3] The following day he met with a group of architects from Spokane who were nationally recognized for their expertise in correctional design and prison security. The architects began combing the institution and documenting its weaknesses.

Spalding's initial reception was uniformly positive. Of course, the governor's office and the DSHS people who appointed him were lavish in their praise. B. J. Rhay, now director of adult corrections in Montana, hailed the appointment of Spalding and called him "an excellent man" who was "very popular with the staff and inmates alike."[4] Parley Edwards called Spalding's appointment "a step in the right direction" and noted that "the morale of the staff is higher than I've seen it in some time."[5] Inmates interviewed by the local paper said that Spalding had a reputation for fairness.[6]

The security improvements to which Genakos had agreed were quickly completed. In addition, metal detectors were installed at cellblock entries and other key locations. All this was completed and the lockdown was over before Spalding finished his first week as superintendent.

Ten days after Spalding took over, Lieutenant Roger Sanders died from the massive wounds suffered when the pipe bomb exploded in his hands. He was the first correctional officer killed by inmates—albeit indirectly—in Washington State prisons in more than forty years. The funeral took place four days later.

Sanders's death and funeral further distilled the frustration and rage of officers over management of the prison and adult corrections in general.

Bob Tropp, along with other dignitaries from Olympia and representatives from law enforcement, attended the funeral. Anticipating the anger of the correctional officers, the state patrol insisted on bodyguards for Tropp.

"I remember sitting in the church service flanked by a couple of people from the state patrol," said Tropp. "The event—going to the church service—would have been an unhappy thing in any case because of the man's death, [but it] had a lot of added drama. You could see knots of officers standing around outside waiting to go in. The atmosphere crackled....There was a lot of steam—justifiably—a lot of heat—on the part of staff. They felt that somehow Olympia was to blame for what had happened."[7]

Unfortunately, the small chapel at the funeral home was not large enough for all the people who came to pay their respects. While strangers from Olympia sat, friends and colleagues had to stand—some of them outdoors.

Jim Hartford was one of the frustrated officers at the funeral. Fifteen years after the fact, as he recalled the funeral of his former colleague, he still couldn't hold back the tears. "You had these people...I didn't even know existed, getting front-row seats at a funeral of one of ours. They got to sit down while there were officers that were standing."[8]

As difficult as the death of a staffer was, there was still a prison to run. As he settled into the job, Spalding wandered around the institution, talking to both inmates and staff.

"It was a hot day, and the smoke that was coming out of People's Park was green marijuana smoke," said Spalding. "There was a big cloud of it. There were three hundred inmates, at least, in that park. They were lying all over the grass in all forms of dress and undress, cat-calling people as they came through. There was no control whatsoever."[9] Spalding went into the Bikers' Club, Chicano Club, the club room of Lifers with Hope, and other areas all over the facility. "Everywhere I turned...I found something wrong," he said. "In effect, the administration didn't own anything inside that facility. It was just operating at the whim of the inmates....If you looked at the staff side of it, it was the same way....I don't think that I came across a [single] process that was workable. I knew that there were some drastic changes that needed to be made, [and] I didn't have a clue how to start dealing with some of that stuff."[10]

Within three weeks of his arrival, Spalding had not only a clue, but a plan of how to deal with some of the most challenging long-term problems. The plan came from the team of architects selected to conduct the security review.

John McGough, the architect who led the review, had already designed a number of state-of-the-art prisons and jails in Washington and elsewhere. He was also a member of the national Commission on

Accreditation for Corrections. The latter position put him in contact with correctional leaders around the country and gave him insight into the thinking behind the recently published first edition of the American Correctional Association's *Standards for Adult Correctional Facilities.* Not since Hal Bradley was fired by Governor Dixy Lee Ray did the division of adult corrections have advice from such a knowledgeable person.

The central feature of the plan was construction of a new circulation system with movement controls that effectively divided the prison into four quadrants of more or less equal size. Two quadrants were for housing, one for food service and recreation, and one for health care, education, visiting, and other inmate services.

The physical implications of the plan were extensive. The old gymnasium, Blood Alley, and the B.P.F.U. clubhouse would be demolished to make room for new functions in the inmate services quadrant. The Bikers' Club would be gutted and remodeled into an inmate program area for arts and crafts and other leisure-time activities. A new gym would be built next to it.

As significant as the physical implications of the plan were, the operational implications were greater. While architecture generally can't compel a specific way of operating, it can make certain behaviors easier or harder. The system of movement controls built into the plan facilitated the use of what is known as a "gate pass" system. An inmate moving from point A to point B would have a pass—a piece of paper—with his name and number, where he was going, and relevant times associated with the move. When he got to a gate, he would be let through— provided he was headed in the right direction at the right time.

But in September 1979, all this was just a plan. There was no money. The first phase of construction would cost $13 million, and since the legislature wouldn't meet for months, there was no guarantee that funds would be appropriated. Even with money, construction would take time, particularly construction inside an operating maximum security prison. It would be years before all the elements of the plan could be realized.

Spalding may have had the start of a long-term plan, but there were serious short-term issues that couldn't, and didn't, wait.

Chapter 34

THE PARTY'S OVER

S PALDING WAS OFF AND RUNNING, but given the dysfunction of much of the staff, he had little support. "I knew I had to establish some semblance of an administrative team," he said. "So I started talking to people. I spent a good deal of time talking with Bob Tropp about what an administrative team should do. It was understood that I was going to do the selection of the associate superintendent [for custody]."[11] Unfortunately, there weren't a lot of choices. There were some captains and lieutenants who had been around for a long time. But most of them were pretty closely tied with Bob Rhay and too "old guard" for Spalding's taste. Larry Kincheloe was still there—nominally an acting associate superintendent, but one with no specific duties. Furthermore, since he'd been handpicked by Vinzant, Kincheloe thought his days were numbered.

"I didn't know Larry Kincheloe from anybody," said Spalding. "He didn't have any institutional experience whatsoever. But one [positive] thing: he was concerned about staff. [He] seemed to get along with staff well. I felt that was something we needed. I felt that we could turn him into an associate superintendent. So I picked him—much to the dismay of [those who were passed over]."[12]

Spalding also addressed the issue of Vinzant's promotion of officers to sergeant in violation of merit system rules. "I took the stripes away from the twelve people that were promoted [inappropriately by Vinzant]," said Spalding. This created twelve vacancies for Spalding to fill. "I went right down the register. That was great. People thought that was wonderful, until the twelfth person [on the register] was a woman. I promoted a female, and [the male correctional officers] just came unglued."[13]

Spalding soon created another situation that brought a similar reaction from the inmates. "I met with a group of inmates and all the club leaders," said Spalding. "It was kind of bizarre." He likened it to a meeting with a mini-Mafia. At one point the head of the Chicano Club snapped his fingers, "and a guy immediately came up with a cigarette, gave it to him, and lit it for him."[14] Spalding recalled what happened next:

> That was the point I announced that we were no longer going to have any escorted outings into the community. This was obviously a big perk that they had. They were running around all over the state. The motorcycle club would take a correctional officer and a couple thousand dollars out of the inmate welfare fund, and Genakos or Vinzant would let them go to Seattle for three or four days. There were stories that they were going in and hitting motorcycle businesses—stealing motorcycles and motorcycle parts and bringing a whole truckload of them back to the pen....It was a big perk.
>
> So I cut off the trips out to the community. It was kind of: "Folks, I'm here, and this is my first action."[15]

The bikers got a double hit. Not only were their outings ended, but the last of their motorcycle shop was finally moved out of the main institution and into the industries area. Their business, which had grown and prospered during Vinzant's tenure, suffered. Membership—and influence—declined.[16]

At least some of the inmates were surprised by Spalding's actions. Those who had been around long enough remembered Spalding from his early days. "They had kind of seen me as having come up through the system—this liberal young person that worked hard with the inmate council and that [had taken] people on escorted trips and was really a pretty nice guy," said Spalding. Now they thought that "I had betrayed 'em." Their attitude was, "'We need to get rid of this jerk, he's going to be causing us some real problems.' I think the battle started right at that point."[17]

The battle lines presumably hardened when, shortly after the announcement about furloughs, Spalding ordered an end to inmate banquets, other than two that had already been scheduled for the following week.[18]

The inmates quickly sounded nostalgic for Vinzant and Genakos. Curtailing outings to the community will hinder rehabilitation, they maintained. Furthermore, the programs created and run by inmates—now threatened by elimination of most furloughs—not only helped rehabilitate convicts, but also reduced violence. "We're the real professionals here," asserted one inmate leader. "We know what's wrong inside this institution, and we are trying to do something about it." In fact, he maintained that had the approach of Vinzant and Genakos been continued, "in another year you would have seen the picture of corrections here."[19]

According to the reporter who interviewed the inmates, "as a result of encouragement from Genakos and Vinzant, inmate leaders claim they have taken a larger role in stopping violence and racial conflict inside." Perhaps they had. Certainly the officers weren't controlling much of anything inside the walls. By the end of the month, however, the inmates' claim that they were holding down the violence sounded pretty hollow.

It started with the last Lifers' Banquet, held on September 17, 1978. Among those attending were two young men who had recently quit their jobs at the local newspaper: a photographer, Ethan Hoffman, and a journalist, John McCoy. Their plan, originally authorized by Vinzant and somewhat miraculously allowed to go forward by Spalding, was to do a photo-essay about the penitentiary. They were given full access to the prison, day or night.

According to the president of Lifers with Hope, something happened at the banquet that caused the lifers to get "into a wreck with the bike shop." In this case, a "wreck" can perhaps best be understood as a conflict with serious consequences. Hoffman and McCoy were at the banquet, as well as a biker who showed them some small bags of marijuana. Hoffman snapped a picture. That was a problem.

Hoffman's photo clashed with the public image the clubs tried to convey: that the banquets were benign, family-oriented affairs. Hoffman and McCoy didn't immediately understand the danger of taking such a picture, but they quickly found out when they were confronted by a group of lifers. Fortunately for them, the immediate issue was resolved when Hoffman turned the negatives over to the lifers.[20] But the lifers interpreted the biker's action as an attempt to discredit Lifers with Hope and cause them trouble. The "wreck" with the Bikers' Club had begun.

In the space of less than two weeks, there were multiple stabbings and other serious assaults. Then, on the last day of September 1978, two lifers were beaten by some bikers outside the chow hall. The members of Lifers with Hope decided to retaliate later that day. One staffer, whose job at the time included internal investigations for the division, said a group of lifers decided they would kill the first biker who came along. It turned out that the first biker they saw was a huge guy—"about three axe handles wide," said the investigator. The lifers reconsidered and decided to kill the second biker who came by. The second man died.[21]

After another murder on the first day of November, the chairman of the inmate Race Relations Committee, who six weeks earlier had claimed that his group worked hard to help curtail violence, told the same reporter that he no longer cared about stopping the killings.[22]

Perhaps the chairman of the Race Relations Committee no longer cared, but other leaders were worried. If the violence continued, there might be another lockdown. The inmate leaders called for a work stoppage and a "peaceful demonstration" for Friday, November 3.

Spalding approved the demonstration, but called out the riot squad just in case. Nine hundred inmates gathered in People's Park to listen to inmate leaders blast Olympia for its "inability to manage the prison" and Spalding for "creating a paralyzing atmosphere of apathy" by cutting back on furloughs and hampering inmate programs.[23] The demonstration was peaceful, and the riot squad wasn't needed.

If the inmates expected the demonstration to change the attitude of Spalding and leaders in Olympia, their hopes were dashed later that month when Bob Tropp was named permanent director of the division of adult corrections. Nonetheless, tensions eased in the penitentiary after the demonstration. The inmate leaders were again controlling the violence. But perhaps they had an ulterior motive.

"We had received intelligence that an escape was coming," said Spalding. Spalding knew it involved a tunnel and a lot of inmates, but he didn't know where or when the breakout would occur.

The inmates' plan was a good one. A short tunnel was dug in the northwest corner of Lifers' Park, which couldn't be seen from any of the towers. The tunnel led under the foundation wall of Eight Wing and into the crawlspace under the building. Once the inmates were in the crawlspace, a longer tunnel could be dug at leisure under the opposite wall of Eight Wing and from there to freedom on the other side of the prison wall. Disposal of dirt was easy—it was just dumped in the Eight Wing crawlspace.

As soon as the tunnelers went to work or came back out, a sheet of plywood was placed over the entrance to the short tunnel that started in Lifers' Park. Then inmates covered the plywood with shoveled dirt and rose bushes. This could be done quickly, but there was one place from which this operation could be seen—several windows in the Classification and Parole office.

The C&P office was on the top floor at the south end of Seven Wing. The inmates knew the schedule of the staff in the C&P office, and there was a short window of time during which the inmates could get into the crawlspace in the morning and leave in the afternoon without being seen. But there was a problem.[24]

The problem was Hoffman and McCoy, the photographer and journalist. Because they had full access to the prison day or night, they could be anywhere at any time. They might just stumble onto the escape plot.

To ensure that Hoffman and McCoy didn't show up in Lifers' Park at an inopportune time, the conspirators voted to select one of their members to act as a decoy. The man selected for the job was the president of Lifers with Hope. Interviews and photo shoots with the decoy were scheduled for times and places that wouldn't cause problems for the tunnelers.[25]

Meanwhile, over time, the information the administration received from inmate informants became more detailed. Prison administrators now knew that the tunnel was in the general area of Eight Wing and the western wall of the penitentiary and that the breakout would happen sometime soon. Following this latest intelligence, they began stationing extra officers on the prison wall and in strategic locations west of the prison. Prison staff used a backhoe to dig a trench between the wall and Eight Wing. On the day of the attempted escape, they probed the area with metal rods. The backhoe was brought in to explore a "soft area," but they missed the tunnel by twenty feet.

After dark on December 5, 1978, with a light dusting of snow on the ground, three men popped out of a hole outside the prison wall. The first man was Arthur St. Peter. He was the convict B. J. Rhay had sent on a "Take a Lifer to Dinner" outing in 1972, when St. Peter had escaped through a bathroom window, killed a pawnbroker, and wounded the pawnbroker's wife. This time, six and a half years later, his escape lasted only moments. The official story is that St. Peter froze in place when he heard a shouted order to halt. He then dropped a loaded .38-caliber revolver and put his hands in the air. According to the report, two other men ran. One of the purported runners was the president of Lifers with Hope. The other was his second-in-command. Both men were shot and received non-life-threatening wounds. A fourth convict, whose head was seen emerging from the hole, ducked back into the tunnel as the first shots were fired.

Jim Hartford wasn't on duty that night, but came to the institution because he felt certain the escape attempt was about to happen. After the dust settled, Hartford and another officer dove into the tunnel. As they crawled through the tight space, they found various objects, but no inmates. Later it was determined that perhaps ten more inmates were in the tunnel when the shots were fired. On the sound of gunfire, these men retreated and scattered.

St. Peter was put in segregation. While having their wounds attended to in the prison hospital, the president of Lifers with Hope and his second-in-command claimed they never ran but were lying on the ground when they were hit. This allegation resulted in an investigation by the FBI, which ultimately sided with the official report.

After short stays in the prison hospital, the two men who had been shot were transferred to segregation. Little did these men know they would soon escape the confines of the Washington State Penitentiary, but not of prison.

Chapter 35

The Midnight Express

S PALDING KNEW SOMETHING HAD TO BE DONE to rein in the inmate
leaders. Resistance was growing and he wanted to send a message.
Bold action was needed, and he took it.

Surprisingly, his motive for reining in the leaders was not solely to
gain more control over the prison. It was also for the sake of some of the
leaders themselves. According to Spalding, some of them "had established such a reputation [that] it was tough for them to make it in the
system." At times they were in danger not only from their peers, but also
from out-of-control officers. There was a legitimate question "whether
or not the correctional officers would ever give 'em a fair shake," said
Spalding.[26] Perhaps they would set the inmate leaders up—plant a gun
in their cell or something. Perhaps they would beat them up (something that happened all too regularly in segregation). And perhaps one
or more officers did try to kill two of the inmates during the failed
escape attempt. Despite the FBI investigation, Spalding had no way to
know for sure.

So Spalding called Tropp with a proposal. He wanted to take a group
of the most troublesome inmate leaders—not just one or two, but most
of them—and get them out of the penitentiary in one fell swoop. Those
who couldn't be controlled in other Washington prisons would be flown
out of state to separate facilities, where they couldn't communicate and
cause more trouble.

"This is well-established procedure," said Bob Tropp. Moving
inmates to other locations was (and is) done for a variety of reasons. For
example, if a particularly troublesome leader is put into a new environment, he doesn't have to live up to his reputation quite as much. Sometimes, just breaking up certain combinations of inmates so they can't
egg each other on eliminates what Tropp called "symbiotic, pathological
behavior."[27]

194

Tropp agreed to Spalding's proposal. Because of the number of people and the nature of the inmates involved, the arrangements were time-consuming and difficult. As Tropp said, "No authority in its right mind really is happy to take on people like this. But there is kind of a quid pro quo. We would take people from elsewhere just to give them a break for a while too."[28] As one of Tropp's assistant directors said, "As I recall, we had to take some real assholes in exchange."[29]

Back at the penitentiary, a select group of staff were briefed on the strategy and they greeted the idea with enthusiasm. Each person in the group was asked to nominate inmates they'd like to see go. A list was started, and certain names kept appearing over and over.

Inevitably, word got out. Some officers probably told their least favorite convicts that they'd soon be gone, and the story spread that transfers out of state were in the works. And, as rumors go in prison, only a few people had all the facts. Rumors were repeated, the details changing with each telling. The governor received at least one letter complaining that certain friends of the letter writer would be moved. In this case, the letter writer got it partly right—one of the three men he named (a leader of the George Jackson Brigade) was among the first to be sent out of state. Perhaps the other two felt slighted by their implied unimportance, but they stayed behind while others left.

As work progressed on the details of the transfers, the importance of the move and the inadequacies of the penitentiary's segregation unit were driven home. Many of the ringleaders and others involved in the attempted escape in early December were in seg. But the men in segregation could still make their wishes known and influence felt through shouting and other means. Accurately or not, many of those involved in the foiled escape believed a certain inmate had snitched on them. In fact, the purported snitch had talked with Larry Kincheloe a few days before the attempted escape. He told Kincheloe that six inmates—including himself—and six officers were on a hit list "developed by a small group of influential inmates who were attempting to take care of loose ends."[30] According to Kincheloe, the man declined an offer of protective custody.

Seven days before Spalding's transfer plan could be put into action, Kincheloe's informant was attacked. The purported snitch was stabbed four times in the chest and twice in the back. He was dead before his body reached the prison hospital. A tower officer saw the presumed assailants run into Lifers' Park, but in the low evening light, he couldn't identify the men.

The next day another inmate—a former president of the Bikers' Club—was stabbed six times while taking a shower. Over the next few days, at least eight beatings were reported along the breezeways. "Life is so cheap in here," one inmate told a newspaper reporter that week, "it's not very safe to be walking around." Spalding confirmed that the prison was on edge. "I'd be crazy to say things are not pretty tense," he said.[31]

It's likely the mounting tension and knowledge of the hit list accelerated the move. Based on the subsequent delay in transferring some of the men to prisons out of state, it was clear that not all the arrangements were finalized. But enough were ready so that after the evening meal on Valentine's Day 1979, a one-day lockdown began. After lights-out, eight inmates were taken from their cells, cuffed and chained, and escorted to a waiting bus parked inside the walls. In the middle of the night, the bus drove across the state to Shelton and the segregation unit of the division's newest prison. Five other inmate troublemakers were placed in administrative segregation at the penitentiary that night.

Built as a reception center and long-term housing for the state's least dangerous offenders, Shelton was, to use the words of one who worked there, "a duck pond." The officers had presumably been briefed, but most of the staff at Shelton had probably never seen anything like the eight men who came to them that night. The inmates transferred from Walla Walla proceeded to tear the segregation cells apart—but their rage was local, unable to infect the prison they'd left behind or the prison to which they were transferred.

The last details were finally worked out a few weeks later. The first three men to be sent out of state were made ready, including one who was shipped to Shelton at the last moment. "They literally had us draped in chains," said the former president of Lifers with Hope, who was on the first plane. Each inmate had two sets of leg irons attached to his ankles like hobbles on a horse. Each had double belly chains to which his hands were handcuffed. The lock holes on the cuffs were taped so the locks couldn't be picked. Another chain secured the handcuffs to the leg irons so the men couldn't raise their arms. After the inmates were seated on the airplane, a chain was put around their necks, between their handcuffed hands, down the crotch, and attached to the leg irons.[32] Add a seat belt, and these guys could hardly move.

Sometimes referred to as "the governor's plane," the airplane was comfortable but small—a six-seat Beechcraft King Air 90. While the governor occasionally used the plane, it belonged to the state patrol and was used for a variety of purposes—this time carrying convicts and their escorts on a flight of thousands of miles. Like the midnight express from Walla Walla, the plane took off at night. Its first destination was the federal penitentiary in Marion, Illinois. After that, it flew to the federal penitentiary in Atlanta, Georgia.

Although the inmates were well restrained, other options for controlling unruly behavior on the governor's plane were limited. A gun, Mace, or other gases were useless in such a confined space. As an extra precaution to ensure a peaceful flight, the pilot made an announcement to those in the passenger compartment. Exact words aside, the gist of what the pilot said, according to several people who were there, was something like this: "Good evening, ladies and gentlemen. Welcome aboard flight such-and-such to Marion, Illinois. We'll be cruising at thirty thousand feet at an airspeed of approximately two hundred twenty-six knots. And if any of you mother-fuckers back there decide to screw around, I'm going to decompress the cabin, and since you can't reach your oxygen masks, you'll be dead in thirty seconds."[33]

The pilot was bluffing. If there was a rapid decompression of the airplane at thirty thousand feet (the service ceiling for this type of aircraft), the incapacitated convicts would likely pass out within a minute or two, but they wouldn't die unless they were without oxygen for several minutes longer. If the pilot actually decompressed the airplane and killed the inmates, he would surely lose his license and probably go to jail. But the men in chains didn't know this. It was an effective ploy, and the flight proceeded without incident.

Back in Walla Walla, the change was immediate. When the brief lockdown ended, the released prisoners were met with a show of force of forty additional officers and a dozen state patrolmen.[34] Tensions lowered, and a brief period of calm descended on the prison.

"It woke the place up," said John Lambert. "The inmates finally realized that they didn't have control anymore."[35]

Chapter 36

POWER VACUUM

S PALDING'S DECISION TO SHIP OUT a small busload of prison leaders drew rare praise from union president Parley Edwards. "The
man had the guts to grab the bull by the horns and do it," he said.
"It's never been done by any administrator we can remember." Then,
perhaps experiencing cognitive dissonance with his praise of Spalding,
Edwards added, "He surprised a lot of us."[36]

Edwards's praise was also tempered by a perceptive note of caution.
The transfer of prison leaders "may take tension off for a week, three
months, maybe four months," he said. But Edwards told the newspaper reporter that power struggles between inmates coveting the power
of those recently removed were likely, and although the prison was now
relatively peaceful, "it can change."[37]

During the lull following removal of the first tier of inmate leaders,
Spalding and Kincheloe took steps to consolidate their recent gains. In
early March 1979, they created a dedicated search team made up of a
sergeant and three officers. They called it the Security Service Team. Jim
Hartford, recently promoted to sergeant, was in charge.

"I was afforded a personal conversation with Jim Spalding," said
Hartford, describing how he came to join the team. The superintendent
told him, "We're going to take this place back. It may take a while, but
we're going to take it back." Spalding went on to say that some people might get hurt—that Hartford might be hurt. "That's acceptable,"
Hartford recalled telling Spalding, "as long as we're trying to do something as opposed to trying to keep the status quo."[38]

Organizing the Security Service Team "was a conscious effort on
Kincheloe's part—with Spalding's blessing, I'm sure—to give the inmates
four guys to hate terrible," explained Hartford. The inmates "couldn't
predict when we'd be at work or where we'd be. All we owed the state
was forty hours a week. We'd come in at night and shake [them] down.

We'd come in early in the morning. We had a preference for afternoons, just because that's when things were happening....[Part of the strategy was] to take some of the heat off the wing officers....Spalding would share information with me from his sources...as far as locations of dope or a stash of weapons or something. He'd call me in and tell me what he knew and say, 'Go find it.' That was fun," said Hartford.[39]

Because lack of visibility into Lifers' Park was a major problem for prison staff—a factor in their failure to find the entrance to the tunnel used in the December escape attempt and in the murder of the purported snitch—Spalding had the fish pond and most of the shrubbery in Lifers' Park removed. A temporary tower was installed on the south wall so that an officer had direct line-of-sight supervision of the area during hours of greatest inmate activity. The park itself was closed to all outside visitors. This last change didn't affect just lifers. All programs involving outside visitors were now confined to the visiting room.

While a comprehensive plan to address outside lighting was on the drawing board, temporary improvements were made by installing mercury vapor floodlights on the west and south walls. These illuminated the area between Eight Wing and the wall, Lifers' Park, and the south end of People's Park. Moveable searchlights were installed at several towers and various locations along the catwalk on top of the wall.

Meanwhile, the architects were developing more detailed proposals, including remodeling each of the cellblocks, and remodeling and repurposing the Lifers with Hope club room, the old auditorium, and other club areas and offices.

Dayrooms for each cellblock and newly constructed office space for on-unit counselors and others were based on a plan to implement "unit team management." Under this operational concept, the same people worked with the same inmates over extended periods of time. In the past, the only people who did this were correctional officers who reported up the chain of command to the associate superintendent for custody. Under unit team management, a non-custody person, called a correctional unit supervisor, was responsible for how the unit ran. The correctional unit supervisor, as well as the counselors and other non-custody personnel, reported up a different chain of command. Each cellblock, or unit, operated somewhat autonomously from all other cellblocks. When unit team management worked effectively, communication between inmates and staff was improved and surprises became less frequent.

Plans were also made to increase staff supervision of inmate movement and program areas. But these plans, along with the major capital initiatives proposed by the architects, would have to wait for additional funding by the legislature.

Unfortunately, as Parley Edwards predicted, the peace brought about by the removal of dysfunctional inmate leaders didn't last. New blood vied to fill the leadership vacuum created by the departure of inmate leaders. According to Larry Kincheloe, "Some of the people who were able to grasp the leadership [during that time] were both untried and unskilled in their roles. Some of them were in fact perhaps more volatile and more dangerous than some of the people that had been transported [out of state]....It was very unsettling."[40]

The first major unsettling event occurred in early May 1979. Spalding was out of town, flying back from a warden's conference in El Paso. Kincheloe was in charge. In a move that took both inmates and staff by surprise, three inmates entered the Classification and Parole building just before one o'clock in the afternoon. One had a large, concealed shank. Another carried a screwdriver modified to make a stabbing instrument. Before he knew what was happening, the officer on the first floor had a knife at his throat. Working from the ground floor up, the inmates systematically took ten staff hostage and put them in a large janitor's closet on the second floor.

While one inmate stood guard over the hostages, the leader of the group sat down at a desk and called the captain's office. He told the sergeant who answered the phone that they had control of the C&P building, they had taken hostages, and he wanted to talk with the captain. But the captain wasn't available. A few minutes later, the inmate called a reporter from the *Walla Walla Union-Bulletin*, who in turn called the superintendent's office at the penitentiary. "Did you know you have a hostage situation?" he asked. A cascade of events quickly followed.

All departments were immediately notified, and steps were taken to get as many inmates as possible back in their cells and the prison locked down. Most of the inmates complied, but several hundred men refused to return to their cells. Officers were dispatched to the C&P building, where they reported seeing a device wired to the door, possibly a bomb. A specially trained disturbance team and SWAT team were assembled. Two trained negotiators were called to the captain's office. Snipers were placed on the roofs of buildings. The Walla Walla police department, the county sheriff, the Richland bomb squad, the state patrol, and the FBI were all notified. The Walla Walla police responded within minutes, the Richland bomb squad a short time later. An FBI negotiator and two other agents joined the prison negotiating team later that afternoon. By evening, personnel were on the ground from every agency contacted.

In May 1979 the penitentiary was better prepared for an incident of this kind than it had ever been in its history. Larry Kincheloe had recently sent two officers for training in disturbance tactics in Los Angeles, started a SWAT team, and sent two officers to both basic and advanced courses in incident negotiation.

"I was pretty well versed in disturbance control from the military," said Kincheloe. "I'd been in the riots in Baltimore after Martin Luther King's assassination and had trained in the military formations and so on. [The officers who went to Los Angeles] learned more appropriate formations down there—a flexible formation to be used in close [quarters] and with other weaponry. They came back and we started training a [tactical squad]. Both a SWAT team and a hostage negotiation team were started at that time. We had been working on that for several months prior to the hostage taking."[41]

Jim Hartford, who seemed to be everywhere in those days, was one of the trained negotiators. "The training was good for a variety [of things]—confrontational diffusing and stuff. But this was the only hostage situation that I [ever] negotiated and, in retrospect, negotiated poorly," he said.[42]

After speaking with Kincheloe, Hartford and the other negotiator went to the captain's office, where Hartford grabbed a phone and cleared off the incredulous assignment officer's desk by sweeping piles of his paperwork onto the floor with his arm and maimed right hand. Before the assignment officer could speak, the other negotiator did the same with the captain's desk.

Back in the C&P building, the convicts told the hostages, "Nobody's going to get hurt. We're just going to take over so we can get our grievances aired. Everybody remain calm, this is going to be nonviolent."[43]

One of the women was brought out of the closet, held at knifepoint, and used as a shield while her captor inspected the first floor and talked with the officers outside the window in People's Park. She was then told to make calls to news media and various custody people. About an hour into the ordeal, she asked whether she could contact some of the hostages' families, because she knew they would be worried. The inmates let her call her family and that of one of the other women. They also allowed her to talk with the prison switchboard operator, to whom she gave the names of all the hostages.[44]

The hostages did their best to remain calm. Outside the door of their makeshift cell, they could hear the agitated sounds of their captors as they alternately talked with the negotiators and media. In the background, the inmates in People's Park who refused to go to their cells could be heard yelling encouragement to the hostage-takers.

Shortly after the call to the switchboard, the hostages were taken out of the closet, one by one, and told to lay face down on the floor, where their hands were tied behind their backs with white adhesive tape. The men were transferred to the bathroom and the women kept in the closet.

The hostage-takers' initial demand "was just for us to back off and not assault the unit," said Hartford. "I was able to talk with a few of the hostages over the phone. [The hostages'] only complaint was that their hands were bound too tight."[45]

Hartford recommended to the convicts that the hostages be freed from their bindings and put into more comfortable handcuffs. "I knew that [the correctional officer who had been taken hostage] had a handcuff key," said Hartford. According to Hartford, "Handcuff keys were not supposed to be inside the walls, but everybody carried them....If anybody in there had a handcuff key, it was [this guy]."[46] So Hartford took a bunch of handcuffs down to People's Park, where the hostage-takers lowered a bucket and hauled them up to their second-story window. The bindings were removed and the cuffs applied. Now, anytime they wanted, the hostages could set themselves free.

As the day wore on, the demands of the hostage-takers became more realistic and tensions eased. They dropped a demand to talk with the governor or lieutenant governor; they no longer wanted to talk with Spalding or Kincheloe. They became hungry and had inmates in People's Park bring them food. They made coffee and tea for the hostages, brought in benches and pillows for them to sit on, and allowed the women to join the men in the restroom. Finally, the only demand from the hostage-takers was a press conference with a TV crew and newspaper reporter. While this was progress, the hostages were still in danger.

"Typically, in a negotiating strategy, you give and take," said Hartford. "You get one hostage out in exchange for a pack of cigarettes [or something]. In this case, we were getting nothing for nothing. It was stalemated."[47]

Meanwhile, Spalding's plane landed at the Tri-Cities Airport, about fifty miles west of Walla Walla. After being briefed by Kincheloe over the telephone, Spalding sped to Walla Walla with a high-speed escort by the state patrol, making it there in record time. When he arrived, the stalemate was still on. Furthermore, there were about 250 inmates in People's Park, preventing any progress toward resolving the crisis. They would have to be moved.

The negotiators told the hostage-takers that the inmates in People's Park were going to be moved to the Big Yard, but that the C&P building would not be assaulted. The hostage-takers were not assured. They saw SWAT team members on the roof of the administration building and feared more were on the roof above their heads. They had one of the male hostages call Spalding and tell him "to pull back the officers outside the walls or they were going to start killing [hostages]."[48] After giving the message to Spalding, the hostage hung up the phone, pushed the phone and a chair at the closest inmate, and rushed into the restroom to join the other hostages. By this time, the correctional officer who was one of the hostages had freed the others from their restraints with his handcuff key.

In a plan they had agreed upon, the hostages quickly barricaded the door with the benches the inmates had thoughtfully provided. From that point on, the inmates no longer had control over their hostages.

No one except the hostages and hostage-takers knew what had happened. The last communication the negotiators heard was that the hostages were going to be killed. According to Hartford, until that point the negotiators had been able to talk to a hostage almost anytime they wanted. Suddenly the hostages were no longer available. "I saw that as an ugly sign," said Hartford, "but I didn't know how to read it."[49]

Meanwhile, People's Park was still crowded with inmates who refused to return to their cells.

The tactical team entered People's Park wearing gas masks and carrying riot batons. They formed a line approximately fifty to sixty-five yards south of the dining hall, opposite a large group of inmates who were shouting, cursing, and throwing rocks, bricks, pieces of pipe, and two-by-fours. An order was given via the public address system for the inmates to go to the Big Yard. This had no effect. The tactical squad was then authorized to use chemical agents. The officers advanced in unison, using a practiced technique of "stomp and shout" intended to convey that they were a no-nonsense team that knew what it was doing. Two rounds of tear gas were fired in their direction and the rioters started moving out of People's Park. The retreating inmates continued to throw projectiles as more gas grenades moved them farther north. When the tactical team entered the area between the dining halls and Big Red, the gas man threw another grenade into the corner by the bike shop to move the rioters to the Big Yard gate. Some of the inmates held their ground in front of the gate and continued to throw projectiles. Finally, the gas man fired two more rounds followed by a cluster grenade that had an explosive charge designed to split three canisters apart and disperse gas in a concentrated area. The last of the diehards moved into the yard.[50] The inmates spent the night under the stars in the Big Yard, where they proceeded to destroy the recreation equipment and set fire to some bleachers.

Back in the restroom, the hostages took steps to protect themselves in the event of an assault on the building by the SWAT team or an attempt by the inmates to break in the door. They put wet paper towels, tissues, and toilet paper in the crack under the door and dampened articles of clothing in case the building was gassed. They filled a trash can with water and stacked coats next to the sink so they could be wetted

Moving inmates to the Big Yard—May 1979

down in case the inmates set fire to the door. The men made weapons out of their belts and handcuffs. One of the women took off her nylons and heels in case she had to run.[51]

"The next thing that happened," said one of the hostages, "was a change of tone of our convict-captors." Instead of ordering the hostages about, the hostage-takers began to plead with them to help in the negotiations. "Every few minutes [one of the inmates] would come back to the door and try to get someone to come out." Each time the hostages declined.[52]

The hostages also detected a change in tone as the inmates talked with the hostage negotiators. The inmates' side of the conversation "changed from a demanding conversation to an asking conversation... [and finally to] whimpering and sniveling," said one of the hostages.[53]

The hostages also noticed that the noise from People's Park had ended and figured that the tactical team had moved the inmates out. They became more confident and agreed to stay barricaded in the restroom until they were rescued or had to fight the inmates.[54]

About eleven o'clock in the evening, one of the inmates told the hostages through the door that they were negotiating their surrender. To the negotiators, the inmates repeated their proposal to release the hostages unharmed if their leader could talk with a TV and newspaper reporter for one hour. The negotiators still had no idea what had become of the hostages, but this seemed like the only nonviolent way out.

Spalding asked Hartford whether he believed the inmates. "I told him that I did," said Hartford. "I said, 'That's my opinion, but it's your call. We aren't getting anywhere without the interview. That's what they want. Let's give it to them and see what happens.'"[55]

Twenty-eight minutes before midnight, the leader of the hostage-takers came out of the C&P building and sat down in front of a TV camera and reporter from the *Walla Walla Union-Bulletin*. He talked for an hour about many of the same grievances the inmates had complained about for years, some of them—like crowding, ongoing brutality in segregation, and poor medical care—definitely legitimate. After an hour, an officer came up and said the interview was over. The other two inmates surrendered peacefully, and all three were escorted to segregation without resistance.

The Richland bomb squad examined the suspicious device wired to the door and determined it was fake. When police officers and others reached the second floor and found the room where the hostages had barricaded themselves, the hostages had to be convinced their rescuers were real. It took a police badge slid under the door to get them to come out. By one o'clock in the morning, twelve hours after it started, the ordeal was over.

Everyone breathed a sigh of relief, but they were ill prepared for what happened next.

Chapter 37

CROSS

REFLECTING ON THE DOWNWARD SPIRAL of events in the spring of 1979, Dick Morgan said, "Usually a club was warned when somebody was going to be disciplined or killed. [The inmate leaders would] hold court in the Lifers' Club and a decision would be made." For example, explained Morgan, if the Chicanos had a beef with the blacks, the leaders of the two clubs would be told, "Lifers and RGC and everybody else [says] it's between you guys. Work it out."[56]

But there was no warning when the Indian was killed.

Perhaps the absence of the former leaders was a stumbling block. It's not clear that anyone was "holding court" in June of '79, when every club was weakened and second-tier inmates vied for leadership. The Chicanos and Confederated Indian Tribes were never large or influential groups, although they would have been at the table in the past. The Native Americans in particular were an independent lot. The CIT was not affiliated with any other group, but members of the various tribes banded together for mutual protection. Their nominal leader exercised little control. Whatever the reason, it appears that no one was put on notice that "discipline" was in the offing.

One of the Indian inmates apparently owed money to the Chicanos—supposedly five dollars for drugs. Perhaps he blew them off once too often or antagonized them in some other way. In any event, shortly after breakfast on a Tuesday morning toward the middle of June, the purported debtor was stabbed twice, once in the chest and once in the groin. The chest wound, near the heart, was quickly fatal.

"The natural order of inmate discipline had disappeared," said Morgan. "I think the Indians felt that it was open season on Indians by the entire population." And this latest killing, unexpected as it was, "had pushed the one button on Indians that you don't want to push—the rest of the world is against you."[57]

In the three days that followed, no one needed to tell the Chicanos that revenge was on its way. The prison was on edge, as both groups were believed to be heavily armed. Larry Kincheloe elaborated: the Indians "had had bad dealings with the Chicano Club for some time over various issues. I think they felt that if they did not retaliate [for this killing], they would be decimated."[58]

At the two o'clock shift change on June 15, 1979, an order was given to the officers. Some men remember the order as "Back off—leave the inmates alone." Others heard it as a recommendation: "Stay out of harm's way. Don't provoke anything." The words and intent of the order are in dispute. But Sergeant William Cross wasn't at the shift change briefing—he'd been held over from the morning shift and was still on assignment in the kitchen. It really doesn't matter what was said, Sergeant Cross never heard the order.

Earlier that day, Sergeant Cross saw some Indians tearing up pallets behind the kitchen—state pallets—to build a fire for their sweat lodge. In a move that won him no favors, he stopped them.[59] Thanks to this action, when Cross next encountered a group of Indians, they were more than ever predisposed to dislike him.

At the evening meal, Cross and a junior officer were assigned to the door of the south dining hall, while Rich Mason and another experienced officer worked inside the north dining hall door. As men filed out, the junior officer saw an inmate who appeared to have something concealed under his shirt. He told the inmate to stand for a search. The inmate refused and a crowd gathered. The officer backed down. Sergeant Cross came over and asked the junior officer what was wrong. When told that the inmate refused a search, Cross said, "Let's get him."[60]

Cross and the other officer stepped outside. Looking to their left, they saw a group of inmates standing about midway between the south dining hall and the admissions wing of Big Red.

As they approached the group, one of the Indians in the crowd stepped in front of Cross. "What the fuck is it to you?" he demanded.[61]

"You're coming with me," said Cross, intending to take both inmates to segregation.

The inmate spat in Cross's face. As Cross tried to grab him, the inmate pulled a knife and stabbed Cross in the chest. Another inmate rushed Cross's partner and knocked him to the ground. As the second officer got to his feet, he saw an inmate with a knife coming at him. He turned and ran toward the north door.[62]

Meanwhile, a black inmate, who could have been a power linebacker in another context, was seen racing into the dining hall past the officers assigned to the north door. To Mason, that meant there was a fight outside. As he and his partner rounded the corner outside the dining hall, Mason saw an inmate trying to hit a fleeing officer. "So I snatched up [the inmate] and introduced him to a steel door and cuffed him up," said Mason.[63] When he started taking the inmate to segregation, Mason saw a man lying on the ground.

In 1979 an officer's uniform consisted of a white shirt, blue pants, and a hat. Many of the inmates, in white T-shirts and jeans, looked much the same. In a fight, where the officer was almost certain to lose his hat, the difference could be slight. Furthermore, Cross was caked in mud from soil saturated with his own blood. The sergeant stripes on his shoulders were obscured.

"I didn't recognize him as an officer at first," said Mason. But Mason had worked with Cross in the forest service before either of them worked at the pen, and he soon realized who it was. Not understanding the gravity of Cross's wounds, Mason tried to pick him up. As he learned later, "he'd been stabbed [multiple] times," said Mason. "One cut the top of the aorta—which was an unsurvivable wound, one went up underneath the bottom of his sternum, one was in his belly—down low, and one was in his back."[64]

Mason immediately radioed the control room and said an officer was down. As he performed CPR, the crowd around him grew larger, leaving an open space maybe twenty feet in diameter around him and the unresponsive body of Bill Cross. Shouts of "Kill 'em, kill 'em all" were heard.

Not all the inmates despised Cross, but many did. One inmate in the crowd said, "When I saw Cross lying on the ground, I looked at him and my first thoughts were, 'Man, I want to kick this guy, I want to spit on him, I want to hit him'—but I'm not [going to do any of that], because that would make me part of this. So I looked at him and walked away."[65]

Jim Hartford and two other men were dispatched to the scene. Calls went out to the cellblocks to lock down. Officers in the TV and recreation rooms were told to lock themselves in. The security booth called an ambulance and the Walla Walla police department. Larry Kincheloe was called at home. (Spalding was in Olympia.) The tower officer overlooking the scene raised his gun and fired three times in the air. Pow! Pow! Pow! "Disperse. Disperse," he yelled. "This institution is on lockdown."

Out in Eight Wing, Sergeant Morgan was about to announce last call for chow. He had just opened the lock box on D-Deck when he heard the telephone ring one floor below. As he hollered "Last call," the officer who answered the telephone shouted, "No! Don't!"

Morgan shouted, "What's the matter?" and the officer yelled back, "Lockdown!"

Morgan closed the lock box and hurried down the two flights of stairs to the officer below. The officer relayed the news. A sergeant had been killed. Two minutes had passed since Mason's radio call.[66]

It was standard procedure that in a lockdown, once a door was locked, it stayed locked until further orders. Almost immediately, scared inmates running from the scene of the stabbing started pounding on the front door of Eight Wing. Soon, fifty to sixty inmates were outside the door, screaming "Let us in! Let us in!"

Morgan and the other officer stood by the locked door. All the inmates inside the wing were locked in their cells. Despite the fact that no inmates could get to them, "that really was one of the scariest moments inside [the prison for me]," said Morgan. "I've been in a lot of close calls, [but] that was probably my first real shot of mortality awareness.... You're wondering, is it over with? Are they still killing people out there or what?"[67]

As inmates piled up outside the locked doors of the cellblocks, Hartford and another officer arrived at the scene of the stabbing on the run, a gurney right behind them. With Mason's help, they got Cross onto the gurney. When some of the inmates tried to block the way, they used the gurney as a battering ram to open a hole through the crowd.[68] When they reached the prison hospital, Cross was immediately transferred to a waiting ambulance.

Six minutes had passed since Mason called Central Control.[69]

According to Rich Mason, the ambulance EMT got one heartbeat out of Cross, and then they raced off to the downtown hospital with sirens blaring. "I pretty much knew he was dead," said Mason, "but you never know. You can always hope."[70]

At the hospital, Cross was pronounced dead on arrival, until then the only Washington State correctional officer to be murdered at the hands of inmates in living memory.

Areas were cleared of inmates throughout the evening and night. Counts were made, and all inmates and staff were accounted for. The SWAT team and state patrol troopers added firepower to the wall.

Once everyone was locked up, Spalding conferred with the leader of the tactical team. From various eyewitness accounts, there were five suspects—all locked in their cells. Spalding knew the suspects were not safe. The danger wasn't from other inmates, but from angry correctional officers.

Spalding told the tactical team leader to pick a few cool-headed officers to remove the suspects from their cells and take them to segregation. He also ordered a special watch to ensure there was no retaliation in the segregation unit.[71]

One of the suspects picked up that night was in Eight Wing.

"They went down on E-Deck," said Morgan, "where [this] obnoxious, foul-mouthed Indian guy [lived]....They went down to 12E and they grabbed him up, brought him out to the head of the tier....He and I locked eyes. I thought, 'You son of a bitch.' By then we knew that Indians had killed Bill Cross. He looked at me and he just started bawling like a baby. He said, 'Morgan, I didn't do it. I didn't do it. I swear to God I didn't do it.' They drug him off down the stairs and out the front door with him yelling he didn't do it."[72]

The tactical team took the five suspects to segregation without incident.

Jim Hartford didn't go home that night. Others stayed late as well, and the roll call room was full when he walked in, his clothes stained with Bill Cross's blood. "There wasn't a lieutenant around, and everybody was talking [about] what had happened and what was going to happen," said Hartford. "There was all sorts of talk. Real crazy talk.... [One guy] had a riot baton in his hand...smacking the wall."

A hush settled over the room, and the expectant officers turned their heads toward Hartford. He surveyed the men and said, "Let's not let Billy's death be in vain."[73]

Chapter 38

SHAKEDOWN

A LINE HAD BEEN CROSSED, and there would be no turning back. Some officers blamed Spalding for the death of one of their own. Some were out for revenge.

The morning after Cross died, Parley Edwards and the union vice president went to Spalding's office. "Pack your stuff and get the hell out of here," they told him. "You're done. You've got one of our people killed, and we're holding you personally responsible."[74]

"[The death of Cross] was pretty devastating to me," said Spalding. "That's something that is very unusual in our system—to have a staff member killed. For somebody to come in and say you're responsible for that—I just about lost it."[75]

But not everyone believed Spalding was responsible. "I was with Parley one hundred percent during the Vinzant and Genakos era," said Jim Hartford. "But then I sided more with Kincheloe and Spalding and distanced myself from Parley, just because he became radical....He was advocating things that would create a riot. I saw that Spalding and Kincheloe at least had a plan."

Hartford explained his motivation. "My target was the inmates," he said. "Take this place back. Hurt the inmates to the point that they can't do the things that they've done in the past." Hartford wasn't advocating violence. What Hartford meant was that he wanted to "hurt them by virtue of [limiting] their freedom of movement inside; hurt them by virtue of [limiting] the property they were previously allowed to have."[76]

There was so much property in the cells that effective searches were difficult, and sometimes impossible. Hartford told Spalding that if he knew a gun was in a particular cell, he might not find it after eight hours of searching.[77]

Four-man cell in Eight Wing

It wasn't just Hartford who complained of too much property in the inmates' cells. Everyone agreed a major shakedown was needed.

Spalding decided to keep the institution on lockdown until the entire facility was searched and excess property removed. "We figured it would take us thirty to forty days to really do it good," said Spalding.[78]

"I can't remember how many of us were on that shakedown crew—twenty to twenty-five of us, somewhere in there," said John Lambert. "There was a lieutenant...that ran it [and] three or four sergeants, I being one of them. We had two, three officers on a team. We left Eight Wing for last, because we figured we would have problems because that's where the worst of the inmates had congregated in the institution."[79] Eight Wing was also the unit with the most excess property, and the search teams used the other cellblocks for practice so they would be more efficient when they got to Eight Wing. In a large unit with huge amounts of excess property, being efficient was important, because once they started searching a wing, they kept searching until the job was done. "It turned out that that would take us sometimes eighteen or twenty hours," said Kincheloe. "That's a long day."[80]

The official procedure was straightforward. A list was prepared of the property each inmate was allowed to keep, and a copy was given to the inmates in each cell before the shakedown began. The search crew would then go cell by cell, starting at the top of a cellblock. At each cell, the search crew had the inmates strip and stand naked with their backs to the bars and their hands behind their backs. The officers applied handcuffs and then locked the inmates in a large broom closet at the head of the tier. The inmates remained in the broom closet until the search crew was finished with their cell. Of course, not everyone went willingly.

"We took everything that was state-owned—state being towels, clothing, whatever was state issue—we saved it and sent it out to the laundry," said Lambert. "All the wood items...that could be readily identified as institution or pirated items that the inmates couldn't have gotten [legitimately] were sent out and stored...behind the firehouse. Any item that was inmate-owned...was put in a box [and] sealed...with [tape]....We marked the cell number on [the box], and we listed who was in the cell by name and number....In some cells there were probably fifty to one hundred boxes [of property]."[81]

The prison also purchased fifteen hundred government surplus footlockers—enough for every inmate at Walla Walla, plus some spares. The lockers could be slid out of the way under the bunk beds in the big cellblocks. The plan was to limit personal property to only what could fit inside the lockers.[82]

At least that was the theory. Much of what was found was considered junk by the officers. For example, there were wooden cabinets that some inmates had made to fix up their cells. If a cabinet couldn't be removed without breaking it, it quickly became junk. There was excess paper that some inmates had stored for years. There were fish tanks, some of which contained black widow spiders. Tons of property items were taken from cells and thrown over the railing to the floor below. Whether because of fatigue, the speed of working, indifference, or malicious intent, personal items such as family photos, letters, and legal documents made it onto the junk heap. There were allegations—some no doubt true—that items of value, such as watches and jewelry, disappeared.

Hartford said, "I was right in on every shakedown. Systematically, we're going wing by wing, cell by cell. So much property's allowed—no questions asked. [It was] 'You just shut the fuck up—this stuff goes and goes now.'" While Hartford says he kept his crew in line, "there was some heavy-handedness by a lot of people. There were officers that were going in and maliciously breaking things....We saw it...but we really didn't do anything [about it]."[83]

Not surprisingly, the prediction that Eight Wing would have the most problems proved true. As they approached the outside of the building for the first time, the search crew could hear inmates pounding on tables and screaming "Kill, kill." Some inmates tried to booby-trap the cells by planting razor blades or attaching hot electrical wires to the bars. "We really had to pay attention," said Lambert.[84]

Dick Morgan, who had worked overtime in Eight Wing during the first part of the lockdown, was on vacation leave during the search of his unit. He came back on July 6, just as the search crews were finishing their work.

Shakedown

"I'd picked up over vacation that they were searching and doing a damn fine job," said Morgan. As he entered Eight Wing and looked down B Tier on the first floor of the building, he saw a ten-foot-high pile of junk extending from the outer wall to the edge of the D Tier catwalk on the second floor. "You could have stepped off of D Tier onto a pile of garbage and dropped maybe six inches," said Morgan. "The image from the front door was a hundred-and-fifty-foot-long pile of garbage about ten feet tall, with a tunnel burrowed through it [under the second-floor catwalk] in front of the [first-floor] cells."[85]

Morgan climbed the stairs to the second floor. From there, he could see some of the debris smoldering where inmates had thrown out matches to try to get it burning. As Morgan watched, the search crew was still working at the far end of D Tier. "Tons and tons of garbage [were] flying out of the cells onto this garbage heap," said Morgan.

Morgan walked through the unit. "I was trying to picture in my mind what [cell] 15B was going to be." This was one of the cells that was "owned" by an inmate who charged rent to those who lived there. "It had ornate cabinetwork in it and good bunks and furniture and stereo and stuff," said Morgan. "It commanded a high price. I was just trying to figure how much of that was going to be left."

"God, there was nothing in the cells," said Morgan. "There were four bunks, four mats, four pillows, three walls, a ceiling, a floor, and that was it. There was nothing left in there. Personal property was gone. Everything was gone."

That's not all that struck Morgan. "I had been conditioned to believe that the inmate's tolerance for control was very low," he said. But as Morgan walked through the unit, "they didn't back talk. It was literally a whipped and humiliated inmate population. I couldn't believe that the place hadn't exploded."[86]

As a final step, a Bobcat loader with a cage to protect the operator was used to move the debris to the front of the wing. Garbage trucks were backed up outside the front door. "I can't remember the figures," said Morgan, "whether it was seventeen tons of garbage or seventeen dump trucks, two tons each, [that] left Eight Wing."

The first purpose of the lockdown was to shake down the entire institution, find the weapons, and get rid of excess property. But Spalding also decided that "we've got to make some major physical changes to this facility so that when people walk out of their cells [when the lockdown ends], they see that this is a different place."[87]

By the summer of 1979, the money for the security package recommended by the architects the previous fall had been appropriated and the first construction contracts let. A decision was made, and the contractor's crew was redirected to a new task. They would pour concrete.

Before the end of June, backhoes and cement trucks were working full-time inside the walls. The grass, dirt, and shrubbery in Lifers' Park, People's Park, and various other locations inside the walls had made handy hiding places for weapons and contraband of all sorts. The two parks and every blade of grass inside the walls disappeared under slabs of concrete. To Spalding, the architectural message of all this concrete was clear: "This is a close custody institution. Some of the most dangerous people in the state are housed here—and we are going to control it."[88]

While hindsight proved that this decision and many others made at the time were good ones, it wasn't at all clear in June 1979. Spalding wondered whether they were on the right course. He was relatively

Preparing People's Park for paving

inexperienced, with just twelve years in the business, and he certainly knew nothing about prison architecture. One of his associate superintendents, Larry Kincheloe, had almost no experience with prisons. His other associate was a former priest who drank a lot.

Spalding talked it over with Bob Tropp, and the two men decided to invite experts from the American Correctional Association to come to the penitentiary to give them advice.

Sometime earlier, Tropp had met American Correctional Association executive director Anthony Travisono at an ACA conference, where he asked Travisono if the ACA did evaluations of institutions. Travisono told him, "Sure we do, we do that all the time. We pick people depending on what the assignment is—all professional people and so forth."[89] When the need was there, Tropp knew who to call.

Tropp reviewed the idea with his superiors at headquarters, who no doubt ran the idea past the governor. With approval secured, Tropp called Travisono. The dates were agreed upon, and Travisono assembled a team of four senior wardens from major correctional facilities around the country.

Some people in DSHS were concerned that the move could be interpreted as lack of confidence in Spalding. But that was the least of their worries. In Bob Tropp's handwritten notes made in preparation for a June 20 interview with the *Walla Walla Union-Bulletin*, he wrote, "I think having outside experts come in should provide everyone with the assurance that we are moving in the best possible direction—it is in everyone's best interest."[90]

The experts arrived on Friday, July 6, 1979. Not everything went according to plan.

Chapter 39

SATURDAY NIGHT LIVE

TEMPERATURES IN THE CELL HOUSES were hot—over a hundred degrees—during the first week of July 1979. In Eight Wing, it had been twenty-one days since any inmate had taken a shower, exercised, or eaten a meal other than a TV dinner. Some correctional officers had worked overtime every day for weeks. Tempers were short—on both sides of the bars.

The review panel from the American Correctional Association arrived on Friday afternoon, July 6. The group first met with Tropp, Spalding, and other prison officials, who presented the experts with a short briefing paper on the current status of the penitentiary. The briefing paper identified six major problems, with plans or projects under way to address the first five. Tropp and Spalding wanted feedback on those five, but it was the sixth item—the role of the local union and the attitudes and demands of correctional officers—that was the sticking point. The paper gave examples.

> Through their union, the line staff have threatened to walk out if their demands are not met....If implemented, a number of these demands would probably cause further trouble with the inmate population....
>
> Officers frequently violate policy and directives by abusing their authority and sometimes by physically and verbally abusing inmates....
>
> The deaths of two officers,...one from attempting to dismantle a bomb...and the other by knife attack,...has charged the staff with tremendous emotion and intransigence....
>
> Training has not affected staff attitudes and staff ability to interact positively with inmates, and to manage routine confrontations and program requirements at a satisfactory level.[91]

Perhaps because of the stated urgency of the matter, the first meeting of the ACA team Saturday morning was with the union. Afterward they talked with prison staff, mainly lieutenants and captains, for most of the day. At four in the afternoon, they met with representatives from a group called United Friends and Families of Prisoners.[92] After that, they went to their hotel, where they met with Spalding and Tropp.

The ACA team never made it to Eight Wing, where the last debris from the shakedown was hauled away Saturday morning. Dick Morgan, who had marveled at the transformation the day before, was back at work.

"We had just served the evening meal," said Morgan. "I usually took two officers and myself, and we'd put those big eighteen-inch-wide floor brooms together and we'd act like a snowplow. We'd start at cell 17, and we'd plow TV dinner [trays] and food and crap up to the front, where we could shovel it into garbage cans."[93]

While Morgan and the officers were plowing the debris from the evening meal, someone threw a chicken bone at Morgan. It hit him in the back of the head. "[That] was the first noncompliant [aggressive] kind of stuff I had witnessed since coming back the day before," said Morgan. He thought, "Well, it's a cheap shot. We'll just keep an eye on what's going on." Then, silently, inmates started throwing more and more things at the officers.

"Fine," thought Morgan, "if they don't want the garbage picked up, we'll just leave it on the floor." Morgan and the other officers retreated to the head of the tier to wait out the throwing of garbage before resuming their sweeping.

It was then that an inmate near the far end of D Tier yelled, "Showers!"

It was a cry that resonated with the hot and sweaty inmates. Pretty soon there was a loud chant of "Showers, showers, showers" throughout the unit. Morgan called the shift lieutenant and said, "I've got something going here in the wing. They're chanting for showers." The chanting was so loud that the lieutenant could hear the inmates over the phone. The lieutenant told Morgan to keep him informed.

According to Morgan, one side of the wing then started chanting "Kill, kill, kill," with phrases like "Kill the pigs" interspersed every now and again. After the other side of the wing picked up the chant, someone started yelling, "Tear your shitter off the wall. Tear your shitter off the wall." Others joined in. With the sound of this long, deafening

Trashed cell in Eight Wing

refrain reverberating off the walls, the banging started. The inmates were destroying their toilets and sinks. Water began to pour out of the cells and cascade to the floor below.

Morgan called the lieutenant. "We've got something serious going on here," he said. In the back of Morgan's mind was the fear that the locking mechanism might fail and the inmates would come for them. Morgan asked the lieutenant for additional officers. He wanted someone at the head of each tier so that any inmate breaching a cell door would be seen immediately.

By the time the additional officers arrived, the noise was so loud that the only way Morgan could tell an officer what to do was to cup his hands over the officer's ear and shout. He told each officer, "Take your whistle, and if you see anybody stick a head out of the cell…blow your whistle and come running fast, because we're going to bail out of this wing if a head comes out."

The officers managed to turn the water off, but there was still water everywhere from broken plumbing. Compounding matters was the fear of electrocution because of jury-rigged wiring in many of the cells. After requesting permission from his lieutenant, Morgan cut the power. It would soon be dark.

While this was going on, the officers had to repeatedly duck as chunks of porcelain were hurled from the cell fronts and toward the head of the tier, where the officers huddled.

Suddenly a huge booming started. "It was like out of *Alien* or something," said Morgan. "I thought the other stuff was loud, but this was amazing. It was a very low-frequency boom. It sounded like a giant [battering ram] on the gates of a castle. It shook the whole wing. You could feel it almost more than you could hear it."

When the booming started, everything else went quiet. In the lull, Morgan heard a voice call out from F-Deck, "We're going through the wall!" Then the booming resumed, to the screams and cheers of the inmates. KA-BOOM!

Morgan assumed the inmates were trying to get into the pipe chase between the back-to-back cells. Once they were in the pipe chase, only a very old steel door stood between the inmates and the officers. Morgan called the lieutenant and said, "Man! They're saying they're going through the wall."

Into this cacophony, Spalding, Kincheloe, and the plant manager showed up. Morgan wasn't interested in what the superintendent and associate superintendent had to say. He wanted to talk to the plant manager. The two men went outside the front door of Eight Wing, where they could at least talk. "You [could] still hear the bricks rattling from this big booming that's going on," Morgan remembered. He jokingly asked the plant manager, "Hey, Walt, how long is it going to hold together?" The plant manager replied, "Not very goddamn long.... They'll have those doors open within the hour if this keeps up."

The big concern was that the cell door locking mechanism in Eight Wing wasn't the stoutest in the world. One fear was that if the inmates acted in unison by tying one end of a sheet to each cell door and the other end to the cell bars, they could twist the sheets with a broom handle (or something similar) and all the doors on a tier would pop open at the same time.

While Morgan and the other officers contemplated this scenario and waited for the tactical team and SWAT team to show up, Spalding and

Kincheloe left the unit. They joined Bob Tropp and others in the superintendent's conference room, now converted to an incident command center for the night.

What Morgan didn't know was that the penitentiary was short-staffed that night. After three weeks of nonstop work, the men on the shakedown crews were given the weekend off. They were down to a skeleton crew, and the lieutenant was trying to marshal forces to help in Eight Wing. Of course, on a Saturday night after weeks of nonstop work, many of the officers were out partying. It took a while before a crew was assembled, and some of those who showed up had partied pretty hard.

In Eight Wing, after more booming, a voice called out, "We're through. We're through." The other inmates cheered, and Morgan thought, "Oh, God, they're into the pipe chase." Morgan called the lieutenant yet again. This time he was assured that the tactical team and SWAT team were on their way.

When the tactical team arrived, Morgan turned the wing over to the team leader. "I told my officers to leave—count all their keys and stuff. I made sure I had the front door key, and I locked both front doors so I would be the last one out—like going down with your ship or something." But Morgan was the chemical weapons man for the tactical team, so he put on his gas gear and got the grenades and gas gun ready to go back inside.

By this time, everyone believed the inmates were in the pipe chase on the top floor between E and F Tiers. Kincheloe denies ever saying this, but several people say he turned to the SWAT team and said something like, "You open the front door of the pipe chase. If there are inmates there, you kill them."

According to Morgan, several people said, "Say what?" and Kincheloe repeated, "You kill 'em."

"That's like throwing meat to a rabid dog," observed Morgan when he was interviewed years later.

In preparation for opening the door to the pipe chase, one of the shotgun men was told to go to the head of the tier and fire a round of plastic bird shot at the far wall. The noise of the riot was deafening until the shotgun man cranked off a round. Things got real quiet.

On cue, the SWAT team opened the pipe chase door and jumped in. Nobody was there.

Starting with the first cell on the top tier, the tactical team started pulling the screaming inmates out of their cells one by one. Inmates would yell, "Come and get us, you punks. We'll cut your throats." As they worked their way down F-Deck, the tactical team discovered a hole, not through the wall to the pipe chase, but between two cells.

According to Morgan, "a guy down in 7B…yelled out this one obscenity [that] I remember just as clear as day. He could see me at the head of the tier with my gas gun and stuff." The inmate yelled, "Morgan, I'm going to come out of this cell, and I'm going to climb over your dead sister to fuck you in the ass, you punk." According to Morgan, the whole tactical team laughed. When more insults were hurled at other officers by the inmate in 7B, members of the tactical team hollered back at him, saying, "We're coming for you, Larry."

Morgan, as the chemical weapons man, had nothing to do at this point except watch. He was there in case they needed chemicals. He described what he saw. "For the most part, [the inmates] were handled very roughly," said Morgan. "It wasn't beatings or thumpings or anything like that…but there was no question in anybody's mind who was in charge. They were throwing guys—slamming [them] up against walls and not allowing [anyone] to talk or they would get whacked. They were taken out of the unit…and then thrown down in the dirt." Despite asserting that there were no beatings or thumpings, Morgan admitted that "some of the crew got a little out of hand." For example, he said he saw one officer "take a cheap shot" on an inmate. Sometime later it was determined that this same officer had taken the inmate's watch.

"I remember stepping out in front of the wing to see what they were doing with these guys," said Morgan. There he saw inmates lying face down in construction dust. The officers had told them not to turn their heads. "You could see little puffs of dust coming out underneath their heads," said Morgan.

At some point, Tropp and other administrators went out on the wall and saw the men being thrown down in the dirt. Tropp told Kincheloe, "Tell those guys to cool it." The abuse—that which could be seen from the wall, at least—apparently stopped.

The process of clearing the wing was time-consuming. When all the inmates on a tier had been removed, the tactical team would leave the building for the next step in the operation.

First, the tactical team lieutenant would order the inmates to stand in line, with each man putting his nose on the guy in front of him. Then the officers would escort the inmates as they walked in lockstep, single file, to the Big Yard. Once in the Big Yard, the inmates were ordered to sit silently as officers with high-powered rifles watched over them. Moving a single tier from cells to the Big Yard took an hour or more.

"As they cleared off tier by tier, it kept getting quieter and quieter," said Morgan. It was dead quiet when they got to B Tier, where Larry, the inmate who shouted the memorable insult to Morgan, was waiting his turn. The silence was broken when Larry hollered, "Tell them we're sorry."

"Those of us who were left in Eight Wing just burst out laughing," recalled Morgan.

It was almost daylight when the last inmates were moved to the Big Yard. Outside Eight Wing, an officer stooped to pick up the cigarettes that had been taken from the inmates.

Morgan's description of what happened in the Eight Wing riot was relatively benign. Robin Moses, called in from his job as captain at the Minimum Security Building, had a different take on what happened.

"It's a good thing they never called me to [testify in] court," said Moses. "Bad, bad things happened that night."[94]

When Moses arrived, the tactical team lieutenant was supervising the removal of inmates from their cells. There were no other supervisors around. No one was watching what happened as inmates were muscled down the stairs, marched out of the building, and thrown to the ground.

Moses saw officers walking across the backs of inmates lying in the construction dust. He ordered them to stop. Moses saw SWAT team members pouring soft drinks from the top of the wall onto the inmates and saying they were peeing on them. He stopped that too. Inside Eight Wing, Moses saw a group of officers forcing inmates to run a gauntlet. When he told them to stop, one of the officers said, "And you call yourself an officer!"[95] Moses told the man to get out.

"Mostly [there was] a lack of enough supervisors—at least for the first hour or two," said Moses. "Some of these brand new macho officers…

After the riot in Eight Wing

thought that this was 'get back' time....It was a very, very confused and difficult situation."[96]

Barbara Miller, paralegal for Prison Legal Services, arrived the next day with an attorney. Miller and the attorney talked with some of the inmates who had spent the night in the Big Yard. Her description of what happened that Saturday night uses stronger words than "confused" and "difficult." Clearly agitated recalling these memories, she said:

> I saw the people. I know what the hell happened to those people. They ran them down a gauntlet inside goddamn Eight Wing and beat them....There were two homosexuals who lived in the first cell on the bottom floor inside of Eight Wing. Not only did they destroy all their stuff, they destroyed their dentures, they beat the shit out of them, they took clubs and rammed them up the anus of the older one of the two.[97]

After a long pause to control her emotions, Miller said, "I still have too much rage....I never cried in that penitentiary. I couldn't stop crying that day."

Chapter 40

BREAKDOWN

THE SUN WAS RISING when the final group of men brought out of Eight Wing was escorted to the Big Yard. When the last inmate was finally inside, the door to the Big Yard was closed and locked. The inmates were seated in rows and told to remain silent. Officers, some armed, observed the scene. When one inmate tried to stand, Officer Mason fired one shot in the air and yelled, "Sit down!" The man sat.[98]

From the wall, Jim Hartford could hear faint sobbing from some of the men seated below. The inmates stayed quiet and didn't move for another forty minutes. Then, when nothing happened after another inmate tried to stand, the men slowly began to rise and move about.[99] With no shelter, the unprotected inmates were about to bake and burn under the hot Walla Walla sun.

Early morning in the Big Yard—July 8, 1979

Exhausted tactical team members—some of whom hadn't slept for at least twenty-four hours—went home to rest before coming back on shift.

Nothing was normal. There was water and debris throughout the trashed cell house. The men from Eight Wing who hadn't destroyed their cells were moved from the Big Yard to cells in other wings. Soon everyone had a pretty good idea of what had happened. No one was happy.

Like everyone else, the men in segregation had heard the riot. Those in cells facing People's Park probably saw shadowed groups of men as they were moved to the Big Yard in the middle of the night. At some point on Sunday, the prisoners in seg began talking of a protest. They discussed what they should do.

"One idea was to throw urine and feces on the guards," said one of the youngest inmates in segregation. Other ideas included writing letters of protest or conducting a hunger strike. But nobody wanted to go hungry, writing letters didn't work, and throwing body waste was hardly a bold new idea. "Another idea was to tear the cells apart like Eight Wing and try to instigate the other tiers [in segregation] to do the same," said the young inmate.[100]

The inmates reasoned that if all the prisoners in segregation destroyed their cells, maybe Six and Seven Wings would follow suit, and pretty soon every inmate in the penitentiary would be in the Big Yard. And that, said the young inmate in segregation, would bring press coverage, public attention, public support, and lawsuits filed by legal service attorneys.[101]

Out in the administration building, no one heard this conversation, but it was exactly what Spalding feared. "I was concerned with the possibility of [cell destruction] spreading," said Spalding. "I certainly didn't want to lose another cell house."[102]

On Sunday the men in segregation had a new grievance: they didn't get lunch. The inmate in the cell at the head of the tier yelled to the shift sergeant and asked why. The sergeant told him there would be only two meals that day because so many officers were involved in trying to straighten things out after the riot the night before. The sergeant also said that full meal coverage would resume the next day. For whatever reason—probably to build incentive for their plan—the inmate at the head of the tier passed word to the other inmates that "they were only going to get two meals a day from that point forward as punishment for what happened in Eight Wing."[103]

Within minutes, inmates were shouting and banging throughout the tier. The prisoner in the first cell shouted to the sergeant, telling him that if they didn't get fed, they were going to tear up their cells. The sergeant reportedly told the inmate that "he knew how they felt, but that kind of action would be worthless." This time, when the inmate passed the word to the others on the tier, the relayed message was, "They don't care."[104]

Now inmates were shouting through the air vents at the back of their cells to spread the rebellion to the rest of the unit. The inmate at the head of the tier explained to the others how to break up a cell. Each cell had a stool bolted to the wall beneath a small metal shelf that served as a table. If an inmate jumped up and down on the stool, the stool would eventually break away. Once that happened, the stool could be used as a mallet to smash the toilet, sink, and bed. Notes were passed, and a decision was made to wait until after the evening meal.[105] After all, they'd missed lunch and could easily miss the next meal too if they acted in haste.

Some of the inmates began to leisurely work at the first part of the task—breaking the stool off the wall. Getting the stool off "was hard work," said the young inmate in segregation. "I had to jump up and down on it to get it to where it would bend all of the way down and touch the floor. Then I'd have to get down on the ground to pry it up with my legs....[Finally the metal] started warming up and loosening up to where it would bend easily. It took quite a while." Before dinner was served, the stool in his cell was nearly off the wall. After dinner, "all I had to do was jerk it a couple of times and it came out," he said.[106]

The attempt to spread rebellion was far from successful. In the end, only six inmates in segregation destroyed their cells that evening. Even the inmate at the head of the tier, the one who had done so much to egg the others on, left his cell intact. Nonetheless, it was obvious from the noise that some inmates were tearing up their cells. When the segregation sergeant informed the shift lieutenant of what was going on, the shift lieutenant sent four or five officers to the unit to secure the cells and handcuff the men to the bars.[107] This was accomplished without significant incident, but somewhere along the line the lieutenant's instructions were either vague, misinterpreted, or ignored. Instead of cuffing the men to the outside of the cell bars, the officers cuffed them to the inside. That meant when it came time to move the men who had destroyed their cells, doing so would require a cell extraction instead of a more straightforward escort. In a cell extraction, if the inmate doesn't cooperate, three or four officers would have to go into the small cell to muscle the struggling man out. It was easy for someone to get hurt when so many people struggled in such a confined space.

Despite the obvious resemblance of the rebellion in seg to the riot in Eight Wing, no one bothered to inform Spalding of what had happened until much later. By chance, associate superintendent for treatment Jim Cummins came into the control room while the situation was being discussed. Investigating no further, but believing there was still a widespread plan to destroy cells in segregation, Cummins and the shift lieutenant decided to call in about a dozen members of the riot squad. Someone also called Kincheloe.

Members of the riot squad were gathering equipment when Kincheloe arrived. Most had riot batons; a few wore lead-lined gloves; some took no special gear. The lieutenant in charge requested, and was granted, permission to carry Mace—something he used liberally later on. He was told by Kincheloe that there were men in segregation cuffed to the bars and that they were to be moved to two large strip cells not far away. The strip cell idea was a logical choice. Although theoretically banned by Conte in 1971, strip cells were still occasionally used. They were certainly good for temporarily holding men who had just destroyed their cells—there was nothing inside to destroy.

Like calling the riot squad in the first place, deploying it to the segregation unit was also a decision made without anyone above the rank of sergeant viewing the situation on the ground. While some members of the squad overheard parts of the conversation between Kincheloe and the team leader, late arrivers heard nothing, and no briefing was made. The squad members just showed up and went into action.

Specific details of what happened next are in dispute, but there is no question that excessive and unnecessary force was used to move inmates from segregation to the strip cells. There were contusions and bruises. One inmate had a chipped tooth. Another had a half-inch piece of skin missing from under his chin. One inmate was seen by the prison doctor, then transferred to Walla Walla General Hospital.

It is also clear that officers were verbally abusive and unprofessional. Two inmates made tape recordings of the incident. Neither tape was particularly clear, but individual comments could be picked out from the constant noise: "Sergeant Cross is here—you bet your fucking ass he is." "You little cocksuckers are finally getting what you deserve." "This is a new institution now, we're running the show." "You want some of this? You want some of this, mother-fucker?"[108] And so on.

Not much was known the next morning about what had happened in segregation during the night. Some inmates had been moved to the strip cells. Force was used. There were some injuries. The biggest issue, however, was that the inmate transferred to Walla Walla General Hospital said he'd been raped repeatedly with a nightstick.

Spalding called the physician who attended the inmate at Walla Walla General. By all accounts a respected and competent doctor, Dr. Eng Saw spoke English with a thick Chinese accent. In what may be the most consequential misunderstanding in this whole sorry incident, it appears that Spalding either misheard or misinterpreted the doctor's use of the word "anterior," which, in the context used by Dr. Saw, meant either "the front part of the anus" or "above the anus." Perhaps Spalding thought the doctor said "interior."

Spalding got it wrong. The doctor had observed a "laceration of the anus" measuring two and a half centimeters in length "at the left anterior quadrant." He then inserted an endoscope to a depth of twenty-five centimeters (about ten inches) into the anal cavity of the inmate. The examination "revealed no evidence of any mucosal laceration or trauma."[109]

Operating on misinformation, Spalding discussed what was known with Bob Tropp. The secretary and the deputy secretary of DSHS were apprised of the situation. The governor was informed. It was quickly decided that an outside investigation by independent observers was needed.

Meanwhile, the five men still in the strip cells had to be moved to someplace safe and secure. The cells on the third floor of the hospital— where prison psychologist Dr. Hunter had run his infamous "regression therapy" program—fit the bill. But Spalding was concerned about possible retaliation against the inmates during the move. More violence would only add fuel to the lawsuit that was surely coming.

Robin Moses, a man who could be trusted to treat the inmates appropriately, was given the job. Moses moved the inmates by himself. "Same ones that fought the night before," said Moses. "Here's what we got, guys," he told the men. "Do I have to cuff you up? We're going to go to the hospital because that's a safer place." The inmates didn't need cuffs and chains. They were ready to move. "Let's go," said Moses. The five inmates walked calmly to the hospital, with Moses following behind.

The outside investigators—Brooks Russell, chief investigator for the office of the attorney general, and James Jackson, chief investigator for the department of licensing—arrived in Walla Walla the next day. Because of the potential for criminal charges, the Walla Walla police department joined the investigation, with oversight by the county prosecutor.

That same day, Spalding put the riot squad lieutenant and the eleven officers who had been in the segregation unit on administrative leave pending the outcome of the investigation.

Others didn't wait for the investigation. By evening, newspapers around the state were reporting that an inmate had been raped with a nightstick by an officer at the penitentiary, and that officers were suspended for brutality. When asked about the incident, Governor Ray said, "We cannot tolerate...any incidents of that kind."[110] Within days, the FBI and the U.S. attorney joined the investigation.

Russell and Jackson spent nearly three weeks in Walla Walla. They interviewed inmates and staff and reviewed evidence. They interviewed Dr. Saw a few days after he had seen the inmate who said he was raped. The doctor confirmed that the tear was "totally exterior and caused by exterior trauma."[111] There was no internal damage. In the doctor's opinion, the tear came from either violent sexual activity or "a blow received while the patient was in the knees to chest position, supine."[112] There was no evidence of sexual activity, so the inmate had undoubtedly been struck. Perhaps he'd been kicked, maybe even struck by a nightstick, but it was all on the outside. The evidence said he wasn't raped.

How the inmate received the tear remained unknown, so sometime later Dick Morgan tried to find out. He talked with those who would, or should, have known, and "I got some wishy-washy answers," he said.

> One [participant] explained that there was talk [or] threats of shoving a night stick up his ass, and thus planted the story in [the inmate's] mind. Another said there were "motions" being made at [the inmate] suggesting it was about to happen to him. Another said [the man] was treated roughly and more than one person was trying to hit him with a stick and the blows could have landed anywhere. Everyone denied that [the alleged rape] happened and one of them said nothing like that could have happened intentionally. So the qualifying statements left me with a bad feeling about it. There were people there I would like to believe wouldn't have tolerated it or covered it up, and there were people there who I believe were capable of it.[113]

In their review of the physical injuries of the other inmates, Russell and Jackson concluded that the inmates exaggerated, and the officers minimized, the amount of force that was used. "The truth obviously is somewhere in the middle," they wrote.[114]

Between the riot on Saturday night and the breakdown of staff discipline the next evening, there was a lot of truth to be discovered. Attorneys for Prison Legal Services began to plan their lawsuit.

Chapter 41

A Victory of Sorts

O NE OF THE OFFICERS SUSPENDED after the incident in segregation was union president Parley Edwards. Edwards, like the other participants, was placed on administrative leave with pay pending the outcome of the investigation. While the other suspended officers declined to comment, Edwards described the suspensions as "demoralizing" and "a slap in the face." However, he added, "if one of us screwed up, we will pay the price."[115]

On Monday, August 16, 1979, Spalding announced that a gradual unlock would start the next day. As a first step, groups of sixteen men at a time would be let out of Four, Five, and Six Wings for thirty-minute exercise periods. If that went well, limited visiting would begin the following week. His "biggest concern," he said, "is the attitude of the guards and how they are going to respond to the inmates when they come out. They've had one of their group killed and that's a pretty difficult obstacle to overcome."[116]

Partly in response to Spalding's announcement, but mainly because of the suspension of the twelve men who were involved in the incident in seg, an estimated 250 officers met after work that evening to discuss whether or not to strike. The meeting lasted nearly two hours. At the end of the meeting, the officers concluded that each individual would decide for himself whether to report to work. The next morning all officers scheduled for duty reported, except for one who showed up and immediately quit.[117]

Spalding wanted to continue the gradual unlock, but "the more I mentioned [it], the more the correctional officers got upset," he said. Spalding realized this resistance could be used to his advantage. He decided to push the recalcitrant correctional officers to the point where they would do something so rash that he could regain control of the situation. As strike threats continued, "I didn't know how it was going to come down," said Spalding, but he decided that "we're going to run [the penitentiary] with them or without them."[118]

Out-of-doors for the first time

The final push turned out to be something other than the end of
the lockdown. "I had a couple of correctional officers escorting a shackled inmate through [a] construction area," said Spalding. "The inmate
slowed down or did something, and the correctional officer kicked
him—kicked him from behind....I heard about that. I called the officer
up to the office and said, 'Did you kick that inmate?' He said, 'Yes, I did,
but....'" Before the man could finish, Spalding fired him.[119]

The officer was fired on Friday. Saturday night, about seventy officers gathered and threatened to walk off their jobs starting at the two
o'clock shift change Sunday afternoon. Pressure was applied to others
who hadn't attended the meeting. Dick Morgan recalled the pressure he
received Sunday morning:

I was acting shift sergeant by that time, filling in for whomever. [As shift sergeant,] you always had to go in to work at least an hour early to figure out who was going...to work where.

Two [officers] off the third shift...met me down in the locker room...."You gonna walk?" they asked. "We really need some sergeants to walk. We need some supervisors to go out with us to give us credibility. What are you gonna do?"

I said, "Man, I don't know. I got kids and family. I don't know what I'm going to do."

[One of the officers] pipes up and says, "Well, we know where you live...."

That, as far as I was concerned, was nothing short of convict behavior. I just didn't want to be associated with anybody who thought like that.[120]

Morgan decided he wouldn't walk. While Morgan and others went to work, forty-two men refused to go on shift that day in defiance of a direct order from the superintendent. It was a wildcat strike not sanctioned by the union.

Spalding asked for a list of the men who walked. After reviewing the list, the conclusion was clear: "There are only about three people on this whole list that we should feel bad about leaving. The rest are the ones that should be going....We're going to be a lot better off without them," said Spalding.[121]

In what sounds a little like spite, Spalding asked union president Parley Edwards to come to the superintendent's office. When he arrived, Spalding said, "Parley, you're on suspension right now. What will you do if I call you back today?"

"You know exactly what I'll do," replied Edwards. "I'll walk out and go on that picket line with those officers. I don't have any choice."

"I'm going to fire them," said Spalding. "But I'm not going to call you back. When I get you, I'm going to get you straight up and down."[122]

Spalding fired all forty-two strikers. There were still problem employees. There were still attitudes and comments that would fan flames rather than extinguish them. But according to Spalding, "It broke the back of that group....From the day I fired those people, things changed. It was clearly administrative control....The union was kind of deflated. That was the turning point of the whole process."[123]

Two weeks later, Spalding fired five of the participants in the segregation incident for brutality. Edwards wasn't one of them. In fact, the investigative report depicted Edwards as one of the calmer and more effective influences that Sunday night. As Spalding said, Edwards "was always a good officer"[124]—he was only a pain in the ass as union president.

Spalding never had to get Edwards "straight up and down." A lot of people lost their jobs under Edwards' leadership, and the union turned against him. Within a few months, he resigned as union president and quit his job at the penitentiary. He worked elsewhere for a few years, then came back to a much changed penitentiary. Eventually, he retired as an employee in good standing.

Chapter 42

DOG DAYS OF SUMMER

WHILE REPAIRS CONTINUED in Eight Wing, inmates camped in makeshift shelters in the Big Yard. State troopers, administrators, staff from other institutions, and officers working overtime filled in for the fired workers. The lockdown dragged on.

Spalding's physical condition deteriorated over the summer of 1979. He'd had back problems ever since a parachute training accident in the early '60s when he was in the military. After enduring pain for years, Spalding had back surgery in 1970 for a herniated disk. In 1979 it flared up again. "It got to the point where I was losing the feeling in my right leg," he said. There were times when he worked flat on his back because he couldn't move. Staffers conferred with him as he lay on the floor of his office. The doctor told him, "I realize you don't have time to have this done. But if you don't [have the operation], you could have some permanent disability." Spalding knew he couldn't put it off any longer.[125]

But before Spalding could have his surgery, August 1979 had its share of drama. The report by the team from the American Correctional Association—the group that was at the penitentiary when Eight Wing rioted—was publicly released on August 1. While the experts' report garnered its share of bad publicity, it was nothing compared to media and public reaction to photos and an essay by Ethan Hoffman and John McCoy, the former *Walla Walla Union-Bulletin* staffers, that appeared in *Life* magazine that same week. Some of the more sensational photos showed a prison queen wearing makeup and a miniskirt, a biker racing a chopper around the Big Yard, and clothed couples engaged in what certainly looked like sexual activity. The text made sure readers understood what the photos were about.[126]

Similar articles and pictures by Hoffman and McCoy appeared in *Paris Match* and *Stern*, a German news magazine, a short time later. Bob

State Patrol monitoring the Big Yard, August '79

Tropp, then a dues-paying member of Amnesty International, began receiving letters from all over the world castigating him and the department for the deplorable conditions portrayed in the pictures and the stories of brutality that accompanied them.

"It couldn't have happened at a worse time," said Jerry Thomas, assistant secretary of DSHS. "My immediate reaction was, 'My God,

that can't be happening now—after everything we've been through.'"[127]
Someone had to tell Thomas that the photos had been shot a year before.

The secretary of DSHS had a more succinct description of the *Life* magazine article. He called it an "aw shit" moment. Nonetheless, the agency had some success turning the photos to their advantage. The pictures were from the past, they explained. This is what the institution was like when we took over. This is what we've been suffering through. And this is what we've been doing to correct the situation.[128] It was a reasonably effective response within the state of Washington, but it didn't stop the international cards and letters to Bob Tropp.

August also saw introduction of a new procedure that quickly paid dividends. Videotape recorders—at least those that could be easily carried and were reasonably affordable—were relatively new in the late 1970s. The penitentiary introduced them to record cell extractions, inmate movements, and other activities where there might be trouble. At first the officers were angry. They saw video recording as an attempt by the administration to catch staff doing bad things.

One of the first uses of video recording occurred when repairs and improvements to Eight Wing were finally completed. After forty-five

Camping in the Big Yard

Weapons found in the Big Yard

days in the Big Yard—living in makeshift tents, eating TV dinners, showering outdoors, and using porta-potties—the men returned to the wing without incident under the watchful eye of the video camera. They were ready for a roof over their heads. A few days later, the last of the state troopers who had manned the walls went home.

When the inmates returned to Eight Wing, it was not just repaired, it was changed. Instead of the old porcelain toilets and sinks that were easily broken, new heavy-duty, stainless steel one-piece prison fixtures had been installed. Bunk beds were bolted to the walls. The building had new wiring, new shatterproof windows, improved ventilation, metal detectors, fresh paint, and various other security improvements. Everything was stronger. Destroying a cell and a cell house had become much harder.

Selling cells—a common practice in the past—also became less common. One inmate, who once paid $150 a month for cell 17D in Eight Wing, explained. "When you bought a cell back then, you got everything that was in it." In the past, "everything" could include a lot:

carpeting, curtains, bedspread, television, stereo, and more. "You can't have any of those things anymore," said the inmate. "So a cell is not worth anything....All of the cells are the same in Eight Wing—they are exactly the same....Wherever they move you, what the hell, you may as well stay there."[129]

At the end of August 1979, Spalding had back surgery. He was out for seven weeks. During this time, his associate superintendent for treatment—Jim Cummins, the former Catholic priest—was acting superintendent. Under Cummins's watch, another batch of inmates was shipped out of state.

During Spalding's absence an incident occurred that changed most officers' opinion about videotaping. One of the officers attempting to move an uncooperative inmate in segregation was stabbed in the arm, and the entire incident was caught on videotape. The evidence was conclusive, and officers began to understand that videotaping worked both ways. Soon, everyone—inmates and staff—were aware when the camera was on.

The institution continued on modified lockdown while Spalding was away. Inmates could leave their cells if they had a visitor. All the inmates could take showers, and they received clean clothing and bedding. With the Big Yard freed up, extended exercise periods began for inmates in Four and Six Wing. A dozen inmates returned to work in the license plate factory. Others began helping with construction and maintenance. Some were allowed to eat in the dining hall. By the middle of September inmates could make collect telephone calls to those on their approved list of contacts. Education classes resumed.

But most inmates still spent hours on end locked in their cells, eating a cold breakfast in the morning and TV dinners twice a day. The length of the lockdown was becoming a concern, not just to the agency, but to attorneys for the inmates.

Chapter 43

HOPTOWIT

THE ORIGINAL REPORT by Russell and Jackson on the incident
in segregation was distributed to a short list of people. Since
DSHS had requested the investigation, its top administrators
and their attorney were on the list. So, too, were representatives of the
partner agencies in the investigation: the Walla Walla police department, the county prosecuting attorney, the FBI, and the United States
attorney in Spokane.

The Russell-Jackson report was an investigation into employee conduct that could result in termination of employment and disciplinary
action under state personnel rules. Because of this, the report was confidential and protected from public disclosure by Washington law. No
one else was supposed to have a copy. This was a nicety not observed
by everyone. The report, along with the diagnosis by the physician who
examined the inmate who said he was raped, was leaked to the media
and attorneys representing the inmates. When the contents of the report
became public, there were widespread charges that DSHS and the governor were involved in a cover-up.

Who leaked the report is unknown. It's unlikely that anyone at the
Walla Walla police department or the county prosecutor's office was
responsible—they were largely sympathetic to the state. That leaves the
FBI and the U.S. attorney's office in Spokane. Between these two, the
prime suspect would be the U.S. attorney's office. This suspicion is suggested not only by the office's role in the subsequent lawsuit, but by the
fact that one of the lead U.S. attorneys later married one of the inmates
who destroyed his cell in segregation that night. That's not proof, but
one might conclude that objectivity was perhaps not her strongest suit.

It is also reasonable to ask whether a true copy of the report was given
to the newspaper. In the first two paragraphs of an article titled "Medical Evidence of Inmate Injury," the reporter wrote: "Medical reports

show that [the] inmate who alleged he was brutalized July 8 by guards at the Washington State Penitentiary in Walla Walla, suffered an injury to the inside of his anus. The medical reports, obtained by the *Seattle Post-Intelligencer*, appear to confirm [the inmate's] allegation that he was raped by a guard's nightstick."[130]

Neither the doctor's report nor the much longer Russell-Jackson report says any such thing. The Russell-Jackson report was unequivocal: "Medical examination by the doctor at Walla Walla General Hospital does not support any penetration of the bowel by any foreign object."[131]

Bad things happened in segregation that night, and five officers were fired for brutality. But the central allegation—the revolting image of a man being sodomized by an officer with a nightstick—was not supported by the medical evidence. Absent this allegation and the misinformation that became part of public perception, there would undoubtedly still have been a major lawsuit against the state of Washington over what happened that weekend in July—but the visceral image of savage brutality would not have been part of it.

Legal services attorneys weren't waiting for the Russell-Jackson report. They began interviewing inmates and collecting evidence almost immediately after the riot in Eight Wing and the chaos in segregation. They were soon joined by several private attorneys and the ACLU. "We plan a joint lawsuit in either federal or state court, asking for immediate injunctive relief from overcrowding and guard brutality, for damages for the beatings and for damages for the loss of personal property," said the executive director of the Washington State chapter of the ACLU. In early September he told a reporter for the *Seattle Post-Intelligencer*, "We expect to file in about four weeks."[132]

On October 12, 1979, attorneys for the inmates filed *Hoptowit v. Ray* in federal district court. According to John Midgley, one of the plaintiff's attorneys, inmate Fredrick Hoptowit was listed as the first name on the complaint because one of the issues in the lawsuit was racism against Native Americans. The fact that Mr. Hoptowit's name (pronounced "hop-TAU-it") could be, and was, easily mispronounced supposedly never entered their minds. But attorneys for the state had no trouble recognizing the irony. They could sometimes be heard joking to each other, saying, "We'd better hop to it."[133]

Three days after the lawsuit was filed, Spalding, having recovered from his back surgery, returned to work. The four-month lockdown ended the following week.

When the inmates left their cells and stepped outside, they saw a changed world. The green grass of Lifers' and People's Park was buried under a sea of concrete. There were additional officers everywhere. If an inmate loitered anywhere except in the Big Yard, he risked a trip to seg. Inmates were patted down at every turn. Stripped bare, the former club areas were shared. No turf belonged to anyone except the officers and prison administration. Inmate businesses were closed. Prison staff, not convicts, ran the inmate store. Curio permits, which before had allowed inmates to have tools like carving knives in their cells, could no longer be obtained. During most hours of the day, a strict gate system kept inmates in one of three places: locked in their cells, locked in a double-guarded dayroom or recreation area, or working in a place like prison industries or the kitchen.

Some older inmates told a newspaper reporter they felt safer because of the tighter rules, but many complained of the new restrictions. For their part, the officers were cautiously optimistic.[134]

Against this backdrop, the lawsuit continued. A federal judge was assigned to the case.

Judge Jack Tanner was new and controversial. One of the attorneys for the inmates, John Midgley, said, "we thought Tanner was our best shot....[He] was very open to our case." On the other hand, Midgley and the other attorneys for the inmates had their concerns. Midgley explained: "Judge Tanner was very unpredictable....He could be fairly arbitrary and he could overdo things. If he was going your way sometimes he would go a little too far your way."[135] While having a sympathetic judge is usually a good thing, going too far can be a problem if the case is appealed. *Hoptowit v. Ray* was a case likely to be appealed.

To the state's attorneys, saying that Judge Tanner "was very open" to the plaintiff's case was like saying the sun comes up in the morning. An example of the judge's openness was provided at one of the very first hearings. On the record, the judge said, "I know things are bad over there because I've read the papers."[136] On another occasion, the judge ruled that nothing the State of Washington did after the lawsuit was filed was admissible. This made no sense, since if the defendant had fixed everything (or anything), the judge was supposed to consider whether the fix was permanent or good enough. Tanner also set a case schedule that was extremely fast. While it was a difficult schedule for the six full-time attorneys representing the inmates, it was doubly difficult for the three assistant attorneys general representing the defendant.

For these and other reasons, the attorneys for the state moved to have the judge recuse himself for prejudice. Tanner refused. He also ordered the penitentiary to stop using brutality.

Spalding was furious. He responded in the press saying the judge's order was one-sided and depressing. Wasn't the purpose of the trial to determine whether or not there was brutality? Spalding said that it was the inmates who were causing the trouble and that he had videotapes to prove it. "My officers are being called 'pigs,' they have feces thrown at them daily." He said an injunction against inmate abuse of officers would be welcomed.[137]

Of course, Spalding's pipe dream of an injunction against inmate abuse of officers amounted to nothing. The case went forward, and in June, Judge Tanner issued a sixty-page opinion.

Spalding had it wrong. *Hoptowit v. Ray* was about much more than brutality. Confinement at the Washington State Penitentiary, wrote the judge, constituted cruel and unusual punishment for a host of reasons. These included overcrowding, racism, harassment, brutality, and negligent and substandard medical, dental, and mental health care. There were physical plant deficiencies, including sanitation, lighting, and cell size. The judge identified staffing levels, staff recruitment, staff training, and inmate idleness as contributing factors that had to be addressed. He said a special master (an overseer for the court) would be appointed and the court would retain jurisdiction.

The judge based his finding of overcrowding primarily on voluntary standards concerning cell size and square feet per inmate published by the American Correctional Association. Under these standards, Wings Four and Five could no longer be used, and the total number of inmates housed at the penitentiary could not exceed 492.

The findings on racism, harassment, and brutality were based on a variety of factors, including inmate testimony, the tape recordings made during the incident in segregation, and Spalding's firing of officers for brutality. The judge also concluded that inmate property had been destroyed or stolen during the shakedown and that inmates sustained significant injuries after the riot in Eight Wing and during the incident in segregation. The state disputed the extent of racism, harassment, and brutality, but Tropp, Spalding, and others concurred that such attitudes and actions were present at the penitentiary.

Health care was another area in which the state could muster little defense. Access to, and the quality of, health care was an issue that had been on every list of inmate grievances since the Christmas strike of 1970, when inmates stopped work and refused to shave or have their hair cut. The problems were not related to convenience or bedside manner, but to matters of life and death.

Inmate Robert Redwine was on the receiving end of egregiously bad medical care. Redwine was admitted to the prison hospital after being stabbed by an unknown assailant. The physician's assistant on duty ordered a chest x-ray and blood study. Before the x-ray and blood work could be done, the attending physician examined the man's wound by separating the cut edges and looking. (The normal procedure in a case like this would be to at least probe the wound.) The physician then cancelled the x-ray and blood tests and directed a supervisor to suture the wound and send the man back to his cell. This inmate, explained the doctor, "had always been a complainer."[138]

Custody refused to move Redwine, and the man remained in the hospital.

In the night, the patient was found covered by a large amount of blood that had soaked through his pajamas and bed linen. The blood was cleaned up and the bleeding stopped. That morning, on her own initiative, the x-ray technician took an x-ray of the man's chest and abdomen. The man's chest looked normal, but the image of his abdomen showed dilation of the small bowel. Despite established procedure to x-ray any stab wound, the attending physician castigated the technician for taking an x-ray without orders from an MD.

Throughout the day, Redwine sat hugging his upper abdomen while complaining of severe pain. At 4:25 in the afternoon he was found dead, sitting on the toilet in an unusual position. He had bled to death from internal hemorrhaging.

Redwine experienced bad medical care. Inmate John Bumphus experienced problems of access to medical care.

It started with an ingrown toenail during the lockdown in the summer of 1979. When a medic visited the wing, Bumphus was given Desenex antifungal medication and Epsom salts. He used these as directed. When the pain grew worse, he asked to see a doctor. His request was ignored. His foot swelled up, and the top of his big toe split open. The swelling reached his ankle, and he had to drag his foot when he walked. In September and again in early October, he thought he was scheduled to see a doctor. Each time, he slowly made his way from Six Wing to the prison hospital, dragging his leg and frequently stopping to catch his breath. Both times, the officers at the control room turned him away because they said he was not on the call sheet for the hospital.

By mid-October, the pain was excruciating. Finally, Bumphus was examined by a nurse and admitted to the hospital. It was too late. Bumphus had gangrene from an ingrown toenail. His leg was amputated just below the knee.[139]

The law calls such medical malpractice "deliberate indifference." On this, and every other issue, the state was soundly defeated in *Hoptowit*.[140]

Even before Judge Tanner's decision in *Hoptowit v. Ray*, the penitentiary had greatly exceeded its operating budget because of the tens of thousands of overtime hours caused by the lockdown, the riot, and the firing of officers due to the wildcat strike and excessive use of force in segregation. But with the Tanner decision and the short time frames the judge required for compliance, "that's about the time we started… throwing money at the institution," said John Shaughnessey, the adult corrections assistant director for management.[141]

To address the budget shortfall, DSHS assistant secretary Jerry Thomas asked Secretary Thompson for additional spending authority. The authority was granted, but the agency didn't really have the money. Instead, Thomas created a paper budget with the intention of asking the legislature, when it was next in session, for a supplemental appropriation to cover the unanticipated expenditures. "Unfortunately," said Thomas, "someone nicknamed the paper budget the 'credit card,'"[142] a choice of words the agency would later regret.

Chapter 44

POLITICAL FALLOUT

THROUGHOUT 1979 AND 1980 adult corrections in Washington was front-page news across the state—perfect cannon fodder for the many politicians who wanted to make Dixy Lee Ray a one-term governor.

Whether in public or private, Governor Ray was always a woman who spoke her mind. Her candor and outspokenness served her well as a candidate, but these same qualities became liabilities when applied to the business of governing. A brilliant woman who liked to show off what she knew, she suffered no fools. In the process, she alienated most of the media and many of her political allies. When the going got tough, she was largely on her own.

The going got tough in 1979. The penitentiary had been a mess for years, but 1979 was in a class by itself. An officer had been murdered. A cell house had been destroyed in a riot. An inmate said he was raped with a nightstick. A major class-action lawsuit was filed.

Months before he declared his candidacy for governor, the Republican speaker of the house repeatedly blasted Governor Ray and Bob Tropp for "inept leadership."[143] Other voices, including Democrats, demanded major changes—including a renewed call to remove corrections from DSHS and create a separate department of corrections.

In the session of the state legislature beginning in January 1980, legislators expressed their displeasure of DSHS by slashing funds requested for adult corrections. They eliminated all money to improve the inmate grievance system and funded only half the amount requested for correctional officer training. All this occurred at a time when DSHS was trying to demonstrate to the court that it was making progress in addressing these and other issues raised in *Hoptowit v. Ray*.

As the political campaigns intensified, "there [were] a couple guys in that equation—notably Tropp—that [got] bloodied unnecessarily," said DSHS secretary Gerald Thompson. Tropp got caught up in the political world, not by his own doing, but by the nature of the times, said Thompson. Part of the problem, he explained, was the personality of Governor Ray, and part was the actions and statements of people in the legislature who wanted her job. "I could see Bob deteriorating under that pressure," said Thompson.[144]

Serious challengers emerged from both parties. By September 1980, Dixy Lee Ray was a lame duck—defeated in the primary by a Democratic state senator from Seattle.

As for Bob Tropp, during 1980 he carried a letter with him at all times addressed to the department of retirement systems announcing his intention to retire within the next sixty days. He had been eligible to retire for several years, and giving advance notice affected the timing of retirement pay. As Tropp explained, you didn't have to retire within the time period, but you had to give notice if you wanted to collect retirement as soon as you quit work. He simply updated the letter every sixty days.

"I was so fed up and so disgusted with the way things were—even though I knew…we were making progress," said Tropp. "Occasionally, when something would happen—a phone call or an event or something came across my desk—[I'd say to myself,] 'How do I go on with this for even another month?' [Then] I would pull this letter from out of my pocket and read it again."[145]

In November 1980, the Republican candidate for governor, John Spellman, prevailed. A few weeks later, Tropp announced his retirement effective at the end of the year.

DSHS secretary Gerald Thompson reminisced about those times. "I look back on…corrections and I kind of have a feeling that [I'm] witnessing this thing…through field glasses. You see the battle, and you can kind of empathize with the participants. You know the fury, and you understand just how difficult it is, but there's not much chance that you're going to get shot.…[But] guys like Tropp and Spalding and some of Spalding's immediate subordinates are right there. The changes that were going on were significant, and those guys were on the front line. They were engaged in the hand-to-hand combat. I think that the people that followed Tropp and Spalding owe those guys a lot of gratitude.

I think that they took a lot of abuse and did a lot of things that were well above what you would expect for people in that position. I think they accomplished a great deal and set the groundwork for what we have today."[146]

PART 6
TRANSFORMATION
1981–1985

A quiet day at the Washington State Penitentiary

Site Plan 1985

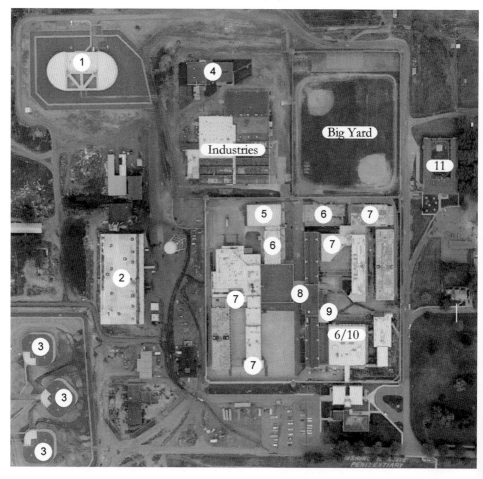

KEY

1. Intensive Management Unit (IMU)
2. Warehouse & Outside Stores
3. Medium Security Complex
4. Vocational Education
5. Gym
6. Inmate Programs

7. Dayrooms and/or Unit
   Management Offices
8. Circulation Control
9. Divided Circulation Corridors
10. Inmate Services / Visiting
11. Minimum Security Building

Image courtesy of the Washington State Department of Transportation, Aerial Photography Branch

Chapter 45

A DEPARTMENT IS BORN

DURING THE ELECTION CAMPAIGN in 1980, it seemed everyone but Governor Ray pushed for a separate department of corrections. A pre-session poll of state legislators found majorities in both parties supported the idea. It was going to happen.

With the decision all but made, governor-elect Spellman needed someone to run the new department. He knew local sheriffs and jail managers from previous political positions, but he wanted someone with a national reputation and expert credentials. He asked Steve Excell, a member of his transition team, to conduct a search. According to Excell, every time he called someone in another state, he was told, "Well, if you want to get your house in order, you might want to take a look at Amos Reed."[1] At the time Reed was the newly elected president of the American Correctional Association and director of corrections in North Carolina. The man who had originally appointed Reed to the latter position, Jim Hunt, had just been reelected to a second term as governor. Despite Hunt's reelection, Reed's position in North Carolina was far from secure.

Excell talked with Reed on the phone, and Reed told him, "My days here are numbered. The governor wants me gone."[2] While Reed was highly recommended by others, Spellman needed to know why Reed was being fired.

"So I had Spellman call Governor Hunt," said Excell. According to Excell, Hunt told Spellman, "You can't quote me, but Amos Reed is the finest head of corrections you can ever have, but I have to fire the son of a bitch because he's not political enough. We do favors for legislators, and we go mow their lawns. I hate to say this, but we got graft and corruption in our procurement, and he's cleaning it all up, and he's pissing off the legislature, he's pissing off some of the companies that use prison industries at ten cents an hour, and he's making changes too fast.

He's doing all the right stuff, but I can't have change that fast or I'm not going to be in office."[3]

What Hunt didn't tell Spellman was that Reed often resisted Hunt's efforts to fill open positions in corrections with patronage appointments.[4]

Even without this last bit of information, Spellman hung up the phone and said to Excell, "Well, that's the best endorsement I've ever heard."[5]

Reed had the reputation and expert credentials that Spellman was looking for, and the deal was cut within a few days. Amos Reed would become the first secretary of the Washington State Department of Corrections.

Spellman wasted no time getting Reed on board. In fact, Reed attended Spellman's first cabinet meeting in January. But Reed was on the cabinet by invitation only. There was no Department of Corrections yet. Technically, Reed replaced Tropp as director of the Division of Corrections within the Department of Social and Health Services. But since Reed reported directly to the governor, the secretary of DSHS had no real authority over him.

At sixty-five, Reed was something of an elder statesman for adult corrections when he came to Washington. A tall, slender man with piercing eyes beneath his prominent forehead, Reed spoke with a hint of a Southern accent. He could be charming, even charismatic, when he addressed legislative committees. According to Steve Excell, Reed "liked everybody to think that he was just a country bumpkin—a little bit of a hick—[who had come] up through the school of hard knocks and knows a thing or two. He had a gift for turning a phrase, and in a way he could mesmerize legislators when they started listening to him." When Reed talked, explained Excell, what he said "came across as just plain, old-fashioned, common sense."[6]

In his first appearance before the House Select Committee on Corrections in early February, Reed described the corrections system in the state of Washington as "sick, very very sick." Perhaps unaware of the true depths of dysfunction inherited by Spalding and Tropp, he told the legislators, "The system is on the precipice. We've virtually given our prisons away."[7]

While Washington's prisons had clearly moved away from the precipice, Reed's concept of "the system" was broad. It wasn't just prisons that

Reed was talking about—it was everything that makes a large organization work. There wasn't even "a skeleton of a budgetary, accounting and management system," Reed told the committee.[8] Reed wasn't talking about the new department of corrections—it didn't exist yet. He was talking about DSHS.

Reed and others started to assemble the pieces needed by the new department. The transfer of employees and physical resources from DSHS to the new department was easy when it came to prisons and community corrections personnel and their field offices. It was in headquarters where things got sticky.

Every headquarters division in DSHS, not just the division of adult corrections, relied on all kinds of centralized services: budget and accounting, personnel and labor relations, legal services and information technology, planning and research, legislative liaison and public relations, word processing and mail, cleaning and building maintenance, and more. It was a very long list. The new department of corrections would need all of these things, and need them under its own control.

Often, when a new function is created within, or in this case carved out of, a bureaucracy, there is an attempt to get the new or departing function to take as much of the agency's deadwood (that is, low-performing employees) as possible. It's a kind of cat and mouse game, with one side knowing more about the quality of resources proposed for transfer than the other. The mouse—in this case the emerging department of corrections—was at something of a disadvantage.

Of course, certain headquarters personnel were obvious transfers, and some of them were talented and knowledgeable. Some of the deadwood refused transfer, and some high performers lobbied for it. As the knowledge base increased on the adult corrections side, the game became more even.

Tropp's assistant director for management, John Shaughnessey, was one of the division's key staff retained by Reed. As Reed began to look into the agency's finances, Shaughnessey suggested that Reed meet with Bob Tropp to get some history behind the cost overruns and the so-called "credit card."

A meeting between the two men took place, although on Tropp's initiative rather than Reed's. During the brief meeting, the message Tropp got was that Reed wasn't interested in anything Tropp had to say because he knew everything already. "Amos didn't want to hear anything," said Tropp, "not what's going on, not who to trust or who not to trust, not anything."[9]

So the credit card issue "just kind of simmered there for a while, and then suddenly it exploded," said Shaughnessey. Reed took Shaughnessey and one or two others to see the chair of the state senate's Ways and Means Committee. He "didn't tell us why we were going or anything of that sort. We get in there, and Amos lays this big turd out on the table" about the cost overruns.[10] The next thing Shaughnessey knew, the overruns were not just "unauthorized," they were "illegal."

Reed gave Spellman this same version of the fiscal situation in adult corrections. The governor announced at a press conference that his new prison director had "uncovered illegal and unauthorized over-expenditures of at least two million dollars, maybe more."[11]

Of course, these "illegal and unauthorized" expenditures were due to the remedies required by the court under *Hoptowit v. Ray*, and for the cost of thousands of hours of overtime. In other words, the excess expenditures were for the very things that, in the normal course of events, would have been in the agency's supplemental budget request.

But there was no normal course of events in 1981. Within weeks, the estimated cost overruns had grown to $7 million, and the state house of representatives voted 98–0 to direct the attorney general to "bring any appropriate civil action or recommend any appropriate criminal action against past or present officials or employees of the department [of Social and Health Services.]"[12] A few days later, the legislature appropriated all the funds for the new department of corrections that the governor and Amos Reed had requested. Nothing ever came of the attorney general's investigation.

The way Reed used the "credit card" issue revealed a lot about his character and how he intended to play the game. Jim Spalding quickly experienced Reed's character firsthand and learned that the game Reed played was hardball. At an early meeting in Olympia, Spalding said something with which Reed disagreed. There is no record of what transpired at this meeting, but when Spalding returned to the penitentiary he told his key staff, "Different story now, folks. Amos Reed will eat your lunch."[13]

How Reed treated John Shaughnessey reinforced this image. "Amos let me get him through the legislative session," said Shaughnessey. But when the legislature adjourned in April, "[Reed] called me into his office and told me he was letting me go." When Shaughnessey asked why, Reed said it was about the cost overruns. He told Shaughnessey, "The legislature is asking for heads on a platter, and yours is one I'm going to give them."[14]

In April, as the time grew closer for the official start of the new department on July 1, 1981, Reed concluded that he wanted someone other than Spalding as penitentiary superintendent. On the last day of the month, Reed announced that Spalding would become the first deputy director of the Division of Prisons in the new department. Spalding would move to Olympia as soon as a replacement for him could take over in Walla Walla.

Spalding recommended that C. R. M. "Bob" Kastama become the next penitentiary superintendent. The two men had worked together as associate superintendents prior to Spalding's move to Walla Walla. Kastama also lobbied for the job, sending Secretary Reed a letter and a copy of a ten-page paper he had written. Reed read the letter and paper and asked Kastama to come to Olympia. Not long after, Kastama was offered the job. "I was told I was hired for my humanitarian ideas, reputation of integrity, and demonstrated management skills," said Kastama.[15] He would start on the first of July.

Kastama met with Reed before going to Walla Walla. Speaking of Spalding's imminent departure from the penitentiary, Reed told Kastama it was time to "bring the boy in."[16] Spalding always considered his appointment as deputy director a promotion, but he had no idea that such a condescending, dismissive attitude—typified by Reed's "bring the boy in" comment—would await him in the secretary's office.

He soon found out. For much of Reed's tenure, Spalding would literally become ill when told to meet with Reed. Before going into the secretary's office, Spalding would take his wastebasket in his hands and vomit. Murders, riots, rebellious staff—all in a day's work for Spalding. The old man in the corner office—that was a different story.

Chapter 46

FIRST STEPS

A FTER SIX MONTHS OF PLANNING, legislative action, and incremental implementation, the department of corrections officially started on July 1, 1981.

Robin Moses's explanation of how Reed built a modern correctional system in Washington State made the process sound easy. Amos Reed, said Moses, was "the first man to take control of the system and run it; the first one to give a directive of 'Here's what I want.'"[17]

Moses was only partly right. Reed wasn't the first person to take control of the system and run it—just the first since the creation of DSHS. And Reed certainly wasn't the first to give a directive of "Here's what I want." Every director since Hal Bradley had tried to move the system in ways he thought right. The difference between Reed and the others is that his directives stuck.

One reason Reed's directives stuck was because he had instant credibility. Not only was Amos Reed president of the American Correctional Association, he was a key player in developing the first set of standards for adult corrections published by ACA in 1977. The ACA standards, taken as a whole, represented the first codified system of best practices for running a correctional system in the United States. Almost everything was covered—from the day-to-day operation of prisons to overall management of an adult corrections agency and its specialized services. Reed knew it all. In 1981 there was probably no one in the country better prepared than Amos Reed to build a new department of corrections.

Reed's directives also stuck because he was never second-guessed. Tropp and his predecessors were two steps removed from the governor. Before Reed, the director of the division of adult corrections reported to the deputy secretary of DSHS, who reported to the secretary, who reported to the governor. Reed sat on the governor's cabinet. Governor

Spellman trusted and relied on Reed, and Reed carefully supported his boss.

Reed was also effective because he and key staffers in his inner circle were controllers. Directly, and indirectly through staff, Reed controlled everything. He knew what he needed to know and had systems put in place to ensure the flow of information he wanted. Superintendents were expected to emulate the same approach in managing their institutions.

There was also the fear factor. It wasn't just Spalding who had trouble with Amos Reed. Charming in public, Reed could be a domineering, difficult man in private. Every employee entering the secretary's office during the Reed administration expected the worst. Furthermore, if a male subordinate wasn't wearing a coat and tie, he could expect to be chewed out for whatever reason he was summoned to see the secretary, and for his casual attire. This created a problem. Since the Department of Corrections headquarters building didn't have air conditioning, many middle management men didn't wear a coat on hot days. To avoid being caught without suitable attire, one of the men bought an extra sports jacket from the local thrift store and hung it in his office for anyone who needed it. Given Reed's usual temperament, over time, the spare jacket became known as the "flogging coat."[18]

More senior managers—those who frequently met with Reed—were no less likely to feel the secretary's wrath. John King, the department's first legislative liaison, said he had irritable bowel syndrome for the entire time Reed was department secretary, a condition that went away when Reed departed.

King's explanation of how Reed created a modern correctional system in Washington State adds another dimension to Robin Moses's contention that Reed was "the first man to take control of the system and run it." According to King, Reed's method of taking control involved brute force and intimidation. "He choked the throat of the organization until it just about passed out," said King. Despite this, King admired the man because of what he accomplished.[19]

Amos Reed knew what he wanted, had the support of the governor, knew what was going on, and would chew you up into little pieces and spit you out if you—or the people you supervised—fell short of his expectations. If you were superintendent, you were responsible for everything at your institution.

When the department of corrections officially got underway on July 1, 1981, Reed didn't give a lot of direction to his newest superintendent, Bob Kastama. At a meeting in which Reed slowly reeled in the line of an imaginary fishing pole, Kastama heard his boss tell him, "I want you to pull in the line. I want you to do it very slowly." Kastama understood. However, unlike Reed, Kastama knew that Spalding had already hooked and landed the biggest fish—the rebellious correctional officers, most of the lead cons, and the dedicated turf controlled by the various clubs. Kastama's assignment was to continue to chip away at the accumulated dysfunctional privileges that compromised the ability of the correctional officers to control the prison.

The penitentiary Kastama inherited from Spalding that July was a far different place than the one Spalding had inherited from Genakos three years earlier. In addition to the paving that buried Lifers' Park and People's Park, other parts of the architect's long-range plan were completed or underway. A strategic movement control point at the center of the

New movement control room and gate

institution, where the four quadrants met, was in operation. Blood Alley was gone, and the building housing the B.P.F.U. was being demolished to completely alter how inmates and staff moved through the southeast quadrant of the institution. Banquets, to which hundreds of outside guests had previously been invited, had ceased. A modern outdoor lighting system eliminated the dark shadows that had previously frustrated nighttime observation of the prison grounds. A new gymnasium was under construction in the area immediately north of the old Bikers' Club. This gym would replace one of the oldest buildings at the penitentiary after the latter was demolished as part of the master plan for the quadrant system. The Bikers' Club itself was gutted, and construction to convert the building into an inmate program area was nearly complete.

Some changes to the architect's long-range plan were also underway. Just after Kastama arrived, a previous decision to create temporary inmate housing in the Big Yard using precast concrete cells was scrapped. The original idea was to rotate the inmates through the temporary housing as each cellblock was being renovated. When work was completed on all the wings, the temporary housing would be removed.

The new plan was to use the precast cells to create a permanent segregation unit outside the prison walls. Segregation inmates would move to the new unit, and other inmates would rotate through the vacated cells in Big Red while their cellblocks were renovated.

It wasn't just the physical plant that had changed. Videotaping was routinely used for cell extractions and other planned uses of force. A closed-circuit television system, known as WSP TV, allowed the superintendent to address the entire prison population with the flip of a switch. At least sixteen inmate troublemakers had been shipped out of state. The union no longer openly defied the superintendent. Most of the rogue officers who had caused problems in the past were gone. Staff turnover was down.

Probably the most important advantage Kastama inherited was the attitude of the sergeants, lieutenants, and some of long-term correctional officers who had experienced the '70s and stuck it out. Many of these survivors had been assaulted; some had been stabbed or taken hostage. While much still needed to be done, this experienced and determined cadre of officers was dead set against any retreat from the progress that had been made since the departure of Vinzant and Genakos. Officers were no longer just punching the clock and trying to get home in one piece at the end of their shift—most did their job with a newfound sense of purpose to help reestablish control of the prison.

Of course, there were still problems. While the cellblocks were generally cleaner, segregation, which could be trashed in minutes, remained a nightmare. Some inmates had shanks and other weapons, although carrying a weapon was not nearly as common as in the past. There were fights, some assaults on staff, and the occasional stabbing.

The weather was also a problem. It was a hot summer in Walla Walla in 1981, and August was one of the hottest months on record. With a high temperature for the month of 107 degrees Fahrenheit, and an average daily high of nearly 96 degrees, August 1981 was a cooker.

Kastama had fans put in the wings and sprinklers turned on in the Big Yard. Ice cream was served at meals, and ice cubes were handed out in the evening.[20] But the relative cool of the night provided little relief in the concrete cellblocks that baked all day.

During his first months on the job, Kastama interviewed six or seven inmates, chosen more or less at random, each Saturday and sometimes on Sunday. He wanted to know what the inmates were thinking. "Most of the inmates wanted the administration to be in charge," he said. "They knew the inmate leaders weren't fair. They told me that the first thing I needed to do was to get rid of the motorcycles. [They said] the bikes were a symbol of inmate power."[21]

Of course, the bike shop had been moved when Spalding arrived in 1978, and the Bikers' Club, like every other group, no longer had a dedicated meeting place to which only they had the keys. But the bikes were still there, out in the industries area.

Kastama took advantage of WSP TV to make an announcement to the inmate population. He said the motorcycles had to go.

A few days later, on September 1, the inmates rioted and burned down the dining hall and kitchen. The majority of rioters were thought to be bikers, and Kastama believed the riot was in reaction to his announcement.

Motorcycles stored in the industries area

Immediately after the riot, three hundred inmates were herded into the Big Yard, where they spent the night under the stars. "In the morning, each inmate was brought out, one at a time, and searched," said Kastama. "I insisted that it all be videotaped—as much out of concern about potential officer behavior as about inmates." Missing kitchen knives and various homemade shanks were recovered. The prison was locked down.[22]

Early in the lockdown, Kastama called a meeting of his associate superintendents. He told them, "Now is the time to get rid of the bikes." A plan was developed. First, the owner of each bike was identified. If the biker acknowledged that the bike was his, he was given a box and a set of tools, then told to dismantle the bike and put it in the box. The box was then shipped to an address chosen by the biker. If the biker denied the bike was his, it was put in storage.[23] The reign of the Bikers' Club was finally over.

Kastama also called Tana Wood during the lockdown. At the time, Wood was working at a small prison near Spokane, Washington, a few hours north of Walla Walla by car. Before that, Wood had been a senior counselor and one of the first correctional unit supervisors under the unit team management concept at the prison in Shelton, Washington. Unit team management was a system the penitentiary planned to implement.

Kastama had been authorized to hire a third associate superintendent that summer, and Wood was ranked number one in the state on the associate superintendent register. Wood was happy where she was, and when Kastama explained why he called, she was sure she didn't want the job. Despite her lack of interest, Wood decided to talk with Kastama on a stopover in Walla Walla while she was driving to eastern Oregon to visit family. Kastama made a great impression on her. "I spent probably less than fifteen minutes with Kastama," said Wood. "When [the interview] was finished, I told him, 'If you accept me, I'll take the job.'... There's something about Kastama," she continued. "It wasn't even a formal interview, and man, I'd walk through rattlesnakes for that guy."[24]

Kastama offered her the job, and on October 1, 1981, Tana Wood became the highest-ranking female to work at the penitentiary since its founding nearly one hundred years earlier.

At the time, Wood was not only experienced in unit team management, but was one of the department's few experts on the subject. "Nobody [at the penitentiary] had even a clue what a unit system looked like," she said.[25]

Although in theory the lockdown was over by the end of September, a modified lockdown continued for months. Inmates could go to school, have visitors, and go to rec, but all meals were in the cell. If an inmate didn't have a reason to be somewhere else, he was locked up.[26]

During the months of modified lockdown, Wood concentrated on implementing unit team management. She, along with Larry Kincheloe, interviewed candidates for the position of correctional unit supervisor—the non-custody person who had the authority and responsibility for how an inmate living unit was run. Most of those selected came from other institutions, thereby increasing the presence of middle management staff uncontaminated by associations—or memories—of what had happened at Walla Walla in years past. Meanwhile, others worked on a long list of initiatives. "We moved like mad to get the quadrant system on line, to implement the pass system, clean the place up physically, implement reduced size of gatherings, and to revise visiting," said Kastama.[27]

And then came Kautzky.

Chapter 47

KAUTZKY

MUCH WAS ACCOMPLISHED IN 1981, but Amos Reed wanted a field marshal to carry his message and instill discipline deep inside the agency. He knew just the man he wanted.

Like many people in this somewhat unusual profession, Walter "Kip" Kautzky came to adult corrections by a circuitous path. He started out studying to be a priest, but in his words, was "done in by epistemology." Kautzky changed his major to psychology.

While in graduate school at Florida State University, Kautzky worked in the state's prison system, partly to earn money and partly as research for his master's thesis. In 1968, while teaching and working on a doctorate, Kautzky was drafted into the army. There someone noticed his prison experience, and he was sent to Fort Leavenworth, Kansas, to become an operations officer at the United States Disciplinary Barracks. A year later, thinking he was going to Vietnam, Kautzky was put in charge of a then-secret Joint Services Stockade located in Thailand.

Kautzky's career path was set. He returned to the United States in 1971, interviewed with two commissioners of corrections, and accepted a job in North Carolina. An intelligent and disciplined workaholic, Kautzky quickly rose through the ranks. By 1975 he was deputy director of the department. A year later newly elected governor Jim Hunt appointed Amos Reed to be director of the North Carolina Department of Corrections. Reed was Kautzky's boss for the next four years. In 1981, ten months after Reed was fired for not being political enough, Kautzky's career in North Carolina ended for similar reasons.

Knowing that his former second-in-command was looking for work, Reed called Kautzky and offered him the job of director of the Division of Prisons in Washington State. Kautzky accepted and came to Olympia the following January.

If Reed had his fear factor, so too did Kautzky. But where Reed was overbearing, Kautzky was just hard to please. Trim, fit, polite, and soft-spoken, his expectations were very high. Unless Amos Reed or the governor was present, there was no question who was in charge when Kautzky walked into a room. Some staff said he had a "command presence," an attribute Kautzky attributes to his time in the army.

A controller like Reed, Kautzky would first assume all the authority and control for a function and then relinquish it to those he thought could handle it properly. One of the first areas over which Kautzky assumed control was the design of the new segregation unit at the penitentiary.

Kautzky took one look at the architect's nearly completed plans—one hundred precast concrete cells arranged in clusters along a linear axis—and said, "Really? We're going to do that?"[28]

Kautzky wanted something different. He wanted a facility that could be run so that no one—not staff, not inmates—would be hurt. He wanted a totally secure and totally clean segregation unit. He wanted a reset button that would change the culture at the Washington State Penitentiary to one in which the officers and leadership would take responsibility for, and ownership of, a new mode of operating segregation.

Some of the implications of these principles were quickly apparent. The segregation facility would be broken down into small components, or pods, with dayrooms and showers. A group of pods would have enough recreation space so that segregation inmates could, if necessary, exercise alone. An officer would be able to see every cell door and every activity from a safe vantage point.

In 1982 there was little or no precedent for what Kautzky was trying to accomplish. However, one facility had most of what he was after: the recently completed Special Offender Center, located next to Washington's second oldest prison. Designed by the same architects now working on the penitentiary improvements, the Special Offender Center didn't have the direct line-of-sight supervision that Kautzky was after; but, Kautzky said, "it definitely had the conceptual framework for subcategorizing various inmates based on risk into separate housing units that then could be managed in a different way."[29]

The idea of using precast cells was thrown out, and the architects started over.

What emerged over the next few months was what Kautzky believes was the first modern supermax—super-maximum security—facility in the country. Other very strong facilities certainly predated the penitentiary's Intensive Management Unit, but the IMU had the capability of handling the most difficult inmates in a highly controlled way.

Under the architect's plans, the building was divided in half; the west end of the building was a mirror image of the east. At the strategic center of each half of the building was a secure control room surrounded by a circulation corridor. On the other side of the corridor—visible through high-security polycarbonate windows—were four pods of cells, two dayrooms and two small outdoor exercise areas with concrete walls and a wire-screened roof. Each dayroom and exercise area served two pods of cells. Each pod had twelve cells—six on the main floor and six on a mezzanine level. From the elevated control room, the officer on duty would have an unobstructed view of every inch of the dayrooms, outdoor exercise areas, and forty-eight electronically controlled sliding steel cell doors.

Each one-man cell was designed to hold a stainless steel prison toilet and sink, a stainless steel mirror embedded in the concrete wall, a small stainless steel writing surface and chair bolted to the wall, and a bed made of poured concrete. Meals would be passed on trays through a wicket in the cell door. If necessary, an officer could override the inmate's control of his light, electrical outlet, and water. An intercom would allow the control room officer to listen in on what was happening in the room or converse with the inmate.

Between the two halves of the building, the designs called for an intake area, noncontact visiting booths, attorney-client rooms, a fully equipped nurses' station, and other support spaces. In theory, ninety-six inmates could have daily exercise periods, showers, and visits without ever seeing another inmate.

But in the spring of 1982, these ideas were only lines on paper. It would be years before the new segregation facility was constructed and operational.

It wasn't just the architects that Kautzky challenged. Tana Wood, Kastama's associate superintendent, explained how Kautzky tested her. "At one point I had to go to headquarters to defend the budget," said Wood, "and Kip *knew* the budget....I found out fairly early on that you could go toe to toe with him if you knew what you were talking about. Once he found out that you wouldn't shine him on, or lie to him, or try to be a yes man, you did very well....He wanted people that knew what they were talking about, that did their homework and that would tell him the truth."[30]

Of course, Kautzky tested Kastama as well. Unfortunately for Kastama, Kautzky—with his military bearing, take-charge personality, and top-down command style—was Kastama's polar opposite.

"I was a participatory management type manager," said Kastama. "[I believed] that I could get things done faster and better with such an approach. I also believed [that a participatory management] approach brings about a transformation among staff over the long haul." For example, when Kastama was asked how he accomplished something, he wouldn't take credit for it. He may have given directions or developed a plan with his key staff, but he gave all the credit to the people who actually did the work. Kastama suspected that for a controller like Kautzky, this was seen as a weakness.[31]

In addition to their different management styles, Kastama had what he called "a rigid set of ethics" that guided his actions. "I said and did some things that got me into a lot of hot water," said Kastama. "I wasn't a company man. There was a feeling in the department that there were too many independent people, and I was one."[32]

Kastama displayed his independence when one of the state's assistant attorneys general asked him to testify at a compliance hearing associated with the Hoptowit case. The attorney wanted Kastama to say that the penitentiary could safely increase the number of inmates inside the walls. Kastama refused. Two of his associate superintendents—Larry Kincheloe being one of them—testified instead. They said it could be done.

On another occasion, Kastama strenuously objected to a cut in the penitentiary's education budget. "This was seen as an act of insubordination," he said.

Philosophically, Kastama was what he called "humanistically oriented." When interviewed about his philosophy of corrections, a newspaper reporter asked Kastama whether he was more in the punishment camp or the inmate rehabilitation camp. Kastama said rehabilitation, but "that wasn't the way the wind was blowing," he said.

With strikes like these against him, Kastama was, in Kautzky's eyes, the wrong person to be penitentiary superintendent. Furthermore, according to Kastama, there was no real communication between Kautzky and himself. "It was a matter of leaving...or be fired," he said.[33]

In May 1982, Kastama resigned. With Kastama gone, Kautzky turned to a fellow military man to lead the penitentiary: Larry Kincheloe.

Chapter 48

BUILDING BLOCKS

THERE IS NOTHING SEXY about training, standards, budgets, and holding people accountable for doing their jobs. But it was with these nuts and bolts that Reed and his staff built a modern correctional system in Washington State.

One of the first areas in which Reed emphasized accountability was cleanliness. While some progress had been made in cleaning up the penitentiary before Reed arrived—for example, by reducing the amount of property inmates could have in their cells—the penitentiary still had a long way to go.

It wasn't just that Reed was appalled by conditions at the penitentiary. Reed knew that the environment of a prison affects the behavior of inmates and staff alike. If the environment says "We don't care" or "You deserve no better," staff gets a good dose of behavior that fits the message. If the environment is clean and bright and well maintained, the message, and behavior, is different. As Robin Moses put it, "That was a major step in [Washington] corrections—a broom and a mop."[34]

Staff uniforms played a similar role. After Sergeant Cross was killed in 1979, the uniforms for correctional officers were changed to make officer and inmate clothing clearly distinguishable. But it took Reed, and especially Kautzky, to turn the uniform from an article of clothing into a message of professionalism.

According to Kautzky, when he first visited the penitentiary he saw correctional officers with wrinkled clothing, unshined shoes, and shirt-tails hanging out. For the meticulous Kautzky with his military background, this wouldn't do. But just as Reed understood that the environment can influence behavior, Kautzky knew that in a prison, pride in appearance was about more than just looking good. "The uniform issue is an interesting one," he said, "because if someone is dressed like a plumber they don't mind getting dirty like a plumber." But, he explained, if an officer looks sharp and has respect for his uniform, the way he interacts with inmates changes.[35] Like cleaning floors, inspection of officer dress raised the bar for everyone's behavior.

In addition to the early messages of professionalism and maintaining an orderly prison environment, a consistent and insistent theme of Reed and Kautzky was that prison operations be conducted in a way to keep people as safe as possible—staff and inmates alike.

Appointing Kincheloe superintendent both reinforced these messages and promoted the concept of a centralized, top-down command structure in which superintendents know that their future depends on satisfying the expectations of their superiors. Kincheloe knew how to follow orders, knew how to give orders and hold subordinates accountable, and commanded the respect of the correctional officers.

Early in Kincheloe's tenure as superintendent, the expectations of Reed and Kautzky began to be standardized and codified through written statements of the principles, rules, and guidelines that expressed the long-term goals of the agency—in other words, agency policy. With clearly expressed goals and expectations, it was up to each institution to develop effective procedures to carry out the agency's policies on a day-to-day basis. All this made perfect sense to a military man like Kincheloe.

After Kincheloe had been superintendent for about six months, Rich Mason, a newly promoted lieutenant, was put in charge of segregation. Within weeks, Mason implemented new procedures in segregation that emphasized safety, professionalism, and order. One of these procedures was how to conduct a cell search. To teach new officers the procedure, Mason would tell them two stories, prefaced with "You tell me which one's best." The first story was:

> You go down and get some inmate and jerk him out of his cell—stand him out on the tier with four or five guys on him with nightsticks. Tell him if he moves they're going to beat the hell out of him. You go in and you basically trash his cell—dump all his bedding on the ground, go through his garbage [and] turn it upside down—dump it in his cell.... [When you] put him back in there and slam the door...he's going to go off.

"That's scenario number one," Mason told the new officers, "and we've been doing that here for years."

Mason's second story began with a pat search of the inmate. After that, the inmate would be taken out of his cell and removed from the area, because the inmate "has no business seeing what you're doing when you do a cell search." In the cell search itself,

> when you…empty the garbage you put a clean sack back in the cell.…
> After you've checked the walls, ceiling, floors, and all the fixtures…you
> fold the mattress in half, fold his blankets up, fold his sheets up. You
> put the mattress at the foot of the bed, you put the blankets on top and
> the sheets on top of that. As you walk out of that cell—you can picture
> what it looks like—it's very clean, very organized, and you've performed
> a security process. When you put [the inmate] back in that cell, one of
> the first things he's gonna do is he's gonna [make his bed]. It's sublim-
> inal, but I've found [that with a cell search like that] you can actually
> have inmates make their own beds every day.[36]

Another new procedure was how to do a cell extraction—that is, how to forcefully remove an uncooperative inmate from his cell. This pro-cedure applied not just to segregation, but to the entire prison. Under the new procedure, all planned uses of force began with a supervisor briefing the officers on the situation and what each person was to do. Because cell extractions were one of the most dangerous procedures in the penitentiary, the intent of the plan was to accomplish the objec-tive while minimizing the likelihood of injury—especially injury to the officers, but also to the inmate, if possible. The entire use of force was videotaped, and the tapes were reviewed by a captain, associate superin-tendent, or superintendent. Officers were disciplined, and occasionally fired, if the tapes showed they had used inappropriate methods.

By the end of Kincheloe's first year as superintendent, other thought-ful approaches were starting to happen all through the adult corrections system. "That was part of the whole procedure thing," explained Tana Wood, one of the principal authors of many agency policies and peni-tentiary procedures. Standard policies and procedures, she said, "were a major, major improvement on a lot of levels."[37]

While new policies and procedures were taking hold, unit team management was growing stronger. In addition to having a non-custody person in charge of each unit, formerly centralized services, like counseling and classification of inmates by security level, now occurred where the inmates lived. Having counselors and other non-custody staff in the unit did several important things. First, it gave inmates greater access to services and potential problem solving. In addition, it gave staff a better idea of what was going on in the lives of inmates and how they behaved in their normal living environment. Regular meetings involving the unit supervisor, counselors, custody staff, the inmate, and relevant specialists took place to develop, monitor, and update individual case management plans. Unit team management began to reduce the "us against them" mentality that had characterized the relationship between inmates and penitentiary staff in the past.

During Kincheloe's second year as superintendent, the quadrant system and movement controls envisioned by the architects were completed. The movement controls and associated gate pass system gave the penitentiary the ability to manage smaller groups of inmates in isolation from one another. People who should be kept apart were kept apart. This system proved a critical factor in reducing violence inside the walls.

While all of these initiatives were important, the cornerstone of changing the culture inside the penitentiary and elsewhere in Washington prisons was surely enhanced training. During the same legislative session that created the department of corrections, the legislature mandated that the state Criminal Justice Training Commission develop new training standards for correctional officers and that all new correctional hires at both the state and local level be required to successfully complete a lengthy and rigorous training regimen. By the time Kincheloe became superintendent, the new curriculum for correctional officers was in place. New training was also created for officers promoted to sergeant, lieutenant, and captain. It didn't happen overnight, but as new hires replaced those who transferred, were promoted, retired, or quit, the correctional officer corps and their leaders became increasingly well trained.

In a similar way, training, mentoring, and job rotations through a newly created Career Executive Program developed management skills for headquarters personnel and created expertise for successive generations of leaders.

Finally, both training and accountability were enhanced through a system of regular inspections by trained staff who reviewed performance at each facility multiple times per year. If the inspectors observed a potential security hazard—inadequate tool control, for example—they would point out the problem, suggest possible solutions, and require a corrective action plan. Subsequent inspections would pay particular attention to areas previously found wanting.

It was a comprehensive system implemented quickly and with skill. And behind it all loomed taskmasters Reed and Kautzky.

Chapter 49

IMU

REMOVING SEGREGATION from the middle of the institution was the final piece of the puzzle. Changing the design of the segregation unit after the architects' original plans had been finalized delayed the start of construction and the date by which the unit could be opened. Not only did the architects have to start over from scratch with a new and very particular client, but the department of corrections had to mollify various influential legislators over what the legislature perceived as a change in use of appropriated funds from one purpose to another. After these delays, construction contracts were let, and work began on the Intensive Management Unit, or IMU, in the summer of 1983.

With construction underway, the design of the IMU was set—but design is just the beginning. How a building is organized and constructed can make certain things harder or easier. How the building is used is up to the user.

Larry Kincheloe approached Dick Morgan and said, "I don't know who's going to end up running the IMU, but I need somebody to start writing the policies and procedures for [how to run it]. Would you like to do it?"[38] Morgan jumped at the chance.

"[Kincheloe] ran down the philosophy of what he wanted," said Morgan. "Larry, I think, would freely admit that he was just parroting what Kautzky had told him he wanted in terms of the procedures [for the] IMU and what the mission...of that unit would be. And pure and simple, that was: 'Don't let anybody ever get hurt.'"

"I went through our current segregation policies and procedures," said Morgan, "and looked at all of the things that we hated that made our lives miserable...and caused inmates to get killed and so on. And those things were just so obvious." For example, segregation staff had routinely allowed four to sixteen people out of their cells at the same time to use a common recreation area. This practice invariably led to fights, confrontations with staff, or inmates refusing to lock up. Sometimes it led to murder. Segregation staffers were so accustomed to operating that way, said Morgan, "that nobody thought you could do things differently."

Morgan devised a policy which made it possible to never have more than one IMU inmate at a time in a dayroom or exercise area. With four dayrooms, four exercise areas, and ninety-six single cells, every inmate could have an hour outside his cell during normal waking hours every day of the week.

Morgan also knew that in the existing segregation unit, confrontations with the officers during any inmate movement were a serious problem. "So we had to have a method of moving inmates from point A to point B that would prevent staff from getting hurt," said Morgan. The solution was to require inmates to be cuffed up whenever they were moved. The procedure Morgan proposed was a new approach that had been successfully used in Big Red for the previous year or two: inmates would place their hands behind their backs and hold them next to the wicket used to pass food trays through the cell door. An officer would apply the cuffs from outside before signaling to the control room officer to open the door. If the inmate didn't cooperate, he could miss his shower, visit, or exercise period.

Morgan reviewed the segregation logs and counted the number of fires that had occurred each month. According to Morgan, "no month went by without at least twenty fires in seg." So Morgan proposed a no-smoking policy.

While he was talking with other officers, the subject of inmates keistering contraband—concealing drugs or weapons in their rectum—came up. Morgan made a mental note. He concluded, "That's something that's got to be taken care of."

While Morgan was working on the IMU policies, he knew one of the department's assistant attorneys general well enough that he could call her directly and ask questions. He wanted to know whether ideas he was proposing would stand up in a court of law. He talked to the AG about the proposed no-smoking policy. He asked her whether it was legal to do a digital probe search of an inmate's rectum as part of the IMU admissions process.

The AG researched the issues and telephoned Morgan. "They don't have a constitutional right to smoke," she told him, "and there's enough case law precedent set that if you can demonstrate that these are really bad guys, it's okay to probe search them."

Morgan reviewed his proposals with the superintendent. According to Morgan, Kincheloe said, "Probe searching, hmm. Well, maybe. What else?" When Morgan told him about the no-smoking plan, Kincheloe told him, "Oh, no. Nobody will go for that....Spalding will never go for that. He's a smoker." But Kincheloe didn't veto the idea, and he took Morgan to meet with Kautzky and Spalding to go over the draft IMU policies.

When Morgan outlined the proposal for rectal probe searches, Kautzky asked why. "I would at least like to start the IMU out contraband-free," replied Morgan. "No weapons, no drugs, no matches, no nothing." Recalling the conversation, Morgan said, "They picked up on 'no matches.'"

Then Kincheloe told them, "And he doesn't want them to smoke out there, either." Spalding was surprised and asked for clarification. "You mean you don't want them to smoke in their rooms," he said. "You'll let them smoke out in the dayrooms and the yard. Right?"

"No," said Morgan.[39]

The meeting stopped, and someone suggested they call one of the department's assistant attorneys general. When the assistant AG walked into Kautzky's office, it was the same one who had researched the issues for Morgan. Kautzky asked about smoking and probe searches and the attorney repeated what she had told Morgan.

There were a few more meetings with Kautzky on the proposed IMU policies. After some additions and modifications, the policies were approved—including no smoking and probe searches.[40]

When it came time to select the officer to run the IMU, Kincheloe told Morgan to apply for captain. Morgan was promoted and put in charge of the unit.

About the same time, Jim Blodgett was hired as a fourth associate superintendent at the penitentiary. A childhood friend of Jim Spalding's,

The Intensive Management Unit (IMU)

Blodgett had been a deputy warden at the Montana State Prison in Deer Lodge. Blodgett's areas of responsibility at the penitentiary included maintenance, some of the cellblocks, and the IMU. Blodgett became Morgan's immediate superior.

Construction on the IMU had just been completed when Blodgett arrived in January 1984. Before the official opening—still months away—a trial run was conducted with inmates in one of the unit's eight pods. Procedures were tested while staff learned how to run the unit, including how to use state-of-the-art electronic controls and communications new to the penitentiary. The trial run didn't go well at first.

"When IMU first opened, there were a lot of [inmates] who were trying to trash it," said Blodgett. Inmates in a pod would throw feces and food out on the tier. They would go on hunger strikes. According to Blodgett, the staff tried a variety of means intended to control the acting-out behavior, including use of force and fire hoses. Nothing really worked. Eventually, the inmates seemed to tire of doing the same things over and over and never making progress. With less acting out and more experienced and better-trained officers, there was less and less need for use of force in the IMU.[41]

After the IMU settled down and more pods were filled, Kautzky arrived for his debut tour. Dick Morgan recalled the event and what Kautzky did and said. "Show me your unit, captain," said Kautzky. Morgan took him through the sparkling new unit, but the tour went faster than expected. Morgan departed from his prearranged tour and asked Kautzky if he would like to see a cell. Kautzky immediately said, "Well, sure, captain."[42]

Morgan knew that a particular cell was empty because the inmate was out in the exercise yard. The control officer popped the door, and Kautzky walked in.

To Morgan's eye, it was a beautiful segregation cell. There was nothing in it but the inmate's bed and properly folded linen. Kautzky went to the sink and saw a stain on the wall where the inmate had apparently splashed a little soup while cleaning his bowl.

"Tell me, captain, how long has this been going on?" asked Kautzky.

Taken aback, Morgan looked at Kautzky and said, "It wasn't there yesterday, sir."[43]

Kautzky stormed out without saying another word.

Morgan was in shock. The director of the Division of Prisons had toured his unit and left in apparent disgust over a day-old soup stain.

Morgan was ready to resign. He told Kincheloe, "I don't know what this man expects, what level of perfection he expects—but I can't live up to that level."

Kincheloe said, "I don't think you get the point."

"So tell me, what *is* the point?" asked Morgan.

"Kautzky didn't go anywhere in that building you didn't offer to take him, and he never will," said Kincheloe. "If you took him somewhere you shouldn't, that's your fault."[44]

From that day forward, as long as Morgan was IMU captain, they never put an inmate in cell 3D. Every time Kautzky visited, Morgan took him to 3D, and it was just as clean every time. "He never asked to see any other cells," said Morgan, "and we got along fine after that."

The IMU was the last big piece of the puzzle in modernization of the Washington State Penitentiary. It solved all the problems that had plagued Big Red. Inmate troublemakers no longer had to be sent out of state. The penitentiary could take care of its own.

Chapter 50

THREE YEARS LATER

Toward the end of 1988, Larry Kincheloe was promoted into the central office. Jim Blodgett, who had left to be superintendent at one of Washington's prison camps, returned to the penitentiary as Kincheloe's replacement.

Blodgett, who had heard stories of the 1970s—many of them from his friend Jim Spalding as they were happening—had only experienced the penitentiary after it was well on the way to recovery. Nonetheless, the penitentiary he took over in 1988 was a different place than the one he had known as associate superintendent only a few years earlier.

"There were still some remnants from the 1970s," said Blodgett. For example, some of the bikers continued to wear their leather chaps and jackets, minus any designation of club affiliation.[45] But the ugliest and most tragic manifestations of the '70s were gone.

By 1988, "assaults on staff were very, very [uncommon]," said Blodgett. About the only staff injuries occurred during use-of-force situations, and because of improved procedures and training, even these were rare. Escapes—which had continued to be a problem at the penitentiary through the middle 1980s—were almost nonexistent. During Blodgett's years as superintendent, only one inmate went missing for twenty-four hours, and he was hiding inside the institution. "That was a great indicator," said Blodgett, "that things were going in the right direction in a lot of different areas."[46] These "things" included unit teams that were able to anticipate problems, experienced and well-trained staff effectively doing their jobs, security systems and procedures that worked, the ability to isolate troublemakers in the IMU, and reduced danger to inmates from the violence that had been so common in the past.

Gone were the factory firearms and ammunition, zip guns, store-bought knives, finely crafted shanks, and homemade bombs. According to Blodgett, the most common weapon found in the late 1980s was a slashing instrument made out of a plastic toothbrush melted to hold a razor blade. Jim Hartford, whose collection of prison-made weapons was now used for training, said there was no longer any "pride in workmanship" in the weapons the inmates made.[47]

The penitentiary and the department of corrections were much bigger when Blodgett took over than at the beginning of the decade. At the penitentiary, a large medium-security complex was in operation west of the main institution. To the east, a vacant building had been converted to house minimum security inmates needed for grounds and building maintenance outside the walls. The department of corrections had opened three new medium security institutions, including a growing presence on McNeil Island, the site of a former federal penitentiary. Part of one of the new institutions could be used as an IMU, and an additional IMU was built at another prison.

Staff turnover, which had exceeded 50 percent per year in the mid-1970s, was greatly reduced. During one six-month period while Blodgett was superintendent, nobody left.

Of course, there were new problems. The Hispanic population was growing, including increasing numbers of Mexican-Americans from the northern and southern California street gangs, the Norteños and Sureños. These archenemies with their creed of "fight on sight" created new challenges. As Jim Hartford said, "There's still a job there. There always will be."[48]

But for the most part, the problems Blodgett and his successors had to deal with were the problems all high-level institutional managers continually face: priorities, budgets, personnel matters, grievances, staff morale, lawsuits, public relations, plant maintenance, service quality, planning. It's a long list.

The job of penitentiary superintendent has never been easy, but by the late 1980s it was becoming routine—just like it's supposed to be.

AFTERWORD

THERE IS STILL A PRISON AT 1313 North Thirteenth Avenue, but change is everywhere. Some buildings sit vacant, slowly deteriorating under the hot summer sun and freezing Walla Walla winters. No one climbs the towers or mans the walls—the ten acres they enclose now demoted to minimum security where such things are no longer needed.

Some old-time inmates claim ghosts roam the halls of the now empty hospital, where naked inmates chained to their beds once wallowed in their own excrement. The corner office of the "new" administration building sits empty. Only memories remain of Spalding conducting business from his office floor while lying flat on his pain-racked back. A nondescript manhole cover in the pavement outside the still massive chow halls marks the approximate spot where Sergeant Cross was killed.

On adjacent land, a gleaming new prison complex dwarfs the institution whose name it has usurped. The state's most dangerous prisoners reside within its miles of sixteen-foot-high double fences and razor wire. The Washington State Penitentiary continues in this new guise, living out chapters not yet written.

Many of the people who cast long shadows during the '70s and early '80s are gone: Bill Conte, B. J. Rhay, Bob Tropp, Jim Spalding, Amos Reed. Others who shared their stories farther from the limelight have also passed away.

In 1992 Tana Wood followed Jim Blodgett as penitentiary superintendent. Later, John Lambert and Dick Morgan occupied the superintendent's office. After leaving Washington in 1987, Kip Kautzky became director of corrections in Colorado for twelve years and in Iowa for six. Robin Moses, along with many others, soldiered on until retirement, doing the unglamorous day-to-day work that contributes so much to the safety, security, and even humanity of prisons.

After his years as penitentiary superintendent, Dick Morgan became director of the Division of Prisons for the Washington State Department of Corrections. As director, Morgan's responsibilities included anticipating problems over the horizon and how they might best be addressed. One such problem was aging inmates, some of whom he'd known since he was a young officer in 1976.

One day, while touring one of the state's more modern prisons, Director Morgan came upon an old biker pushing a broom as part of his job to keep the area clean. Morgan stopped to talk. "Tommy," he said, "I've been thinking about creating a unit at the pen where the old-timers can live and not be bothered by all these youngsters. What do you think of that?"

The inmate paused as he leaned on his broom, memories no doubt flashing through his mind. Perhaps he saw youthful faces of men he'd fought, or recalled unsettled scores. Whatever his thoughts, he let Morgan know his idea might present some problems. "I don't know, Mr. Morgan," he said as he stroked his chin. "We may be old, but we ain't forgot."[1]

APPENDICES

APPENDIX A
List of Persons Mentioned
With positions held during time period of book

NAME	POSITION(S)
Blodgett, James	Associate Superintendent, Superintendent, WSP
Browne, John Henry	Assistant Attorney General, DSHS
Chadek, Steve	Correctional Officer, Union President, WSP
Conte, William R. (Bill)	Director, Department of Institutions
Cross, William (Bill)	Sergeant, WSP
Crowley, Arthur (Art)	Associate Superintendent for Custody, WSP
Cummins, James (Jim)	Chaplain, Associate Superintendent for Treatment, WSP
Edwards, Parley	Correctional Officer, Union President, WSP
Emery, Richard	Director, Prison Legal Services
Evans, Daniel J.	Governor, Washington State
Excell, Steve	Deputy Chief of Staff, Chief of Staff, Governor John Spellman
Freeman, Robert (Bob)	Associate Superintendent for Treatment, WSP
Genakos, Nicholas	Associate Superintendent for Custody, Superintendent, WSP
Graham, Gordon (Gordy)	Inmate, RGC President, WSP
Harris, John (Johnnie)	Inmate, RGC President, WSP
Hartford, James (Jim)	Correctional Officer, Sergeant, WSP
Harvey, James (Jim)	Associate Superintendent for Custody, WSP
Hoffman, Ethan	Professional photographer
Horowitz, Donald (Don)	Senior Assistant Attorney General, DSHS
Kastama, C. R. M. (Bob)	Superintendent, WSP
Kautzky, Walter L. (Kip)	Director, Division of Prisons, Department of Corrections
Kincheloe, Lawrence (Larry)	Associate Superintendent, Superintendent, WSP
Lambert, John	Correctional Officer, Sergeant, Lieutenant, WSP
Macklin, William (Bill)	Associate Superintendent for Custody, WSP
Mason, Richard (Rich)	Correctional Officer, Sergeant, Lieutenant, WSP
McCoy, John	Journalist, Author

NAME	POSITION(S)
McCoy, Steve	Inmate, WSP
McGough, John	Architect, Walker McGough Foltz Lyerla
McNutt, Harlan	Secretary, DSHS
Miller, Barbara	Paralegal, Prison Legal Services
Morgan, Richard (Dick)	Correctional Officer, Sergeant, Lieutenant, Captain, WSP
Morris, Charles R. (Charlie)	Secretary, DSHS
Moses, Carol	Classification Counselor; Supervisor, Classification and Parole, WSP
Moses, Robin	Correctional Officer, Union President, Sergeant, Lieutenant, Captain, WSP
Ray, Dixy Lee	Governor, Washington State
Reed, Amos	Secretary, Department of Corrections
Ressler, Allen	Attorney, Prison Legal Services
Rhay, B. J. (Bob, Bobby)	Superintendent, WSP
Rosellini, Albert	Governor, Washington State
Shaughnessey, John	Assistant Director for Management, Division of Adult Corrections, DSHS
Smith, Sidney (Sid)	Secretary, DSHS
Spalding, James C. (Jim)	Correctional Officer, Sergeant, Lieutenant, Captain, Superintendent, WSP; Deputy Director, Division of Prisons, Department of Corrections
Spellman, John D.	Governor, Washington State
St. Peter, Arthur	Inmate, WSP
Tanner, Jack	Judge, United Stated District Court for Western Washington
Thomas, Gerald (Gerry)	Deputy Secretary, Acting Secretary, DSHS
Thompson, Gerald (Gerry)	Secretary, DSHS
Travisono, Anthony	Executive Director, American Correctional Association
Tropp, Robert (Bob)	Deputy Director, Director, Division of Adult Corrections, DSHS
Vinzant, Douglas (Doug)	Superintendent, WSP; Director, Division of Adult Corrections, DSHS
Wood, Tana	Associate Superintendent, WSP

APPENDIX B

List of Persons Interviewed
With highest position held during time period of book

NAME	POSITION(S)	INTERVIEW DATE(S)
Agtuca, Kenneth	Inmate	Mar 15, 2011
Anderson, Michael	Inmate	Aug 18, 2010
Anonymous	Inmate	Aug 17, 2010
Bender, Paul*	Chief of Staff, Governor Dixy Lee Ray	Jun 28, 1994
Blodgett, James (Jim)**	Superintendent, WSP	Aug 12, 2014
Bradley, Richard *	Chief, DOC Capital Programs	Mar 15, 1993
Browne, John Henry	Assistant Attorney General, DSHS	Jul 29, 1994 Aug 12, 1994
Burfitt, Walter	Plant Manager, WSP	Feb 07, 1994
Chadek, Steve	Corr. Officer/Union Pres., WSP	Jun 21, 1994
Collins, William*	Asst. Attorney General, DSHS Senior Asst. Attorney General, DOC	Jun 08, 1994
Conte, William R. (Bill)	Director, Dept. of Institutions	Jan 18, 1994 Feb 11, 1994
Dellaire, Greg	Director, Prison Legal Services	Jan 13, 1995
Edwards, Parley	Corr. Officer/Union President, WSP	Jun 22, 1994
Eggers, Arthur (Art)	Prosecuting Attorney, Walla Walla County	May 17, 1993
Emery, Richard**	Director, Prison Legal Services	Jul 15, 1994
Evans, Daniel J. (Dan)	Governor, Washington State	Jul 12, 1994 Jul 25, 1994
Excell, Steve	Chief of Staff, Gov. John Spellman	Aug 27, 2014
Freeman, Robert (Bob)	Associate Superintendent, WSP	Aug 13, 1993 Aug 14, 1993
Graham, Gordon (Gordy)*	Inmate, RGC President	Jul 28, 1994
Grisby, Henry	Inmate	Aug 17, 2010
Hall, Frank **	Commissioner, Massachusetts DOC	Apr 28, 1994
Hartford, James (Jim)	Sergeant, WSP	Aug 14, 1993
Harvey, James (Jim)	Assoc. Superintendent, WSP	Feb 18, 1994

NAME	POSITION(S)	INTERVIEW DATE(S)
Horowitz, Donald (Don)	Sr. Assistant Attorney General, DSHS	Feb 10, 1994 Feb 23, 1994 April 01, 1994
Johnson, Curtis (CJ)	Inmate	Aug 16, 2010
Kastama, C. R. M. (Bob)	Superintendent, WSP	Mar 29, 1993
Kautzky, Walter L. (Kip)**	Director, DOC Division of Prisons	Apr 03, 2012
John King	Legislative Liaison, DOC	Aug 13, 2012
Kincheloe, Lawrence (Larry)	Superintendent, WSP	May 02, 03, 09, 12, 1994
Lambert, John	Lieutenant, WSP	Aug 13, 1993
Mason, Richard (Rich)**	Lieutenant, WSP	Sep 29, 2011
Masten, George *	Executive Director, Washington Federation of Public Employees	May 06, 1993
McNutt, Harlan	Secretary, DSHS	Mar 22, 1994
Midgley, John	Attorney, Prison Legal Services	Mar 23, 1994 Apr 12, 1994
Miller, Barbara	Paralegal, Prison Legal Services	Apr 22, 1994 Jun 08, 1994
Morgan, Richard (Dick)	Captain, WSP	Aug 15, 1993
Morris, Charles R. (Charlie)**	Secretary, DSHS	Mar 27, 1994 Mar 31, 1994 Apr 09, 1994
Moses, Carol	Supervisor, Classification and Parole, WSP	Jan 14, 1994
Moses, Robin	Captain, WSP	Jan 14, 1994
Prater, Harry	Inmate, WSP	Aug 16, 2010
Ressler, Allen	Attorney, Prison Legal Services	Jun 01, 1994
Rhay, B. J. (Bob)	Superintendent, WSP	Aug 13, 1993 Aug 14, 1993
Riggens, David	Inmate, WSP	Sep 27, 1994
Rosellini, Albert	Governor, Washington State	Apr 26, 1994
Shaughnessey, John	Deputy Director, Adult Corr. Div., DSHS	Jul 30, 1993 Aug 18, 1993
Smith, Sidney (Sid)	Secretary, DSHS	Sep 28, 1993
Spalding, James C. (Jim)	Deputy Director, DOC Division of Prisons	Apr 20, 1993 Apr 29, 1993
Thatcher, James*	Administrator, DSHS/DOC	May 20, 1993

NAME	POSITION(S)	INTERVIEW DATE(S)
Thomas, Gerald (Gerry)	Deputy Secretary, DSHS	May 10, 1993 Aug 19, 1993 Oct 06, 1993
Thompson, Gerald (Gerry)	Secretary, DSHS	Mar 03, 1994 Mar 16, 1994
Todd, Eddie	Inmate	Aug 18, 2010
Travisono, Anthony**	Executive Director, American Correctional Association	Jul 16, 1993
Tropp, Robert (Bob)	Director, Div. of Adult Corrections, DSHS	May 06, 1993 May 20, 1993 Jun 10, 1993
Vernon, Richard (Dick)	Director, DOC Division of Prisons	Jul 05, 1994
Vinzant, Douglas (Doug)**	Director, Div. of Adult Corrections, DSHS	Apr 22, 1994 Apr 29, 1994
Wood, Tana **	Assoc. Superintendent, WSP	May 18, 2012

* Notes only (not tape recorded)
** Telephone interview

NOTES

Preface

1. Douglas Lipton, Robert Martinson, Judith Wilks, *Effectiveness of Correctional Treatment: A Survey of Treatment Evaluation Studies* (Westport: Praeger Publishers, 1975).

2. Holt v. Sarver, 309 F. Supp. 362 (E.D. Ark. 1970).

Part 1: Super Custody Before 1970

1. Gordon Graham, *The One-Eyed Man Is King*, 1982, p. 61. © Instar Performance LLC.

2. James Spalding (former correctional officer, sergeant, lieutenant, captain, and superintendent, Washington State Penitentiary), in discussion with the author, April 20, 1993.

3. Jim Cummins, Washington State Penitentiary Catholic priest, videotape transcript, "Walla Walla," King-TV, 1972, Washington State Archives, Records of the Department of Social and Health Services, Division of Adult Corrections, 1971–81.

4. Ibid.

5. B. J. Rhay (former superintendent, Washington State Penitentiary), in discussion with the author, August 13, 1993.

6. Ibid.

7. Erle Stanley Gardner is perhaps best known for creating the detective character featured in novels, short stories, films, radio dramas, and several TV series, Perry Mason.

8. Spalding, April 1993.

9. "Possible Medical Career Changes to Penology," *Walla Walla Union-Bulletin*, November 28, 1971.

10. Carol Moses (former administrator, Washington State Penitentiary), in discussion with the author, January 14, 1994.

11. Parley Edwards (former correctional officer, Washington State Penitentiary), in discussion with the author, June 22, 1994.

12. William R. Conte (former director, Department of Institutions), in discussion with the author, January 18, 1994.

13. Ibid.

14. Ibid.

15. Ibid.

16. Daniel J. Evans (Washington State governor, 1965–77), in discussion with the author, July 12, 1994.

17. Conte, January 1994.

Part 2: Changes 1970–1973

1. Rhay, August 1993.

2. William R. Conte, letter to Charles Stastny, Ph.D., Harvard University, July 9, 1981; personal papers of William R. Conte.

3. Conte, January 1994.

4. B. J. Rhay, "Observations on European Correctional Systems," *Planning Prospectus*, Department of Social and Health Services Division of Institutions, Adult Corrections, 1970.

5. Ibid.

6. Ibid.

7. Conte, January 1994.

8. *Minutes*, Adult Corrections Leadership Conference, July 28/29, 1970 and October 5/6, 1970; personal papers of William R. Conte.

9. "Chicano" was the term used at the penitentiary during the 1970s.

10. "Prison Begins Unique Program of Minority Group Culture Sessions," *Walla Walla Union-Bulletin*, November 1, 1970.

11. Rhay, August, 1993.

12. "B.P.F.U. Past and Present," *Voice of Prison*, September, 1974.

13. *Washington Public Employee*, March 1970, Washington Federation of State Employees, Council 28, AFL-CIO.

14. Letter to Richard Hemstad from William R. Conte, January 13, 1970.

15. Evans, July 1994.

16. Sidney Smith (former secretary, Washington State Department of Social and Health Services), in discussion with the author, September 28, 1993.

17. Ibid.

18. Stastny & Tyrnauer, *Who Rules the Joint*, Lexington Books, 1982, page 85.

19. Memorandum #70-4 to All Superintendents from L. Delmore Jr., Chief, Office of Adult Corrections, November 6, 1970; personal papers of William R. Conte.

20. Memorandum #70-5 to All Superintendents from L. Delmore, November 6, 1970; personal papers of William R. Conte.

21. Memoranda #70-6 and #70-7 to All Superintendents from L. Delmore, November 6, 1970; personal papers of William R. Conte.

22. Audio tape, March 1, 1972, Whitman College, Penrose Library Archives, Washington State Penitentiary Collection.

23. William R. Conte, Discussion in Depth, Seattle Center, November 18, 1970; personal papers of William R. Conte.

24. Ibid.

25. Ibid.

26. Memorandum #70-7 to All Superintendents from L. Delmore, November 6, 1970; personal papers of William R. Conte.

27. Donald Horowitz (former senior assistant attorney general, Washington State Department of Social & Health Services), in discussion with the author, February 10, 1994.

28. Donald Horowitz, Discussion in Depth, Seattle Center, November 18, 1970; personal papers of William R. Conte.

29. Rhay, August 1993.

30. "Inmate Strike Slows Prison," *Walla Walla Union-Bulletin*, December 22, 1970.

31. "Letters Indicate Beards Not Only Prison Issue," *Walla Walla Union-Bulletin*, December 24, 1970.

32. Letter from Don Wesley Cole to William R. Conte, December 17, 1970, personal papers of William R. Conte.

33. Letter from William R. Conte to Don Wesley Cole, December 7, 1970, personal papers of William R. Conte.

34. Letter to William R. Conte from Don Wesley Cole, et al., December 19, 1970, personal papers of William R. Conte.

35. Conte, February 1994.

36. Letter from William R. Conte to B. J. Rhay, December 22, 1970, personal papers of William R. Conte.

37. Letter to Don Wesley Cole, et al., from William R. Conte, December 24, 1970.

38. Confidential memo to the file "A Tragedy at Walla Walla," William R. Conte (undated), personal papers of William R. Conte.

39. "Prisoners' Strike Begins 2nd Week," *Walla Walla Union-Bulletin*, December 29, 1970.

40. Horowitz, February 1994.

41. "Conte, Inmates, Air Prison Topics, Plans," *Walla Walla Union-Bulletin*, January 10, 1971.

42. Robert Freeman (former associate superintendent, Washington State Penitentiary), in discussion with the author, August 13, 1993.

43. "Prison Inmate Killed in Stabbing; No Weapon Found," *Walla Walla Union-Bulletin*, February 2, 1971.

44. Rhay, August 1993.

45. Ethan Hoffman and John McCoy, *Concrete Mama: Prison Profiles from Walla Walla* (Columbia, University of Missouri Press, 1981), 6.

46. "Guards Wary of Liberalization," *Walla Walla Union-Bulletin*, April 19, 1971.

47. Ibid.

48. Ibid.

49. Gordon Graham, *The One-Eyed Man Is King* (Gordon Graham & Co., 1982), 93. Permission to quote is gratefully acknowledged to the copyright holder, Instar Performance LLC.

50. "Penal Democratization, the Story of Self-Government in Prison," *Voice of Prison*, February 8, 1972.

51. Harold Allen, inmate, videotape transcript, "Walla Walla," King-TV, April 17, 1972, Washington State Archives, Records of the Department of Social and Health Services, Division of Adult Corrections, 1971-81.

52. Johnnie Harris, inmate, videotape transcript, "Walla Walla," King-TV.

53. "Penal Democratization," *Voice of Prison*, February 8, 1972.

54. Allen, videotape transcript, "Walla Walla," King-TV.

55. Gordon Graham (former inmate, Washington State Penitentiary) in discussion with the author, July 28, 1994.

56. Graham, *The One-Eyed Man Is King,* 94-96.

57. Ibid.

58. Rhay, videotape transcript, "Walla Walla," King-TV.

59. "Penal Democratization," *Voice of Prison,* February 8, 1972.

60. "A new way to run the Big House," *Life,* September 8, 1972.

61. Superintendent's Memorandum, May 5, 1971, Washington State Archives, Daniel J. Evans Papers, 1965-77.

62. Governor's undated notes, 1971, Washington State Archives, Daniel J. Evans Papers, 1965-77.

63. *The One-Eyed Man Is King,* 96.

64. "'Lifers With Hope' One of Four Organizations in U.S.," *Walla Walla Union-Bulletin,* August 8, 1971.

65. "Indian Inmates Powwow at Pen," *Walla Walla Union-Bulletin,* August 1, 1971.

66. Governor Evans's undated notes, 1971.

67. "Letter Rules Tightened," *Walla Walla Union-Bulletin,* July 18, 1971.

68. Freeman, August 1993.

69. "At Washington Prisons, Letter Rules Tightened," *Walla Walla Union-Bulletin,* July 18, 1971.

70. "Inmates Make Own Rules," *Walla Walla Union-Bulletin,* August 1, 1971.

71. Letter from William R. Conte to Daniel J. Evans, June 3, 1971, Washington State Archives, Daniel J. Evans Papers, 1965-77.

72. Letter from William R. Conte to Charles Stastny, July 9, 1981, personal papers of William R. Conte.

73. Smith, September 1993.

74. Horowitz, February 1994.

75. Gerald Thomas (former assistant secretary, Washington State Department of Social and Health Services), in discussion with the author, August 19, 1993.

76. Evans, July 25, 1994.

77. Rhay, August 1993.

78. Evans, July 25, 1994.

79. Rhay, August 1993.

80. "Narcotics, Homosexuality Charged By Former Prison Custody Chief," *Walla Walla Union-Bulletin,* September 12, 1971.

81. The death toll at Attica prison would later to rise to forty-three.

82. "The Hill: 'Long Way From Attica,'" *Walla Walla Union-Bulletin,* September 15, 1971.

83. "Inmate Council Banquet Draws 200," *Walla Walla Union-Bulletin,* October 13, 1971.

84. "Prisons Take a Giant Step," *Newsweek,* November 1, 1971.

85. "Rhay Defends Pen, Blasts Brockett," *Walla Walla Union-Bulletin,* January 28, 1972.

86. Audio tape, March 1, 1972, Whitman College, Penrose Library Archives, Washington State Penitentiary Collection.

87. "State's Prison 'Most Significant'—Rhay," *Walla Walla Union-Bulletin,* April 7, 1972.

88. Barry Farrell, "A New Way to Run the Big House," *Life,* September 8, 1972.

89. Rhay, August 1993.

90. Smith, September 1993.

91. Anonymous (inmate, Washington State Department of Corrections), in discussion with the author, August 17, 2010.

92. Kenneth Agtuca (inmate, Washington State Department of Corrections), in discussion with the author, March 15, 2011.

93. William Conte, unpublished manuscript, "Comments and Recommendations—Visit to Walla Walla on January 8, 1971."

94. "Inmates Issue 'Shutdown' Ultimatum Over Hospital," *Walla Walla Union-Bulletin,* December 9, 1971.

95. *Walla Walla Union-Bulletin,* December 9, 1971.

96. "Prison Conditions Substandard, Doctor Tells Olympia Committee," *Walla Walla Union-Bulletin,* January 14, 1972.

97. Ibid.

98. "Inmates Cite Reduction In Pill Line in Letter," *Walla Walla Union-Bulletin,* February 21, 1972.

99. Anonymous, in discussion with the author, August 17, 2010.

100. Ibid.

101. "Prison Inmate on Furlough Held In Shooting Death of Trooper," *Walla Walla Union-Bulletin,* February 7, 1972.

102. "Governor Announces Eight-Point Plan to Tighten Furlough Program at Prison," *Walla Walla Union-Bulletin*, February 11, 1972.

103. "Arthur St. Peter Charged in Slaying," *Walla Walla Union-Bulletin*, May 7, 1972.

104. Ibid.

105. "Reform in Interest of Public Safety," *Walla Walla Union-Bulletin*, May 22, 1972.

106. Barry Farrell, "A New Way to Run the Big House," *Life*, September 8, 1972.

107. Ibid.

108. "Inmate Stabbed to Death," *Walla Walla Union-Bulletin*, April 25, 1972.

109. "Black Manifesto—22," undated.

110. "Outline of Agreement," signed July 27, 1972, Washington State Archives, Daniel J. Evans Papers, 1965-77.

111. Barbara Miller (former paralegal, Prison Legal Services, Washington State), in discussion with the author, June 8, 1994.

112. Freeman, August 1993.

113. Walt Burfitt (former plant manager, Washington State Penitentiary), in discussion with the author, February 7, 1994.

114. Anthony Travisono (Executive Director, American Correctional Association), in discussion with the author, July 16, 1993.

115. *Walla Walla Union-Bulletin*, September 15, 1972.

116. Ibid.

117. Telegram, Arthur Klundt and A. L. Watts to the Honorable Daniel J. Evans, September 12, 1972, Washington State Archives, Daniel J. Evans Papers, 1965-77.

118. "Rosellini Gets Support From Guards at 'Deteriorating' Prison," *Walla Walla Union-Bulletin*, October 25, 1972.

119. "Rosellini Attacks Administration of State's Penal Reform Programs," *Walla Walla Union-Bulletin*, November 2, 1972.

120. "Prison Self-Government Halted," *Walla Walla Union-Bulletin*, November 27, 1972.

121. Rhay, August 1993.

122. "Penal Democratization," *Voice of Prison*, February 8, 1972.

123. George Jackson, *Soledad Brother* (Coward-McCann, 1970).

124. Robin Moses (former correctional officer, sergeant, lieutenant and captain, Washington State Penitentiary), in discussion with the author, January 14, 1994.

125. Steve Chadek (former correctional officer and union president, Washington State Penitentiary), in discussion with the author, June 21, 1994.

126. Ibid.

127. Ibid.

128. Ibid.

129. John Henry Browne (former Assistant Attorney General, Washington State Department of Social and Health Services), in discussion with the author, July 29, 1994.

130. Ibid.

131. Donald Horowitz (former senior assistant attorney general, Washington State Department of Social & Health Services), in discussion with the author, April 1, 1994.

132. Richard Emery (former director, Prison Legal Services, Washington State), in discussion with the author, July 15, 1994.

133. Browne, July 1994.

134. Ibid.

135. Emery, July 1994.

136. Horowitz, February 1994.

137. Ibid.

138. Allen Ressler (former attorney, Prison Legal Services, Washington State), in discussion with the author, June 1, 1994.

Part 3: Descent 1973–1977

1. Evans, July 1994.

2. Ibid.

3. Charles Morris (former secretary, Washington State Department of Social and Health Services), in discussion with the author, March 27, 1994.

4. Ibid.

5. Ibid.

6. Ibid.

7. Rhay, August 1993.

8. Ibid.

9. Ibid.

10. Morris, March 1994.

11. Ibid.

12. Ibid.

13. Ibid.

14. "Guards Wary of Liberalization," *Walla Walla Union-Bulletin*, April 19, 1971.

15. MO-Instruction 330.2A, Department of Institutions, March 1, 1965.

16. MO-Instruction 334.1A, Department of Institutions, March 1, 1965.

17. Chadek, June 1994.

18. John Lambert (former correctional officer, Washington State Penitentiary), in discussion with the author, August 1993.

19. Ibid.

20. Ibid.

21. R. Moses, January 1994.

22. Dick Morgan (former correctional officer, Washington State Penitentiary), in discussion with the author, August 1993.

23. Edwards, June 1994.

24. R. Moses, January 1994.

25. David Riggins (inmate, Washington State Department of Corrections), in discussion with the author, September 27, 1994.

26. Carol Moses, January 1994.

27. Earl Warren was governor of California before being appointed Chief Justice of the United States Supreme Court in 1953 by President Dwight Eisenhower.

28. Morris, March 1994.

29. Ibid.

30. Robert Tropp (former director, Division of Adult Corrections, Washington State Department of Social and Health Services), in discussion with the author, May 6, 1993.

31. Barbara Miller (former paralegal, Prison Legal Services), in discussion with the author, April 1994.

32. Jim Harvey (former associate superintendent, Washington State Penitentiary), in discussion with the author, February 18, 1994.

33. Ibid.

34. Memo, J. R. Harvey to B. J. Rhay, September 6, 1974, Washington State Archives, Records of the Department of Social and Health Services, Division of Adult Corrections, 1971-81.

35. Ibid.

36. Ibid.

37. Morris, March 1994.

38. "Rap Session Ends Rumor," *It's Happening at WSP / V. O. P.*, November 1974. [Formerly, *Voice of Prison*]

39. Ibid.

40. Harvey, February, 1994.

41. Ibid.

42. "Lack of Treatment Facilities Caused Convict Outburst," *It's Happening at WSP / V. O. P.*, January 1975.

43. Ibid.

44. Harvey, February 1994.

45. Ibid.

46. Ibid.

47. Ibid.

48. Rhay, August 1993.

49. Letter from Charles Morris to B. J. Rhay, January 7, 1975, Washington State Archives, Records of the Department of Social and Health Services, Division of Adult Corrections, 1971-81.

50. Interdepartmental memorandum from R. E. Jones to J. Harvey, January 1, 1975, Washington State Archives, Records of the Department of Social and Health Services, Division of Adult Corrections, 1971-81.

51. Letter from B. J. Rhay to Bill Collins, March 5, 1975, Washington State Archives, Records of the Department of Social and Health Services, Division of Adult Corrections, 1971-81.

52. Memo from Hal Bradley to B. J. Rhay, March 17, 1975, Washington State Archives, Records of the Department of Social and Health Services, Division of Adult Corrections, 1971-81.

53. Harvey, February 1994.

54. Ibid.

55. Harry Prater (inmate, Washington State Penitentiary), in discussion with the author, August 2010.

56. Eddie Todd (inmate, Washington State Department of Corrections), in discussion with the author, August 18, 2010.

57. Curtis Johnson (inmate, Washington State Department of Corrections), in discussion with the author, August 16, 2010.

58. "Breezing in the Breezeway," *Voice of Prison*, November 1975.

59. B. J. Rhay, "Observations on European Correctional Systems," *Planning Prospectus*, Department of Social and Health Services Division of Institutions, Adult Corrections, 1970.

60. *The Challenge of Crime in a Free Society*, President's Commission on Law Enforcement and Criminal Justice, February 1969.

61. "Hill Should Be Replaced by Small Treatment Centers," *Walla Walla Union-Bulletin*, October 18, 1971.

62. B. J. Rhay, "The Need for Innovation," *Institute I: A Search for the Prison of Tomorrow*, Resident Government Council, January 10, 1972.

63. "Days of Walled Prison on Way Out, Superintendent Feels," *Walla Walla Union-Bulletin*, January 16, 1972.

64. "Governor Says Prisons Should Be Torn Down," *Walla Walla Union-Bulletin*, August 10, 1972.

65. "Prison Shutdown in Next 10 Years?," *Walla Walla Union-Bulletin*, December 6, 1972.

66. "Massachusetts warden to study state prisons," *Walla Walla Union-Bulletin*, June 20, 1974.

67. Ibid.

68. Ibid.

69. *Three Thousand Years and Life*, a film by Randall Conrad, copyright 1973.

70. Frank Hall (former commissioner, Massachusetts Department of Corrections), in discussion with the author, April 28, 1994.

71. Morris, April 1994.

72. Ibid.

73. Ibid.

74. Freeman, August 1993.

75. Morgan, August 1993.

76. Morgan, August 1993.

77. Charles R. Morris, *A Time of Passion: America 1960–1980* (New York: Harper & Row, 1984), 194-95.

78. Ibid.

79. Transcript of commission meeting of December 13, 1975. Washington State Archives, Records of the Department of Social and Health Services, Division of Adult Corrections, 1971-81.

80. Ibid.

81. "Psychologist swears by his theory," *Walla Walla Union-Bulletin*, June 15, 1975.

82. Ibid.

83. Browne, July 1994.

84. Emery, June 1994.

85. Ressler, June 1994.

86. Complaint for Declaratory Judgment and Injunctive Relief, Superior Court of the State of Washington in and for the County of Walla Walla, April 7, 1975.

87. Ressler, June 1994.

88. Ibid

89. Todd, August 2010.

90. Ibid.

91. Jim Hartford (former correctional officer and sergeant, Washington State Penitentiary), in discussion with the author, August 14, 1993.

92. "Injured guard prefers to live close to danger," *Walla Walla Union-Bulletin*, May 4, 1977.

93. Ibid.

94. Ibid.

95. Harvey, February 1994.

96. Hartford, August 1993.

97. Harvey, February 1994.

98. Ibid.

99. Anonymous, in discussion with the author, August 2010.

100. Prater, August 2010.

101. Hartford, August 1993.

102. Anonymous, in discussion with the author, August 2010.

103. Johnson, August 2010.

104. Anonymous, in discussion with the author, August 2010.

105. Morgan, August 1993.

106. Hartford, August 1993.

107. Anonymous, in discussion with the author, August 2010.

108. Johnson, August 2010.

109. Ibid.

110. Ibid.

111. Morgan, August 1993.

112. R. Moses, January 1994.

113. Memo from Harold Bradley to B. J. Rhay, January 12, 1976, Washington State Archives, Records of the Department of Social and Health Services, Division of Adult Corrections, 1971-81.

114. Memo from B. J. Rhay to H. B. Bradley, January 13, 1976, Washington State Archives, Records of the Department of Social and Health Services, Division of Adult Corrections, 1971-81.

115. Rhay, August 1993.

116. Miller, June 1994.

117. Harvey, February 1994.

118. Riggins, September 27, 1994.

119. Rhay, August 1993.

120. Burfitt, February 7, 1994.

121. Harvey, February 1995.

122. General Order, signed by J. R. Harvey, January 19, 1976.

123. Memo from Harold Bradley to B. J. Rhay, October 21, 1975, Washington State Archives, Records of the Department of Social and Health Services, Division of Adult Corrections, 1971-81.

124. Memo to Harold Bradley from William McKelvey, September 19, 1975, Washington State Archives, Records of the Department of Social and Health Services, Division of Adult Corrections, 1971-81.

125. "Prison officers may sue over women guards," *Walla Walla Union-Bulletin*, May 7, 1976.

126. Riggins, September 1994.

127. Miller, April 1994.

128. Harvey, February 1994.

129. Ibid.

130. Rhay, August 1993.

131. Ibid.

132. "Warden wants to head corrections," *Walla Walla Union-Bulletin*, January 5, 1977.

133. Harlan McNutt, M.D. (former Secretary, DSHS), in discussion with the author, March 22, 1994.

134. Hartford, August 1993.

135. "Other guard avoids bomb by just a few steps," *Walla Walla Union-Bulletin*, April 8, 1977.

136. Agtuca, March 2011.

137. Email, James Hayner, March 30, 2011; personal communication, Jerry Votendahl, April 12, 2011.

138. There are prisons in the United States where Mace is frequently used. This was not the case in Washington in the 1970s and for some decades thereafter. Policy required that Mace be kept in the armory and issued only when authorized by the superintendent or associate superintendent.

139. Agtuca, March 2011.

140. Undated report on segregation by Tom Farrugia, Resident Government Councilman #1, Washington State Archives, Records of the Department of Social and Health Services, Division of Adult Corrections, 1971-81.

141. Memo to J. R. Harvey from Acting Lt. B. L. Moreland, April 10, 1977, Washington State Archives, Records of the Department of Social and Health Services, Division of Adult Corrections, 1971-81.

142. Memo to Mr. Harvey from Officer J. Meyer, April 11, 1977, Washington State Archives, Records of the Department of Social and Health Services, Division of Adult Corrections, 1971-81.

143. Memo to Mr. Harvey from Officer R. Mason, April 11, 1977, Washington State Archives, Records of the Department of Social and Health Services, Division of Adult Corrections, 1971-81.

144. "Prison search yields more barrels of contraband," *Walla Walla Union-Bulletin*, April 18, 1977.

145. Internal review, William McKelvey, April 27, 1977, Washington State Archives, Records of the Department of Social and Health Services, Division of Adult Corrections, 1971-81.

146. "Prison guards oppose ouster move," *Walla Walla Union-Bulletin*, May 5, 1977.

147. Letter from Samuel Kelly to Harlan McNutt, May 9, 1977, Washington State Archives, Daniel J. Evans Papers, 1965-77.

148. "Prison lockdown will continue indefinitely," *Walla Walla Union-Bulletin*, May 3, 1977.

149. "Prison guards oppose ouster move," *Walla Walla Union-Bulletin*, May 5, 1977.

150. "Prison, not state, to decide lockdown end," *Walla Walla Union-Bulletin*, May 6, 1977.

151. "Prison official to be transferred," *Walla Walla Union-Bulletin*, May 8, 1977.

152. Letter from J. R. Harvey to Harold Bradley, April 27, 1977, Washington State Archives, Records of the Department of Social and Health Services, Division of Adult Corrections, 1971-81.

153. Harvey, February 1994.

154. R. Moses, January 1994.

155. "Lawmakers 'confused' about prison," *Walla Walla Union-Bulletin*, May 25, 1977.

156. John Shaughnessy (former assistant director, Division of Adult Corrections, Department of Social and Health Services), in discussion with the author, July 30, 1993.

157. Dick Bradley (former chief, Office of Capital Programs, Department of Corrections), in discussion with the author, March 15, 1993.

158. Rhay, August 1993.

159. Chadek, June 1994.

160. "New WSP warden will end programs in minimum security," *Walla Walla Union-Bulletin*, June 28, 1977.

161. "Ray vetoes mini-prison proposal," *Walla Walla Union-Bulletin*, July 1, 1977.

162. "Rhay doesn't figure in shakeup," *Walla Walla Union-Bulletin*, August 26, 1977.

163. "B.J. Rhay takes corrections job in Montana," *Walla Walla Union-Bulletin,* October 16, 1977.

Part 4: Nadir 1977–1978

1. McNutt, March 1994.

2. Douglas Vinzant (former superintendent, Washington State Penitentiary, former director, Division of Adult Corrections, Department of Social and Health Services), in discussion with the author, April 22, 1994.

3. Ibid.

4. "Task force may recommend smaller prisons in state," *Walla Walla Union-Bulletin*, October 25, 1974.

5. "State official irks prison employees," *Walla Walla Union-Bulletin*, October 28, 1974.

6. Vinzant, April 1994.

7. Ibid.

8. R. Moses, January 1994.

9. Hall, April 1994.

10. R. Moses, January 1994.

11. Ibid.

12. Chadek, June 1994.

13. Ibid.

14. Ibid.

15. Vinzant, April 1994.

16. Ibid.

17. Vinzant, April 1994.

18. R. Moses, January 1994.

19. Agtuca, March 2011.

20. Prater, August 2010.

21. Anonymous, August 2010.

22. Vinzant, April 1994.

23. Ibid.

24. Ibid.

25. R. Moses, January 1994.

26. Ibid.

27. Ibid.

28. Morgan, August 1993.

29. Ibid.

30. Tropp, May 1993.

31. Prater, August 16, 2010.

32. Ibid.

33. Johnson, August 2010.

34. Prater, August 2010.

35. Henry Grisby (inmate, Washington State Department of Corrections), in discussion with the author, August 17, 2010.

36. Prater, August 2010.

37. Ibid.

38. Ibid.

39. Anonymous, August 2010.

40. Agtuca, March 2011.

41. Grigsby, August 2010.

42. Tropp, May 1993.

43. Chadek, June 1994.

44. Lambert, August 1994.

45. Ibid.

46. "Shotgun blast at penitentiary startles officials, prisoners," *Walla Walla Union-Bulletin*, February 21, 1978.

47. "Prison shotgun misfired before," *Walla Walla Union-Bulletin*, February 22, 1978.

48. Vinzant, April 22, 1994.

49. Ibid.

50. Johnson, August 2010.

51. Agtuca, March 2011.

52. Johnson, August 2010.

53. Vinzant, April 1994.

54. Chadek, June 1994.

55. Lambert, August 1994.

56. R. Moses, January 1994.

57. Prater, August 2010.

58. Lambert, August 1994.

59. The governor didn't like what was happening in adult corrections, but the secretary of DSHS had many responsibilities, and McNutt was fired over problems involving nursing homes.

60. Shaughnessy, July 1993.

61. Thomas, August 1993.

62. "Prison overcrowding 'shocks' Ray," *Walla Walla Union-Bulletin*, May 24, 1978.

63. Gerald Thompson (former secretary, Washington State Department of Social and Health Services), in discussion with the author, March 3, 1994.

64. Ibid.

65. "Vinzant will name successor at penitentiary within 45 days," *Walla Walla Union-Bulletin*, May 24, 1978.

66. Hartford, August 1993.

67. Morgan, August 1993.

68. Ibid.

69. Ibid.

70. Hartford, August 1993.

71. Thompson, March 1994.

72. Ibid.

73. Ibid.

74. Interdepartmental memorandum, August 11, 1978, "Pipe Bomb Explosion in Control," Washington State Archives, Records of the Department of Social and Health Services, Division of Adult Corrections, 1971-81.

75. Larry Kincheloe (former associate superintendent, superintendent, Washington State Penitentiary), in discussion with the author, May 2, 1994.

76. Lambert, August 1993.

77. Investigative report, August 16, 1978, "Bomb Incident of 8-11-78 in Major Control Room," Washington State Archives, Records of the Department of Social and Health Services, Division of Adult Corrections, 1971-81.

78. R. Moses, January 1994.

79. Tropp, May 1993.

80. "Lockdown may end Friday," *Walla Walla Union-Bulletin*, August 21, 1978

81. Shaughnessy, July 1993.

82. "Locals favor Vinzant firing," *Walla Walla Union-Bulletin*, August 16, 1978.

83. "Chief of State Prisons Quits," *Seattle Post-Intelligencer*, August 16, 1978.

84. "Locals favor Vinzant firing," *Walla Walla Union-Bulletin*, August 16, 1978.

85. Tropp, May 1993.

86. Spalding, April 1993.

87. Spalding, April 1993.

88. Thompson, March 1994.

89. "Guards Threaten Walkout," *Seattle Post-Intelligencer*, August 19, 1978.

90. "Penitentiary guards threaten walkout," *Seattle Times*, August 19, 1978.

91. "Prison guards to stay on job," *Seattle Times*, August 20, 1978.

92. Tropp, May 1993.

93. Kincheloe, May 1994.

94. "Walla Walla prison chief quits," *Seattle Times,* August 22, 1978.

95. "WSP inventory a control measure," *Walla Walla Union-Bulletin*, November 28, 1978.

96. Memo, James E. Thatcher to R. Tropp, August 29, 1978, Washington State Archives, Records of the Department of Social and Health Services, Division of Adult Corrections, 1971-81.

97. "State lawmakers agree prison inmates should be put to work," *Walla Walla Union-Bulletin*, April 17, 1978.

98. *Performance Audit of Washington State Penitentiary Motorcycle Association and Seven Arts Club*, Report Number S-ACF-7-79, May 1979, Washington State Archives, Records of the Department of Social and Health Services, Division of Adult Corrections, 1971-81.

99. Ibid

100. "Prison begins $1-million security work," *Walla Walla Union-Bulletin*, June 25, 1978.

101. Memo from Lloyd J. Trefry to Robert E. Neilson, Director, Office of Special Investigations, November 6, 1978, Washington State Archives, Records of the Department of Social and Health Services, Division of Adult Corrections, 1971-81.

102. Tropp, May 1993.

Part 5: War 1978–1981

1. Spalding, April 1993.

2. Tropp, May 1993.

3. "Spalding: Limit 'permissive' policies," *Walla Walla Union-Bulletin*, August 23, 1978.

4. "Former prison chief B.J. Rhay hails Spalding's appointment," *Walla Walla Union-Bulletin*, August 24, 1978.

5. "Feelings mixed about Genakos' resignation," *Walla Walla Union-Bulletin*, August 23, 1978.

6. "Inmates feel Spalding will treat them fairly," *Walla Walla Union-Bulletin*, August 25, 1978.

7. Tropp, May 1993.

8. Hartford, August 1993.

9. Spalding, April 1993.

10. Ibid.

11. Spalding, April 1993.

12. Ibid.

13. Ibid.

14. Ibid.

15. Ibid.

16. Hoffman and McCoy, *Concrete Mama*, 61.

17. Spalding, April 1993.

18. "Inmate leaders say curtailment will hinder rehabilitation," *Walla Walla Union-Bulletin*, September 17, 1978.

19. Ibid.

20. Hoffman and McCoy, *Concrete Mama*, 11.

21. James Thatcher (former administrator, Washington State Department of Social and Health Services and Washington State Department of Corrections), in discussion with the author, May 20, 1993.

22. "Warden, inmates agree on tension cause," *Walla Walla Union-Bulletin*, November 5, 1978.

23. "Prison officials order alert," *Walla Walla Union-Bulletin*, November 3, 1978.

24. Agtuca, March 2011.

25. Ibid.

26. Spalding, April 1993.

27. Tropp, May 1993.

28. Ibid.

29. Shaughnessey, July 1993.

30. "Twelve inmates, guards on prison 'hit list,'" *Walla Walla Union-Bulletin*, March 16, 1979.

31. "More violence expected at WSP," *Walla Walla Union-Bulletin*, February 14, 1979.

32. Agtuca, March 2011.

33. Shaughnessy, August 1993; Agtuca, March 2011.

34. "Lockdown ends quietly," *Walla Walla Union-Bulletin*, February 16, 1979.

35. Lambert, August 1994.

36. "Lockdown brings reprieve from unrest at penitentiary," *Walla Walla Union-Bulletin*, February 18, 1979.

37. Ibid.

38. Hartford, August 1993.

39. Ibid.

40. Kincheloe, May 1994.

41. Ibid.

42. Hartford, August 1993.

43. Stanley Sturgill, Incident Report, May 9, 1979, Washington State Archives, Records of the Department of Social and Health Services, Division of Adult Corrections, 1971-81.

44. Jeannie Hall, Incident Report, May 9, 1979, Washington State Archives, Records of the Department of Social and Health Services, Division of Adult Corrections, 1971-81.

45. Hartford, August 1993.

46. Ibid.

47. Ibid.

48. Aurelio Gonzales, Incident Report, May 9, 1979, Washington State Archives, Records of the Department of Social and Health Services, Division of Adult Corrections, 1971-81.

49. Hartford, August 1993.

50. Paraphrased from a memo from Larry Kincheloe to Robert Tropp, May 21, 1979.

51. Hall, Incident Report, May 9, 1979.

52. Sturgill, Incident Report, May 9, 1979.

53. Ibid.

54. Ibid.

55. Hartford, August 1993.

56. Morgan, August 1993.

57. Ibid.

58. Kincheloe, May 1994.

59. Edwards, June 1994.

60. Interdepartmental memo from Officer E. Jordan to ASC Kincheloe, June 15, 1979, Washington State Archives, Records of the Department of Social and Health Services, Division of Adult Corrections, 1971-81.

61. Ibid.

62. Ibid.

63. Richard Mason (correctional officer, sergeant, lieutenant, Washington State Penitentiary), in discussion with the author, September 29, 2011.

64. Ibid.

65. Prater, August 2010.

66. Control room log, June 15, 1979, Washington State Archives, Records of the Department of Social and Health Services, Division of Adult Corrections, 1971-81.

67. Morgan, August 1993.

68. Hartford, August 1993.

69. Control Room log, June 15, 1979, Washington State Archives, Records of the Department of Social and Health Services, Division of Adult Corrections, 1971-81.

70. Mason, September 2011.

71. Deposition, Donald Talbot, *Hoptowit v. Ray*, December 19, 1979.

72. Morgan, August 1993.

73. Hartford, August 1993.

74. Spalding, April 1993.

75. Ibid.

76. Hartford, August 1993.

77. Ibid.

78. Spalding, April 1993.

79. Lambert, August 1994.

80. Kincheloe, May 1994.

81. Lambert, August, 1993.

82. "New prison stance: No more parks," *Walla Walla Union-Bulletin*, June 29, 1979.

83. Hartford, August 1993.

84. Lambert, August 1994.

85. Morgan, August 1993.

86. Ibid.

87. Spalding, April 1993.

88. Ibid.

89. Travisono, July 1993.

90. Tropp, undated handwritten notes, Washington State Archives, Records of the Department of Social and Health Services, Division of Adult Corrections, 1971-81.

91. Current Status of Washington State Penitentiary, June 5, 1979, Washington State Archives, Division of Adult Corrections, 1971-1981.

92. "Penitentiary search ends, lockdown continues," *Walla Walla Union-Bulletin*, July 8, 1979.

93. Until otherwise indicated, Morgan, August 1993.

94. R. Moses, January 1994.

95. Ibid.

96. Ibid.

97. Miller, June 1994.

98. Mason, September 2011.

99. Hartford, August 1993.

100. Deposition of Manuel Rampola, *Hoptowit v. Ray*, November 29, 1979.

101. Ibid.

102. Deposition, James Spalding, *Hoptowit v. Ray*, January 11–12, 1980.

103. Investigative Report, Brooks Russell and James Jackson, August 2, 1979, Washington State Archives, Records of the Department of Social and Health Services, Division of Adult Corrections, 1971-81.

104. Ibid.

105. Ibid.

106. Deposition of Rampola, November 29, 1979.

107. Investigative Report, Russell and Jackson.

108. Ibid.

109. Affidavit, Dr. Eng C. Saw, *Hoptowit v. Ray*, April 22, 1980.

110. "13 at prison taken off jobs for 'brutality,'" *Spokesman Review*, July 11, 1979. The number was reduced to twelve a few days later due to an incorrect identification.

111. Investigative Report, Russell and Jackson.

112. Ibid.

113. Dick Morgan, email message to the author, September 4, 2012.

114. Investigative Report, Russell and Jackson.

115. "Guards 'fed up' with prisoners who claim brutality," *Spokesman Review*, July 11, 1979.

116. "Guard walkout threat is ended temporarily," *Walla Walla Union-Bulletin*, July 17, 1979.

117. Ibid.

118. Spalding, April 1993.

119. Ibid.

120. Morgan, August 1993.

121. Spalding, April 1993.

122. Ibid.

123. Ibid.

124. Ibid.

125. Spalding, April 1993.

126. "Shocking Pictures from the Big House: A Prison that Prisoners Run," *Life*, August 1979.

127. Thomas, August 1993.

128. Thompson, March 1994.

129. Deposition, John Wait, *Hoptowit v. Ray*, March 18, 1980.

130. "Medical Evidence of Inmate Injury," *Seattle Post-Intelligencer*, September 3, 1979.

131. Investigative Report, Russell and Jackson.

132. "Medical Evidence of Inmate Injury," *Seattle Post-Intelligencer*, September 3, 1979.

133. John Midgley (attorney for the plaintiffs, *Hoptowit v. Ray*), in discussion with the author, March 23, 1994.

134. "Guards in Charge Again at the Prison," *Seattle Post-Intelligencer*, January 13, 1980.

135. Midgley, March 1994.

136. Ibid.

137. "Spalding: Injunction 'depressing, one-sided," *Walla Walla Union-Bulletin*, December 9, 1979.

138. Internal investigation, W. Edward Naugler, MD, Medical Director, Adult Corrections Division, May 30, 1978, Washington State Archives, Records of the Department of Social and Health Services, Division of Adult Corrections, 1971-81.

139. Affidavit of John Bumphus, *Howtowit v. Ray*, March 31, 1980.

140. Memorandum Opinion, Finding of Facts, Conclusions of Law, and Order, *Hoptowit v. Ray*, United States District Court for the Eastern District of Washington, June 23, 1980.

141. Shaughnessey, July 1994.

142. Thomas, August 1993.

143. "GOP House leader wants Tropp out," *Walla Walla Union-Bulletin*, August 24, 1979.

144. Thompson, March 1994.

145. Tropp, May 1993.

146. Thompson, March 1994.

Part 6: Transformation 1981–1985

1. Steve Excell (Governor Spellman's deputy chief of staff), in discussion with the author, August 28, 2014.

2. Ibid.

3. Ibid.

4. Walter "Kip" Kautzky (Director, Division of Prisons, Washington State Department of Corrections), in discussion with the author, April 3, 2012.

5. Excell, August 2014.

6. Ibid.

7. "State prison chief: Give us time," *Walla Walla Union-Bulletin*, February 13, 1981.

8. Ibid.

9. Tropp, May 1993.

10. Shaughnessey, July 1994.

11. "Spellman finds $2 million surprise," *Walla Walla Union-Bulletin*, February 13, 1981.

12. "Solons question DSHS spending," *Walla Walla Union-Bulletin*, March 13, 1981.

13. R. Moses, January 1994.

14. Shaughnessey, July 1994.

15. C. R. M. Kastama (former superintendent, Washington State Penitentiary), in discussion with the author, March 29, 1993.

16. Ibid.

17. R. Moses, January 1994.

18. Personal communication, Jim Thatcher, July 2015.

19. John King (legislative liaison, Washington State Department of Corrections), in discussion with the author, August 13, 2012.

20. "Meetings seek to cool tension at prison," *Walla Walla Union-Bulletin*, August 17, 1981.

21. Kastama, March 1993.

22. Ibid.

23. Ibid.

24. Tana Wood (former associate superintendent and superintendent, Washington State Penitentiary), in discussion with the author, May 18, 2012.

25. Ibid.

26. Kastama, March 1993.

27. Ibid.

28. Kautzky, April 2012.

29. Ibid.

30. Wood, May 2012.

31. Kastama, March 1993.

32. Ibid.

33. Ibid.

34. R. Moses, January 1994.

35. Kautzky, April 2012.

36. Mason, September 2011.

37. Wood, May 2012.

38. Morgan, August 1993.

39. Ibid.

40. Ibid.

41. James Blodgett (former associate superintendent and superintendent, Washington State Penitentiary), in discussion with the author, August 12, 2014.

42. Morgan, August 1993.

43. Ibid.

44. Ibid.

45. Blodgett, August 2014.

46. Ibid.

47. Hartford, August 1993.

48. Ibid.

Afterword

1. Personal communication, Dick Morgan, April 2012.

INDEX

References to illustrations are in italic type

ACLU, 245

Adjustment committee, 8, 78. *See also* disciplinary hearings

admissions, 3, 124

American Correctional Association, 61, 120, 219–21, 239; and Reed, 255, 260; standards of, 78, 187, 247

Attica, 62, 64, 98, 157; effect on penitentiary, 50, 51

Auditorium, 123–24, 199; incidents in, 40–42, 59; location of, *xviii*, 4

banquets: by Bikers, 59, 164; by Confederated Indian Tribes, 46; description of, 59; by Lifers with Hope, 190; locations of, 59; by Men against sexism, 168, 170, 171; by Resident Government Council, 50, 51; Spalding ends, 189

Big Red: abuses in, 112; description of, 3; location of *xviii*, 3. *See also* Segregation

Big Yard, 10, 60, 227, *240*, 243, 246, 263, 264; banquets in, 46, 59; inmates living in, 239, *241, 242, 265*; location of *xviii*, 4, *136, 254*; moving inmates to, 203–4, *205*, 226, 227, *228*

Bikers, 60, 111, *135*, 186, 187, 189, 196, 263, *265*, 282; banquets, 59; and conflict with Lifers, 117–18, 190–91; and enforcement activities, 117; and financial irregularities, 164, 179; and heroin ring, 114; and Kastama, 264–65; unity of, 118–19; and Vinzant, 144, 164–65

Bikers' Club, location of, 59, *136*

Black Dragon Communiqué, 170

Black Manifesto, 58

Black Prisoners Forum Unlimited. *See* B.P.F.U.

Blodgett, James (Jim): as associate superintendent, 279–81; as superintendent, 282–83

Blood Alley, *123*, 155, 187; description of, 122–23; location of, *136*

bombs, 86, 170, 172, 175, 201, 206; and adult corrections headquarters building, 94; and Hartford, 127–28; and Sanders, 173–74, 175, 176; types of, 156

B.P.F.U., 59, 123; and Black Manifesto, 58; and breezeway bandits, 151–52; and heroin, 114; and Pride in Culture, 26

B.P.F.U. clubhouse, 58; activities in, 90, 125; dismantled, 123; demolished, 187, 263; location of, *136*

Bradley, Harold (Hal), 76, 101, 130; and bombing of adult corrections headquarters building, 94; hiring of, 74–75; and Harvey, 83–84, 85–87, 124; resignation of, 126, 133, 142; and Rhay, 89, 94, 120, 122, 133

Brookshire, Michael, 107–8

Brown, "Cadillac," 55, 114, 117–18, 121

Browne, John Henry, 66–67, 68, 69, 78, 106

budget, 249, 257–58

Bumphus, John, 249

Burdman, Milton, 75, 130, 137; hiring of, 73–74; firing of, 126, 133

Central control: bomb in, 173–76; location of, *xviii*, 4

Chadek, Steve, 62, 65–66, 84, 131, 165; on futility of writing infractions, 79; and Genakos, 164; and Hartford, 127–28; and Rhay, 66, 132; and Vinzant, 139, 141–42, 159–61

CIT. *See* Confederated Indian Tribes

Citizens Advisory Council, 61, 90

Confederated Indian Tribes, 26, 46, 207

Conte, William, 25, 28, 29, 30, 34, 53, 66, 285; announces four reforms, 31–33; as director of department of institutions, 18; as director of mental health, 17; resigns, 47; and Rhay, 23–24, 35–37

convict code, 8; defined, 7; erosion of, 64, 151

credit card. *See* budget

Cross, William (Bill), 208–11, 213, 232, 285

Crowley, Art, 63, 83

Cummins, Jim, 96, 231, 243

deadlock. *See* lockdown

Department of Corrections, 126, 250, 256, 258, 283; creation of, 255, 260

Department of Institutions, 16, 18, 30

Department of Social and Health Services (DSHS), 30, 54, 63, 65, 73, 98, 244; and cost overruns, 249, 250, 251; creation of, 27–28; and legal team, 66–69; organization of, 29, 74

THE COVER PHOTOGRAPH—
ABOUT THE PHOTOGRAPHER

 The cover photo for this book was shot by Ethan Hoffman in the Big Yard of the Washington State Penitentiary on a Friday afternoon in September 1978. The inmate riding the motorcycle was the current president of the Washington State Penitentiary Motorcycle Association, better known as the "Bikers' Club."

Hoffman (1949–1990) was an American photographer who was named the College Photographer of the Year, and awarded the World Understanding Award, from Nikon and the University of Missouri School of Journalism, "In recognition of the application of photography toward a deeper unity and understanding among the people of the world." His photo essays appeared prominently in magazines around the world, including *Fortune, Life, Esquire, The New York Times Magazine,* and magazines in England, France, and Germany. His work was shown in leading museums, including the Smithsonian in Washington, D.C. Ethan Hoffman died in 1990 in an accident while on a photo assignment. Prior to his death he opened the Picture Project in New York City, a unique publishing company focused on promoting creative photojournalism books.

Early in his career, Hoffman worked for the *Walla Walla Union-Bulletin* where the biggest story in town was the Washington State Penitentiary. In August 1978 he, and a fellow journalist from the newspaper, quit their paying jobs to do an in-depth report on the prison. The cover photo for *Unusual Punishment* was selected from the many startling images Hoffman captured for the book *Concrete Mama: Prison Profiles from Walla Walla,* published in 1981. Collections of Hoffman's work may also be found in the books *Butoh: Dance of the Dark Soul,* and *Flesh and Blood: Photographers' Images of Their Own Families.*